Professional Examina

Managerial Level

Paper P1

Management Accounting Performance Evaluation

Exam Kit

CIMA

British Library Cataloguing-in-Publication Data

A catalogue record for this book is available from the British Library.

Published by Kaplan Publishing UK
Unit 2 The Business Centre
Molly Millars Lane
Wokingham
Berkshire
RG41 2QZ

ISBN 978-1-84710-441-0

© Kaplan Financial Limited, December 2007

Printed and bound in Great Britain

Acknowledgements

We are grateful to the Chartered Institute of Management Accountants, the Association of Chartered Certified Accountants and the Institute of Chartered Accountants in England and Wales for permission to reproduce past examination questions. The answers have been prepared by Kaplan Publishing.

All rights reserved. No part of this publication may be reproduced, stored in a retrieval system, or transmitted, in any form or by any means, electronic, mechanical, photocopying, recording or otherwise, without the prior written permission of Kaplan Publishing.

INTRODUCTION

We have worked closely with experienced CIMA tutors and lecturers to ensure that our Kits are exam-focused and user-friendly.

This Exam Kit includes an extensive selection of questions that entirely cover the syllabus – this ensures that your knowledge is tested across all syllabus areas. Wherever possible questions have been grouped by syllabus topics.

Questions are of exam standard and format – this enables you to master the exam techniques. Section 1 contains Section A-type questions you will come across in your exam, Section 2 contains Section B-type questions and Section 3 contains Section C-type questions.

May and November 2007 exams are at the back of the book – try these under timed conditions and this will give you an exact idea of the way you will be tested in your exam.

CONTENTS

	Page
Index to questions and answers	vi
Syllabus and learning outcomes	ix
Revision guidance	xiii
The exam	xiv
Mathematical tables and formulae	xv

Section

1	Section A-type questions	1
2	Section B-type questions	53
3	Section C-type questions	65
4	Answers to Section A-type questions	99
5	Answers to Section B-type questions	147
6	Answers to Section C-type questions	179
7	May 2007 exam questions	249
8	Answers to May 2007 exam questions	259
9	November 2007 exam questions	271
10	Answers to November 2007 exam questions	283

INDEX TO QUESTIONS AND ANSWERS

Page number

Section A-type questions

	Question	Answer
Cost accounting systems (Questions 1 – 54)	1	99
Standard costing (Questions 55 – 94)	17	114
Budgeting (Questions 95 – 140)	28	126
Control and performance measurement of responsibility centres (Questions 141 – 172)	41	136

Section B-type questions

Cost accounting systems

		Question	Answer
173	Marginal cost profit and cash flow	53	147
174	Process costing	53	147
175	Throughput accounting	53	148
176	Throughput accounting ratio	53	148
177	Improving the throughput accounting ratio	53	148
178	ABC cost drivers	53	149
179	ABC and profitability	53	149
180	Manufacturing resource planning	53	150
181	Just-in-time	54	150
182	TQM and JIT (Pilot Paper)	54	151
183	Quality cost	54	151
184	Marginal and absorption costing (May 06 Exam)	54	151
185	Marginal costing and throughput accounting (May 06 Exam)	54	152

Standard costing

		Question	Answer
186	Ideal standards	54	152
187	Fixed production overhead volume variance	54	152
188	Labour variances (November 05 Exam)	55	153
189	Criticisms of standard costing	55	154
190	Standard costing and the new management accounting	55	154
191	Ritzer's Mcdonaldization model	55	155
192	Diagnostic related groups	55	155
193	Mix and yield variances	55	155
194	Labour rate variance	55	156

INDEX TO QUESTIONS AND ANSWERS

Page number

			Question	Answer
195	Investigation of variances (November 05 Exam)		56	156
196	Interpreting variances (1)		56	157
197	Interpreting variances (2)		56	157
198	Centrally set standards		56	158
199	Benchmarking		56	158
200	Hospital care (May 06 Exam)		56	159
201	C plc (May 06 Exam)		57	159
202	Modern business environment (May 06 Exam)		57	160

Budgeting

		Question	Answer
203	Purpose of budgets	57	160
204	Controllability (Pilot Paper)	57	161
205	Budget slack	57	161
206	Zero-based budgeting	57	162
207	J Limited (November 05 Exam)	58	162
208	ZBB v ABB	58	163
209	Incremental budgets v ZZB	58	163
210	Rolling budget	58	164
211	'What if' analysis	58	164
212	Feedback and feedforward (Pilot Paper)	58	165
213	Fixed v flexible budgets	58	165
214	Service-based organisations	58	166
215	McDonaldization and budgets (November 05 Exam)	59	166
216	ST plc (November 05 Exam)	59	167
217	Behavioural factors	59	167
218	W Limited (November 05 Exam)	59	168
219	Participation in budget setting (1) (Pilot Paper)	59	168
220	Balanced scorecard (1)	59	169
221	Beyond budgeting (1)	59	170
222	Time series in forecasting	59	170
223	Balanced scorecard (2) (May 05 Exam)	60	171
224	Participation in budget setting (2) (May 05 Exam)	60	171
225	Beyond budgeting (2) (May 05 Exam)	60	172
226	X plc (November 06 Exam)	60	173

Control and performance measurement of responsibility centres

		Question	Answer
227	Decentralisation	62	175
228	Residual income v economic value added (Pilot Paper)	62	175
229	Transfer pricing (1)	62	176
230	International transfer pricing (Pilot Paper)	62	176
231	Marginal costs and transfer pricing	62	176
232	EVA® (May 05 Exam)	62	177
233	Organisation structure (May 05 Exam)	63	177
234	Transfer pricing (2) (May 05 Exam)	63	178
235	T plc (May 06 Exam)	63	178

PAPER P1 : MANAGEMENT ACCOUNTING – PERFORMANCE EVALUATION

Section C-type questions

Page number

Cost accounting systems

			Question	Answer
236	Hensau		65	179
237	Brunti		66	181
238	Trimake		67	183
239	A paint manufacturer		68	186
240	Chemical processing (Pilot Paper)		69	189
241	Biotinct (November 05 Exam)		70	190
242	Pharmaceutical drugs (May 05 Exam)		70	192
243	MN Ltd		72	194

Standard costing

244	RS		72	196
245	DL Hospital Trust		74	199
246	RBF Transport		75	202
247	ABC		76	204
248	ZED		77	206
249	Sales/overhead variances		78	209
250	FB		79	211
251	Satellite navigation systems (May 05 Exam)		79	215
252	X Ltd (November 06 Exam)		81	218

Budgeting

253	Public sector organisation		82	221
254	AHW		83	223
255	ST		84	225
256	Products R, S and T		85	226
257	PMF		86	228
258	Marshall (Pilot Paper)		87	229
259	Key metrics		88	231
260	M plc (May 06 Exam)		89	233

Control and performance measurement of responsibility centres

261	KDS		91	234
262	Y and Z (November 05 Exam)		92	237
263	CTD		92	239
264	Division A		93	241
265	Mobile phones		94	243
266	FP (May 06 Exam)		95	244
267	ZZ Group (November 06 Exam)		96	246

SYLLABUS AND LEARNING OUTCOMES

Learning aims

This syllabus aims to test the student's ability to:

- apply both traditional and contemporary approaches to cost accounting in a variety of contexts and evaluate the impact of 'modern' data processing and processing technologies such as MRP, ERP and JIT;

- explain and apply the principles of standard costing, calculate variances in a variety of contexts and critically evaluate the worth of standard costing in the light of contemporary criticisms;

- develop budgets using both traditional and contemporary techniques, evaluate both interactive and diagnostic uses of budgets in a variety of contexts and discuss the issues raised by those that advocate techniques 'beyond budgeting';

- prepare appropriate financial statements for cost, profit and investment centre managers, calculate appropriate financial performance indicators, assess the impact of alternative transfer pricing policies and discuss the behavioural consequences of management control systems based on responsibility accounting, decentralisation and delegation.

Learning outcomes and syllabus content

A - COST ACCOUNTING SYSTEMS – 25%

Learning outcomes

On completion of their studies students should be able to:

- compare and contrast marginal and absorption costing methods in respect of profit reporting and stock valuation;

- apply marginal and absorption costing approaches in job, batch and process environments;

- prepare ledger accounts according to context: marginal or absorption based in job, batch or process environments, including work-in-progress and related accounts such as production overhead control account and abnormal loss account;

- explain the origins of throughput accounting as 'super variable costing' and its application as a variant of marginal or variable cost accounting;

- apply standard costing methods within costing systems and demonstrate the reconciliation of budgeted and actual profit margins;

- compare activity-based costing with traditional marginal and absorption costing methods and evaluate its potential as a system of cost accounting;

- explain the role of MRP and ERP systems in supporting standard costing systems, calculating variances and facilitating the posting of ledger entries;

- evaluate the impact of just-in-time manufacturing methods on cost accounting and the use of 'back – flush accounting' when work-in-progress stock is minimal.

Syllabus content

- Marginal (or variable) costing as a system of profit reporting and stock valuation.
- Absorption costing as a system of profit reporting and stock valuation.
- Throughput accounting as a system of profit reporting and stock valuation.
- Activity-based costing as a potential system of profit reporting and stock valuation.
- The integration of standard costing with marginal cost accounting, absorption cost accounting and throughput accounting.
- Process accounting including establishment of equivalent units in stock, work-in-progress and abnormal loss accounts and the use of first-in-first-out, average cost and standard cost methods of stock valuation.
- MRP and ERP systems for resource planning and the integration of accounting functions with other systems, such as purchase ordering and production planning.
- Back-flush accounting in just-in-time production environments. The benefits of just-in-time production, total quality management and theory of constraints and the possible impacts of these methods on cost accounting and performance measurement.

B - STANDARD COSTING – 25%

Learning outcomes

On completion of their studies students should be able to:

- explain why and how standards are set in manufacturing and in service industries with particular reference to the maximisation of efficiency and minimisation of waste.
- calculate and interpret material, labour, variable overhead, fixed overhead and sales variances;
- prepare and discuss a report which reconciles budget and actual profit using absorption and/or marginal costing principles;
- calculate and explain planning and operational variances;
- prepare reports using a range of internal and external benchmarks and interpret the results;
- discuss the behavioural implications of setting standard costs.

Syllabus content

- Manufacturing standards for material, labour, variable overhead and fixed overhead.
- Price/rate and usage/efficiency variances for materials, labour and variable overhead. Further subdivision of total usage/efficiency variances into mix and yield components. (Note: The calculation of mix variances on both individual and average valuation bases is required.)
- Fixed overhead expenditure and volume variances. (Note: the subdivision of fixed overhead volume variance into capacity and efficiency elements will not be examined.)
- Planning and operational variances.
- Standards and variances in service industries, (including the phenomenon of 'McDonaldization'), public services (e.g. Health), (including the use of 'diagnostic related' or 'reference' groups), and the professions (e.g. labour mix variances in audit work). Criticisms of standard costing in general and in advanced manufacturing environments in particular.
- Sales price and sales revenue/margin volume variances (calculation of the latter on a unit basis related to revenue, gross margin and contribution margin). Application of these variances to all sectors, including professional services and retail analysis.
- Interpretation of variances: interrelationship, significance.
- Benchmarking.
- Behavioural implications of setting standard costs.

C - BUDGETING - 30%

Learning outcomes

On completion of their studies students should be able to:

- explain why organisations prepare forecasts and plans;
- calculate projected product/service volumes employing appropriate forecasting techniques;
- calculate projected revenues and costs based on product/service volumes, pricing strategies and cost structures;
- evaluate projected performance by calculating key metrics including profitability, liquidity and asset turnover ratios;
- describe and explain the possible purposes of budgets, including planning, communication, co-ordination, motivation, authorisation, control and evaluation;
- evaluate and apply alternative approaches to budgeting;
- calculate the consequences of 'what if' scenarios and evaluate their impact on master profit and loss account and balance sheet;
- explain the concept of responsibility accounting and its importance in the construction of functional budgets that support the overall master budget;
- identify controllable and uncontrollable costs in the context of responsibility accounting and explain why 'uncontrollable' costs may or may not be allocated to responsibility centres;
- explain the ideas of feedback and feed-forward control and their application in the use of budgets for control;
- evaluate performance using fixed and flexible budget reports;
- discuss the role of non-financial performance indicators and compare and contrast traditional approaches to budgeting with recommendations based on the 'balanced scorecard';
- evaluate the impact of budgetary control systems on human behaviour;
- evaluate the criticisms of budgeting particularly from the advocates of techniques that are 'beyond budgeting'.

Syllabus content

- Time series analysis including moving totals and averages, treatment of seasonality, trend analysis using regression analysis and the application of these techniques in forecasting product and service volumes.
- Fixed, variable, semi-variable and activity-based categorisations of cost and their application in projecting financial results.
- What-if analysis based on alternate projections of volumes, prices and cost structures and the use of spreadsheets in facilitating these analyses.
- The purposes of budgets and conflicts that can arise (e.g. between budgets for realistic planning and budgets based on 'hard to achieve' targets for motivation).
- The creation of budgets including incremental approaches, zero-based budgeting and activity-based budgets.
- The use of budgets in planning: 'rolling budgets' for adaptive planning.
- The use of budgets for control: controllable costs and variances based on 'fixed' and 'flexed' budgets. The conceptual link between standard costing and budget flexing.
- Behavioural issues in budgeting: participation in budgeting and its possible beneficial consequences for ownership and motivation; participation in budgeting and its possible adverse consequences for 'budget padding' and manipulation; setting budget targets for motivation etc.
- Criticisms of budgeting and the recommendations of the advocates of the balanced scorecard and 'beyond budgeting'.

D - CONTROL AND PERFORMANCE MEASUREMENT OF RESPONSIBILITY CENTRES – 20%

Learning outcomes

On completion of their studies students should be able to:

- discuss the use of cost, revenue, profit and investment centres in devising organisation structure and in management control;
- prepare cost information in appropriate formats for cost centre managers, taking due account of controllable/uncontrollable costs and the importance of budget flexing;
- prepare revenue and cost information in appropriate formats for profit and investment centre managers, taking due account of cost variability, attributable costs, controllable costs and identification of appropriate measures of profit centre 'contribution';
- calculate and apply measures of performance for investment centres (often 'strategic business units' or divisions of larger groups);
- discuss the likely behavioural consequences of the use of performance metrics in managing cost, profit and investment centres;
- explain the typical consequences of a divisional structure for performance measurement as divisions compete or trade with each other;
- identify the likely consequences of different approaches to transfer pricing for divisional decision making, divisional and group profitability, the motivation of divisional management and the autonomy of individual divisions.

Syllabus content

- Organisation structure and its implications for responsibility accounting.
- Presentation of financial information including issues of controllable/uncontrollable costs, variable/fixed costs and tracing revenues and costs to particular cost objects.
- Return on investment and its deficiencies; the emergence of residual income and economic value added to address these.
- Behavioural issues in the application of performance measures in cost, profit and investment centres.
- The theory of transfer pricing, including perfect, imperfect and no market for the intermediate good.
- Use of negotiated, market, cost-plus and variable cost based transfer prices. 'Dual' transfer prices and lump sum payments as means of addressing some of the issues that arise.
- The interaction of transfer pricing and tax liabilities in international operations and implications for currency management and possible distortion of internal company operations in order to comply with Tax Authority directives.

REVISION GUIDANCE

Planning your revision

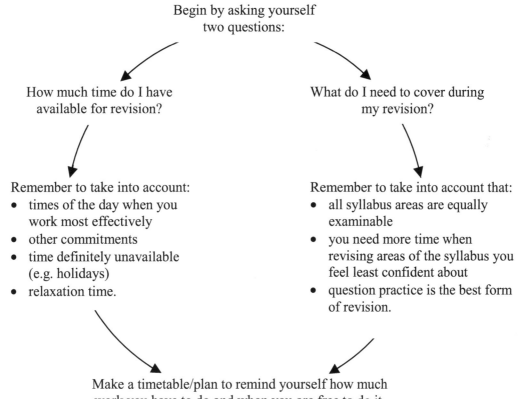

Revision techniques

- Go through your notes and textbook **highlighting the important points**
- You might want to produce your own set of **summarised notes**
- **List key words** for each topic to remind you of the essential concepts
- **Practise exam-standard questions**, under timed conditions
- **Rework questions** that you got completely wrong the first time, but only when you think you know the subject better
- If you get stuck on topics, **find someone to explain** them to you (your tutor or a colleague, for example)
- **Read recent articles** on the CIMA website and in *Financial Management*
- **Read** good newspapers and professional journals.

THE EXAM

Format of the exam

There will be a written exam paper of three hours, with the following sections: *Number of marks*

Section A	A variety of compulsory objective test questions, each worth 2 to 4 marks.	40
Section B	Six compulsory short answer questions, each worth 5 marks.	30
Section C	One question, from a choice of two, each worth 30 marks.	<u>30</u>
	Total:	100

About the exam

- You are allowed 20-minutes' **reading time** before the examination begins.
- Where you have a **choice of question**, decide which questions you will do. Unless you know exactly how to answer the question, spend some time **planning** your answer.
- **Divide the time** you spend on questions in proportion to the marks on offer. One suggestion is to allocate 1½ minutes to each mark available, so a 10-mark question should be completed in 15 minutes.
- Stick to the question and **tailor your answer** to what you are asked.
- If you do not understand what a question is asking, **state your assumptions**. Even if you do not answer in precisely the way the examiner hoped, you should be given some credit, if your assumptions are reasonable.
- If you **get completely stuck** with a question, leave space in your answer book and **return to it later.**
- Spend the last **five minutes** reading through your answers and **making any additions or corrections**.
- You should do everything you can to make things easy for the marker. The marker will find it easier to identify the points you have made if your **answers are legible**.
- **Objective test questions** include true/false questions, matching pairs of text and graphic, sequencing and ranking, labelling diagrams and single and multiple numeric entry**,** but could also involve paragraphs of text which require you to fill in a number of missing blanks, or for you to write a definition of a word or phrase, or to enter a formula. With multiple choice questions you have to choose the correct answer (and there is only *one* correct answer) from a list of possible answers.
- **Essay questions**: Your essay should have a clear structure. It should contain a brief introduction, a main section and a conclusion. Be concise. It is better to write a little about a lot of different points than a great deal about one or two points.
- **Computations**: It is essential to include all your workings in your answers. Many computational questions require the use of a standard format: company income statement, balance sheet and cash flow statement for example. Be sure you know these formats thoroughly before the examination and use the layouts that you see in the answers given in this book and in model answers.
- **Scenario-based questions:** read the scenario carefully, identify the area in which there is a problem, outline the main principles/theories you are going to use to answer the question, and then apply the principles/theories to the scenario.
- **Reports, memos and other documents**: some questions ask you to present your answer in the form of a report or a memo or other document. So use the correct format – there could be easy marks to gain here.

MATHEMATICAL TABLES AND FORMULAE

Area under the normal curve

This table gives the area under the normal curve between the mean and a point Z standard deviations above the mean. The corresponding area for deviations below the mean can be found by symmetry.

$Z = \frac{(x-\mu)}{\sigma}$	0.00	0.01	0.02	0.03	0.04	0.05	0.06	0.07	0.08	0.09
0.0	.0000	.0040	.0080	.0120	.0159	.0199	.0239	.0279	.0319	.0359
0.1	.0398	.0438	.0478	.0517	.0557	.0596	.0636	.0675	.0714	.0753
0.2	.0793	.0832	.0871	.0910	.0948	.0987	.1026	.1064	.1103	.1141
0.3	.1179	.1217	.1255	.1293	.1331	.1368	.1406	.1443	.1408	.1517
0.4	.1554	.1591	.1628	.1664	.1700	.1736	.1772	.1808	.1844	.1879
0.5	.1915	.1950	.1985	.2019	.2054	.2088	.2123	.2157	.2190	.2224
0.6	.2257	.2291	.2324	.2357	.2389	.2422	.2454	.2486	.2518	.2549
0.7	.2580	.2611	.2642	.2673	.2704	.2734	.2764	.2794	.2823	.2852
0.8	.2881	.2910	.2939	.2967	.2995	.3023	.3051	.3078	.3106	.3133
0.9	.3159	.3186	.3212	.3238	.3264	.3289	.3315	.3340	.3365	.3389
1.0	.3413	.3438	.3461	.3485	.3508	.3531	.3554	.3577	.3599	.3621
1.1	.3643	.3665	.3686	.3708	.3729	.3749	.3770	.3790	.3810	.3830
1.2	.3849	.3869	.3888	.3907	.3925	.3944	.3962	.3980	.3997	.4015
1.3	.4032	.4049	.4066	.4082	4099	.4115	.4131	.4147	.4162	.4177
1.4	.4192	.4207	.4222	.4236	.4251	.4265	.4279	.4292	.4306	.4319
1.5	.4332	.4345	.4357	.4370	.4382	.4394	.4406	.4418	.4430	.4441
1.6	.4452	.4463	.4474	.4485	.4495	.4505	.4515	.4525	.4535	.4545
1.7	.4554	.4564	.4573	.4582	.4591	.4599	.4608	.4616	.4625	.4633
1.8	.4641	.4649	.4656	.4664	.4671	.4678	.4686	.4693	.4699	.4706
1.9	.4713	.4719	.4726	.4732	.4738	.4744	.4750	.4756	.4762	.4767
2.0	.4772	.4778	.4783	.4788	.4793	.4798	.4803	.4808	.4812	.4817
2.1	.4821	.4826	.4830	.4834	.4838	.4842	.4846	.4850	.4854	.4857
2.2	.4861	.4865	.4868	.4871	.4875	.4878	.4881	.4884	.4887	.4890
2.3	.4893	.4896	.4898	.4901	.4904	.4906	.4909	.4911	.4913	.4916
2.4	.4918	.4920	.4922	.4925	.4927	.4929	.4931	.4932	.4934	.4936
2.5	.4938	.4940	.4941	.4943	.4945	.4946	.4948	.4949	.4951	.4952
2.6	.4953	.4955	.4956	.4957	.4959	.4960	.4961	.4962	4963	.4964
2.7	.4965	.4966	.4967	.4968	.4969	.4970	.4971	.4972	.4973	.4974
2.8	.4974	.4975	.4976	.4977	.4977	.4978	.4979	.4980	.4980	.4981
2.9	.4981	.4982	.4983	.4983	.4984	.4984	.4985	.4985	.4986	.4986
3.0	.49865	.4987	.4987	.4988	.4988	.4989	.4989	.4989	.4990	.4990
3.1	.49903	.4991	.4991	.4991	.4992	.4992	.4992	.4992	.4993	.4993
3.2	.49931	.4993	.4994	.4994	.4994	.4994	.4994	.4995	.4995	.4995
3.3	.49952	.4995	.4995	.4996	.4996	.4996	.4996	.4996	.4996	.4997
3.4	.49966	.4997	.4997	.4997	.4997	.4997	.4997	.4997	.4997	.4998
3.5	.49977									

Present value table

Present value of $1 i.e. $(1 + r)^{-n}$ where r = interest rate, n = number of periods until payment or receipt.

Periods (n)	1%	2%	3%	4%	5%	6%	7%	8%	9%	10%
1	.990	.980	.971	.962	.962	.943	.935	.926	.917	.909
2	.980	.961	.943	.925	.907	.890	.873	.857	.842	.826
3	.971	.942	.915	.889	.864	.840	.816	.794	.772	.751
4	.961	.924	.888	.855	.823	.792	.763	.735	.708	.683
5	.951	.906	.863	.822	.784	.747	.713	.681	.650	.621
6	.942	.888	.837	.790	.746	.705	.666	.630	.596	.564
7	.933	.871	.813	.760	.711	.665	.623	.583	.547	.513
8	.923	.853	.789	.731	.677	.627	.582	.540	.502	.467
9	.914	.837	.766	.703	.645	.592	.544	.500	.460	.424
10	.905	.820	.744	.676	.614	.558	.508	.463	.422	.386
11	.896	.804	.722	.650	.585	.527	.475	.429	.388	.350
12	.887	.788	.701	.625	.557	.497	.444	.397	.356	.319
13	.879	.773	.681	.601	.530	.469	.415	.368	.326	.290
14	.870	.758	.661	.577	.505	.442	.388	.340	.299	.263
15	.861	.743	.642	.555	.481	.417	.362	.315	.275	.239
16	.853	.728	.623	.534	.458	.394	.339	.292	.252	.218
17	.844	.714	.605	.513	.436	.371	.317	.270	.231	.198
18	.836	.700	.587	.494	.416	.350	.296	.250	.212	.180
19	.828	.686	.570	.475	.396	.331	.277	.232	.194	.164
20	.820	.673	.554	.456	.377	.312	.258	.215	.178	.149

Periods (n)	11%	12%	13%	14%	15%	16%	17%	18%	19%	20%
1	.901	.893	.885	.877	.870	.862	.855	.847	.840	.833
2	.812	.797	.783	.769	.756	.743	.731	.718	.706	.694
3	.731	.712	.693	.675	.658	.641	.624	.609	.593	.579
4	.659	.636	.613	.592	.572	.552	.534	.516	.499	.482
5	.593	.567	.543	.519	.497	.476	.456	.437	.419	.402
6	.535	.507	.480	.456	.432	.410	.390	.370	.352	.335
7	.482	.452	.425	.400	.376	.354	.333	.314	.296	.279
8	.434	.404	.376	.351	.327	.305	.285	.266	.249	.233
9	.391	.361	.333	.308	.284	.263	.243	.225	.209	.194
10	.352	.322	.295	.270	.247	.227	.208	.191	.176	.162
11	.317	.287	.261	.237	.215	.195	.178	.162	.148	.135
12	.286	.257	.231	.208	.187	.168	.152	.137	.124	.112
13	.258	.229	.204	.182	.163	.145	.130	.116	.104	.093
14	.232	.205	.181	.160	.141	.125	.111	.099	.088	.078
15	.209	.183	.160	.140	.123	.108	.095	.084	.074	.065
16	.188	.163	.141	.123	.107	.093	.081	.071	.062	.054
17	.170	.146	.125	.108	.093	.080	.069	.060	.052	.045
18	.153	.130	.111	.095	.081	.069	.059	.051	.044	.038
19	.138	.116	.098	.083	.070	.060	.051	.043	.037	.031
20	.124	.104	.087	.073	.061	.051	.043	.037	.031	.026

Cumulative present value of $1

This table shows the Present Value of $1 per annum, Receivable or Payable at the end of each year for n years $\dfrac{1-(1+r)^{-n}}{r}$.

Periods (n)	\multicolumn{10}{c}{Interest rates (r)}									
	1%	2%	3%	4%	5%	6%	7%	8%	9%	10%
1	0.990	0.980	0.971	0.962	0.952	0.943	0.935	0.926	0.917	0.909
2	1.970	1.942	1.913	1.886	1.859	1.833	1.808	1.783	1.759	1.736
3	2.941	2.884	2.829	2.775	2.723	2.673	2.624	2.577	2.531	2.487
4	3.902	3.808	3.717	3.630	3.546	3.465	3.387	3.312	3.240	3.170
5	4.853	4.713	4.580	4.452	4.329	4.212	4.100	3.993	3.890	3.791
6	5.795	5.601	5.417	5.242	5.076	4.917	4.767	4.623	4.486	4.355
7	6.728	6.472	6.230	6.002	5.786	5.582	5.389	5.206	5.033	4.868
8	7.652	7.325	7.020	6.733	6.463	6.210	5.971	5.747	5.535	5.335
9	8.566	8.162	7.786	7.435	7.108	6.802	6.515	6.247	5.995	5.759
10	9.471	8.983	8.530	8.111	7.722	7.360	7.024	6.710	6.418	6.145
11	10.368	9.787	9.253	8.760	8.306	7.887	7.499	7.139	6.805	8.495
12	11.255	10.575	9.954	9.385	8.863	8.384	7.943	7.536	7.161	6.814
13	12.134	11.348	10.635	9.986	9.394	8.853	8.358	7.904	7.487	7.103
14	13.004	12.106	11.296	10.563	9.899	9.295	8.745	8.244	7.786	7.367
15	13.865	12.849	11.938	11.118	10.380	9.712	9.108	8.559	8.061	7.606
16	14.718	13.578	12.561	11.652	10.838	10.106	9.447	8.851	8.313	7.824
17	15.562	14.292	13.166	12.166	11.274	10.477	9.763	9.122	8.544	8.022
18	16.398	14.992	13.754	12.659	11.690	10.828	10.059	9.372	8.756	8.201
19	17.226	15.679	14.324	13.134	12.085	11.158	10.336	9.604	8.950	8.365
20	18.046	16.351	14.878	13.590	12.462	11.470	10.594	9.818	9.129	8.514

Periods (n)	\multicolumn{10}{c}{Interest rates (r)}									
	11%	12%	13%	14%	15%	16%	17%	18%	19%	20%
1	0.901	0.893	0.885	0.877	0.870	0.862	0.855	0.847	0.840	0.833
2	1.713	1.690	1.668	1.647	1.626	1.605	1.585	1.566	1.547	1.528
3	2.444	2.402	2.361	2.322	2.283	2.246	2.210	2.174	2.140	2.106
4	3.102	3.037	2.974	2.914	2.855	2.798	2.743	2.690	2.639	2.589
5	3.696	3.605	3.517	3.433	3.352	3.274	3.199	3.127	3.058	2.991
6	4.231	4.111	3.998	3.889	3.784	3.685	3.589	3.498	3.410	3.326
7	4.712	4.564	4.423	4.288	4.160	4.039	3.922	3.812	3.706	3.605
8	5.146	4.968	4.799	4.639	4.487	4.344	4.207	4.078	3.954	3.837
9	5.537	5.328	5.132	4.946	4.772	4.607	4.451	4.303	4.163	4.031
10	5.889	5.650	5.426	5.216	5.019	4.833	4.659	4.494	4.339	4.192
11	6.207	5.938	5.687	5.453	5.234	5.029	4.836	4.656	4.486	4.327
12	6.492	6.194	5.918	5.660	5.421	5.197	4.968	4.793	4.611	4.439
13	6.750	6.424	6.122	5.842	5.583	5.342	5.118	4.910	4.715	4.533
14	6.982	6.628	6.302	6.002	5.724	5.468	5.229	5.008	4.802	4.611
15	7.191	6.811	6.462	6.142	5.847	5.575	5.324	5.092	4.876	4.675
16	7.379	6.974	6.604	6.265	5.954	5.668	5.405	5.162	4.938	4.730
17	7.549	7.120	6.729	6.373	6.047	5.749	5.475	5.222	4.990	4.775
18	7.702	7.250	6.840	6.467	6.128	5.818	5.534	5.273	5.033	4.812
19	7.839	7.366	6.938	6.550	6.198	5.877	5.584	5.316	5.070	4.843
20	7.963	7.469	7.025	6.623	6.259	5.929	5.628	5.353	5.101	4.870

Formulae

Probability

$A \cup B$ = **A or B**. $A \cap B$ = **A and B** (overlap)

$P(B/A)$ = probability of B, **given** A

Rules of Addition

If A and B are mutually exclusive: $\quad P(A \cup B) = P(A) + P(B)$

If A and B are **not** mutually exclusive: $\quad P(A \cup B) = P(A) + P(B) - P(A \cap B)$

Rules of Multiplication

If A and B are independent: $\quad P(A \cap B) = P(A)*P(B)$

If A and B are **not** independent: $\quad P(A \cap B) = P(A)*P(B/A)$

$E(X)$ = expected value = probability*payoff

Quadratic Equations

If $ax^2 + bx + c = 0$ is the general quadratic equation, then the two solutions (roots) are given by:

$$x = \frac{-b \pm \sqrt{b^2 - 4ac}}{2a}$$

Descriptive statistics

Arithmetic Mean

$$\bar{x} = \frac{\Sigma x}{n} \text{ or } \bar{x} = \frac{\Sigma fx}{\Sigma f} \text{ (frequency distribution)}$$

Standard Deviation

$$SD = \sqrt{\frac{\Sigma(x-\bar{x})^2}{n}} \quad SD = \sqrt{\frac{\Sigma fx^2}{\Sigma f} - \bar{x}^2} \text{ (frequency distribution)}$$

Index numbers

Price relative = $100*P_1/P_0$ $\qquad$ Quantity relative = $100*Q_1/Q_0$

Price: $\quad \dfrac{\Sigma w * \left(\dfrac{P_1}{P_0}\right)}{\Sigma w} \times 100$

Quantity: $\quad \dfrac{\Sigma w * \left(\dfrac{Q_1}{Q_0}\right)}{\Sigma w} \times 100$

Time series

Additive Model

Series $\quad = \quad$ Trend + Seasonal + Random

Multiplicative Model

Series $\quad = \quad$ Trend * Seasonal * Random

MATHEMATICAL TABLES AND FORMULAE

Linear regression and correlation

The linear regression equation of y on x is given by:

$y = a + bx$ or $y - \bar{y} = b(x - \bar{x})$

where

$$b = \frac{\text{Covariance}(xy)}{\text{Variance}(x)} = \frac{n\Sigma xy - (\Sigma x)(\Sigma y)}{n\Sigma x^2 - (\Sigma x)^2}$$

and $\quad a = \bar{y} - b\bar{x}$

Or solve

$$\Sigma y = na + b\Sigma x$$
$$\Sigma xy = a\Sigma x + b\Sigma x^2$$

Coefficient of correlation

$$r = \frac{\text{Covariance}(xy)}{\sqrt{\text{Var}(x).\text{Var}(y)}} = \frac{n\Sigma xy - (\Sigma x)(\Sigma y)}{\sqrt{\{n\Sigma x^2 - (\Sigma x)^2\}\{n\Sigma y^2 - (\Sigma y)^2\}}}$$

$$R(\text{rank}) = 1 - \frac{6\Sigma d^2}{n(n^2 - 1)}$$

Financial mathematics

Compound Interest (Values and Sums)

Future value of S, of a sum X, inverted for n periods, compounded at r% interest

$S = X[1 + r]^n$

Annuity

Present value of an annuity of £1 per annum receivable or payable for n years, commencing in one year, discounted at r% per annum:

$$PV = \frac{1}{r} - \left[1 - \frac{1}{[1+r]^n}\right]$$

Perpetuity

Present value of $1 per annum, payable or receivable in perpetuity, commencing in one year, discounted at r% per annum.

$$PV = \frac{1}{r}$$

Section 1

SECTION A-TYPE QUESTIONS

All questions in this section carry two marks each, unless otherwise stated.

COST ACCOUNTING SYSTEMS

1   A business reported a marginal costing profit of $45,000 last period. Its inventory values for the period were as follows:

	$
Opening inventory	16,000
Closing inventory	20,800

If the business had used absorption costing, the inventory values would have been as follows:

	$
Opening inventory	28,000
Closing inventory	36,400

What would have been the reported profit using absorption costing?

A $41,400

B $48,600

C $57,000

D $60,600

2   A company has a budget to produce 5,000 units of Product B in December. The budget for December shows that, for Product B, the opening inventory will be 400 units and the closing inventory will be 900 units. The monthly budgeted production cost data for Product B for December is as follows:

Variable direct costs per unit	$6.00
Variable production overhead costs per unit	$3.50
Total fixed production overhead costs	$29,500

The company absorbs overheads on the basis of the budgeted number of units produced.

The budgeted profit for Product B for December, using **absorption costing**, is:

A $2,950 lower than it would be using marginal costing

B $2,950 greater than it would be using marginal costing

C $4,700 lower than it would be using marginal costing

D $4,700 greater than it would be using marginal costing.

PAPER P1 : MANAGEMENT ACCOUNTING – PERFORMANCE EVALUATION

3   The following details have been extracted from the budget papers of LK for June:

Selling price per unit $124
Variable production costs per unit $54
Fixed production costs per unit $36
Other variable costs per unit $12
Sales volume   12,500 units
Production volume   13,250 units
Opening inventory of finished items   980 units

If budgeted profit statements were prepared by using absorption costing and then by using marginal costing:

A   marginal costing profits would be higher by $27,000

B   absorption costing profits would be higher by $27,000

C   absorption costing profits would be higher by $35,000

D   absorption costing profits would be higher by $62,000.

4   A plumbing company uses absorption costing within its job costing environment. Overheads are absorbed at a rate of 150 per cent of direct labour cost.

An extract from the production records for the latest week is as follows:

Job number	Opening balance	Costs incurred during week		Status at end of week
		Direct material	Direct labour	
	€	€	€	€
427	87	190	200	Complete
428	194	318	152	Incomplete
429	–	79	40	Incomplete
430	–	188	420	Complete

Which of the following entries would be made in the cost ledger?

	Debit		Credit	
A	Work-in-progress	€1,085	Cost of sales	€1,085
B	Work-in-progress	€2,015	Cost of sales	€2,015
C	Cost of sales	€1,085	Work-in-progress	€1,085
D	Cost of sales	€2,015	Work-in-progress	€2,015

5   A manufacturing business uses absorption costing and absorbs production overhead using a direct labour hour rate of €7 per hour. Data for last period are as follows:

Direct labour hours worked   4,744
Production overhead incurred   €34,789

Which of the following entries would be recorded in the cost ledger?

	Debit		Credit	
A	Production overhead control	€1,581	Work-in-progress	€1,581
B	Work-in-progress	€1,581	Production overhead control	€1,581
C	Costing income statement	€1,581	Production overhead control	€1,581
D	Production overhead control	€1,581	Costing income statement	€1,581

6   XYZ manufactures its product through a series of processes. The FIFO method of valuing opening work-in-process is used, and the following details relate to September.

Opening work-in-process was 600 units, each 80% processed as to materials and 60% processed as to conversion costs.

Normal loss was 500 units, fully completed.

Finished output was 14,500 units; there were no abnormal losses or gains.

Closing work-in-process was 800 units, each 70% processed as to materials and 40% processed as to conversion costs.

When calculating the costs per equivalent unit, the number of equivalent units to be used are:

	Materials	Conversion
A	14,580	14,460
B	14,940	14,580
C	15,180	15,060
D	15,540	15,180

7   In process costing, where losses have a positive scrap value, when an abnormal gain arises the abnormal gain account is:

A   debited with the normal production cost of the abnormal gain units

B   debited with the normal production cost of the abnormal gain units and credited with the scrap value of the abnormal gain units

C   credited with the normal production cost of the abnormal gain units and debited with the scrap value of the abnormal gain units

D   credited with the normal production cost of the abnormal gain units and credited with the scrap value of the abnormal gain units.

8   In process costing, if an abnormal loss arises, the process account is generally:

A   debited with the scrap value of the abnormal loss units

B   debited with the full production cost of the abnormal loss units

C   credited with the scrap value of the abnormal loss units

D   credited with the full production cost of the abnormal loss units.

9   KL Processing has identified that an abnormal gain of 160 litres occurred in its refining process last week. Normal losses are expected and have a scrap value of $2.00 per litre. All losses are 100% complete as to material cost and 75% complete as to conversion costs.

The company uses the weighted average method of valuation and last week's output was valued using the following costs per equivalent unit:

    Materials $9.40
    Conversion costs $11.20

The effect on the income statement of last week's abnormal gain is:

A   Debit $2,528
B   Debit $2,848
C   Credit $2,528
D   Credit $2,848

PAPER P1 : MANAGEMENT ACCOUNTING – PERFORMANCE EVALUATION

10 Explain in less than 50 words three circumstances where the FIFO valuation method of process costing will give very similar results to the Weighted Average valuation method. **(3 marks)**

11 Three products P, Q and R are produced together in a common process. Products P and Q are sold without further processing, but Product R requires an additional process before it can be sold. No inventories are held. There is no loss of volume in the additional process for Product R.

The following data apply to March:

Output	Product P	3,600 litres
	Product Q	4,100 litres
	Product R	2,800 litres
Selling prices	Product P	$4.60 per litre
	Product Q	$6.75 per litre
	Product R	$10.50 per litre

Costs incurred in the common process $42,500
Costs incurred in the additional process for R $19,600

Calculate the value of the common process costs that would be allocated to Product R using the sales proxy method (notional sales value method). **(3 marks)**

12 S, a food processing company, uses the First In First Out method when costing its monthly output. The following details relate to October:

Opening work-in-progress	10,000 kgs	90% complete as to raw ingredients and 40% converted
Raw ingredients added	34,880 kgs	
Output	30,500 kgs	
Normal loss		15% of raw ingredients added in the period
Closing work-in-process	9,700 kgs	85% complete as to raw ingredients and 35% converted

The number of equivalent kgs that would be used when calculating the cost per kg in relation to raw ingredients and conversion costs for October would be nearest to:

	Raw ingredients	Conversion
A	38,200	27,300
B	29,200	29,300
C	29,700	29,900
D	30,300	30,300

SECTION A-TYPE QUESTIONS : SECTION 1

13 A plastics company operates a process in which all materials are added at the beginning of the process. At the beginning of March, the work-in-process in a plastic moulding machine was 200 units, which were 25% complete with respect to conversion costs. During March, 1,400 units were completed and transferred to the next process. Also during March, 50 units were scrapped due to an operator error at the end of the process, although it is unusual for this to occur. At the end of March, there were 200 units in process, which were 50% complete with respect to conversion costs.

Using the First In First Out (FIFO) method, calculate the equivalent units of production for the month of March that would be used in the computation of the cost per equivalent unit for:

(a) material costs **(2 marks)**

(b) conversion costs. **(2 marks)**

(Total: 4 marks)

14 A is a food processing company. The following data have been produced for one of its processes for April. There were no inventories in the process at the beginning or end of the month.

	$
Inputs: 2,400 kg at $8 per kg	19,200
Process costs	4,800
Transferred to packing department: 2,060 kg	22,889

There is usually a loss of 10% by weight of inputs during the process. The normal loss does not have a sale value.

During April there was an abnormal loss that was sold for $400.

Prepare the process account and the abnormal loss account to record the events that occurred in this process during April. **(4 marks)**

15 Company B uses a throughput accounting system. The details of product X per unit are as follows:

Selling price	€50
Material cost	€16
Conversion costs	€20

Time on bottleneck resource   8 minutes

The return per hour for product X is:

A €105
B €225
C €255
D €375

16 A company produces two products, S and T, which pass through two production processes, X and Y. The time taken to make each product in each process is:

	Product S	Product T
Process X	5 mins	7.5 mins
Process Y	18 mins	12 mins

The company operates a 15-hour day and the processes have an average downtime each day of:

Process X	1.5 hours
Process Y	1.0 hours

The costs and revenue for each unit of each product are:

	Product S $	Product T $
Direct materials	20.00	20.00
Direct labour	18.00	14.00
Variable overhead	4.00	4.00
Fixed costs	5.00	4.00
Total cost	47.00	42.00
Selling price	$95.00	$85.00

Sales demand restricts the output of S and T to 50 and 80 units a day respectively.

(a) Identify which of the processes is the bottleneck process. **(2 marks)**

(b) Determine the daily production plan that would maximise the throughput contribution. **(3 marks)**

(Total: 5 marks)

17 What is defined as 'an activity within an organisation which has a lower capacity than preceding or subsequent activities, thereby limiting throughput'?

A   Bottleneck
B   Constraint
C   Limiting factor
D   Restraint

18 MB manufactures a product that requires 3.75 hours per unit of machining time. Machine time is a bottleneck resource, because there is a limited number of machines.

There are just seven machines, and each is available for up to 15 hours each day, five days a week. The product has a selling price of $100 per unit, a direct material cost of $40 per unit, a direct labour cost of $10 per unit and a factory overhead cost of $30 per unit. These costs are based on a weekly production and sales volume of 140 units.

What is the throughput accounting ratio?

A   0.67
B   1.50
C   1.67
D   5.33

SECTION A-TYPE QUESTIONS : SECTION 1

The following data relate to Questions 19 and 20.

A company produces three products using three different machines. The following data is available for December:

Product	A	B	C
Contribution per unit	$12	$10	$6
Machine hours required per unit			
Machine 1	6	2	1
Machine 2	9	3	1.5
Machine 3	3	1	0.5
Estimated sales demand (units)	200	200	200

Maximum machine capacity is 1,600 hours per machine.

Total factory cost for December is $3,200.

19 (a) Calculate the machine utilisation rates for each machine for December. **(2 marks)**

(b) Identify which of the machines is the bottleneck machine. **(2 marks)**

(Total: 4 marks)

20 (a) State the recommended procedure given by Goldratt in his 'Theory of Constraints' for dealing with a bottleneck activity. **(2 marks)**

(b) Calculate the optimum allocation of the bottleneck machine hours to the three products. **(3 marks)**

The following data relate to Questions 21 and 22.

The following data relate to a manufacturing company. At the beginning of August there was no inventory. During August 2,000 units of Product X were produced, but only 1,750 units were sold. The financial data for Product X for August were as follows:

	$
Materials	40,000
Labour	12,600
Variable production overheads	9,400
Fixed production overheads	22,500
Variable selling costs	6,000
Fixed selling costs	19,300
Total costs for X for August	109,800

21 The value of inventory of X at 31 August using a marginal costing approach is:

A $6,575
B $7,750
C $8,500
D $10,562 **(2 marks)**

22 The value of inventory of X at 31 August using a throughput accounting approach is:

A $5,000
B $6,175
C $6,575
D $13,725 **(2 marks)**

KAPLAN PUBLISHING

PAPER P1 : MANAGEMENT ACCOUNTING – PERFORMANCE EVALUATION

The following data relate to Questions 23 to 25.

SM makes two products, Z1 and Z2. Its machines can only work on one product at a time. The two products are worked on in two departments by differing grades of labour. The labour requirements for the two products are as follows:

	Minutes per unit of product	
	Z1	Z2
Department 1	12	16
Department 2	20	15

There is currently a shortage of labour and the maximum times available each day in Departments 1 and 2 are 480 minutes and 840 minutes, respectively.

The current selling prices and costs for the two products are shown below:

	Z1	Z2
	$ per unit	$ per unit
Selling price	50.00	65.00
Direct materials	10.00	15.00
Direct labour	10.40	6.20
Variable overheads	6.40	9.20
Fixed overheads	12.80	18.40
Profit per unit	10.40	16.20

As part of the budget-setting process, SM needs to know the optimum output levels. All output is sold.

23 Calculate the maximum number of each product that could be produced each day, and identify the limiting factor/bottleneck. **(3 marks)**

24 Using traditional contribution analysis, calculate the 'profit-maximising' output each day, and the contribution at this level of output. **(3 marks)**

25 Using a throughput approach, calculate the 'throughput-maximising' output each day, and the 'throughput contribution' at this level of output. **(3 marks)**

26 A business manufactures a single product which sells for $45 per unit. The budgeted data for the latest period are as follows:

Production and sales volume	2,000 units
	$
Material cost	13,500
Direct labour cost	11,800
Production overhead	32,400
Non-production overhead	21,900

Actual production volume and costs were as budgeted for the period but the actual sales volume achieved was 1,800 units. There was no inventory at the beginning of the period. Calculate the profit for the period using:

(a) absorption costing **(2 marks)**

(b) marginal costing **(2 marks)**

(c) throughput accounting. **(2 marks)**

(Total: 6 marks)

27 When building up the cost of a product or service using activity-based costing, which of the following would be used as levels of classification?

   (i)   Facility
   (ii)   Product
   (iii) Batch
   (iv)   Unit
   (v)   Value added
   (vi)   Non-value added

   A   All of them
   B   (ii), (iii) and (v) only
   C   (i), (iv) and (vi) only
   D   (i), (ii), (iii) and (iv)

28 A food-processing company operates an activity based costing (ABC) system. Which of the following would be classified as a facility-sustaining activity?

   (i)   General staff administration
   (ii)   Plant management
   (iii) Technical support for individual products and services
   (iv)   Updating of product specification database
   (v)   Property management

   A   (i) and (ii)
   B   (i), (ii) and (v)
   C   (ii), (iii) and (iv)
   D   (ii), (iii), (iv) and (v)
   E   All of them

29 P operates an activity based costing (ABC) system to attribute its overhead costs to cost objects.

   In its budget for the year ending 31 August 20X6, the company expected to place a total of 2,895 purchase orders at a total cost of $110,010. This activity and its related costs were budgeted to occur at a constant rate throughout the budget year, which is divided into 13 four-week periods.

   During the four-week period ended 30 June 20X6, a total of 210 purchase orders were placed at a cost of $7,650.

   The over-recovery of these costs for the four-week period was:

   A $330
   B $350
   C $370
   D $390

30 Which of the following statements are correct?

(i) A cost driver is any factor that causes a change in the cost of an activity.

(ii) For long-term variable overhead costs, the cost driver will be the volume of activity.

(iii) Traditional absorption costing tends to under-allocate overhead costs to low-volume products.

A (i) and (iii) only

B (ii) and (iii) only

C (i) and (ii) only

D (i), (ii) and (iii)

The following data relate to Questions 31 and 32.

DRP has recently introduced an Activity Based Costing system. It manufactures three products, details of which are set out below:

	Product D	Product R	Product P
Budgeted annual production (units)	100,000	100,000	50,000
Batch size (units)	100	50	25
Machine set-ups per batch	3	4	6
Purchase orders per batch	2	1	1
Processing time per unit (minutes)	2	3	3

Three cost pools have been identified. Their budgeted costs for the year ending 31 December 20X4 are as follows:

Machine set-up costs $150,000

Purchasing of materials $70,000

Processing $80,000

---

31 Calculate the annual budgeted number of:

(a) batches

(b) machine set-ups

(c) purchase orders

(d) processing minutes. **(4 marks)**

32 Calculate the budgeted overhead unit cost for Product R for inclusion in the budget for 20X4.

(4 marks)

33 Explain in less than 50 words, why the costs absorbed by a product using an activity based costing approach could be higher than those absorbed if a traditional labour-based absorption system were used, and identify TWO implications of this for management.

(4 marks)

SECTION A-TYPE QUESTIONS : SECTION 1

34 Which of the following statements about JIT is correct?

- A JIT protects an organisation against risks of disruption in the supply chain.
- B A narrow geographical spread in a business makes JIT more difficult to apply.
- C With JIT, there is a risk that stocks could become obsolete.
- D JIT is more difficult to implement when it is not easy to predict patterns of demand.

35 Which of the following are aspects of a successful JIT system?

- (i) Demand-driven production
- (ii) Savings in total machine set-up time
- (iii) Grouping machines or workers by product or component rather than by the type of work performed

- A (i) only
- B (i) and (ii) only
- C (i) and (iii) only
- D (ii) and (iii) only

36 Which of the following are usually elements of a JIT system?

- (i) Machine cells
- (ii) High levels of raw materials and work-in-progress
- (iii) Close relationship with major suppliers

- A (i) and (ii) only
- B (i) and (iii) only
- C (ii) and (iii) only
- D (iii) only

37 In the context of quality costs, training costs and reworking costs are classified as:

	Training costs	Reworking costs
A	internal failure costs	external failure costs
B	prevention costs	external failure costs
C	external failure costs	internal failure costs
D	prevention costs	internal failure costs

38 MN uses a Just-in-Time (JIT) system and backflush accounting. It does not use a raw material stock control account. During April, 1,000 units were produced and sold. The standard cost per unit is $100: this includes materials of $45. During April, conversion costs of $60,000 were incurred.

What was the debit balance on the cost of goods sold account for April?

- A $90,000
- B $95,000
- C $105,000
- D $110,000

KAPLAN PUBLISHING

39

Which feature distinguishes backflush accounting from other systems?

A Costs are attached when output is completed or sold.

B Cost records reflect the flow of work through the production process.

C Entries are not made until the customer pays for goods purchased.

D Material entries are made when the material is received and moved.

40

A company operates a just-in-time purchasing and production system and uses a backflush accounting system with a single trigger point at the point of sale. A summary of the transactions that took place in June (valued at cost) is:

	$
Conversion costs incurred	890,000
Finished goods produced	1,795,000
Finished goods sold	1,700,000
Conversion costs allocated	840,000

The two items debited to the cost of goods sold account in June would be:

	$	$
A	890,000 and	95,000
B	1,700,000 and	50,000
C	1,700,000 and	95,000
D	1,795,000 and	50,000

41

Summary results for Y Limited for March are shown below:

	$000	Units
Sales revenue	820	
Variable production costs	300	
Variable selling costs	105	
Fixed production costs	180	
Fixed selling costs	110	
Production in March		1,000
Opening inventory		0
Closing inventory		150

Using *marginal costing*, the profit for March was:

A $170,000

B $185,750

C $197,000

D $229,250

42 Definition A: 'A technique where the primary goal is to maximise throughput while simultaneously maintaining or decreasing inventory and operating costs.'

Definition B: 'A system whose objective is to produce or procure products or components as they are required by a customer or for use, rather than for inventory.'

Which of the following pairs of terms correctly matches definitions A and B above?

	Definition A	Definition B
A	Manufacturing resource planning	Just-in-time
B	Enterprise resource planning	Material requirements planning
C	Optimised production technology	Enterprise resource planning
D	Optimised production technology	Just-in-time

43 Which of the following statements is/are true?

(i) Computer-integrated manufacturing (CIM) brings together advanced manufacturing technology and modern quality control into a single computerised coherent system.

(ii) Flexible manufacturing systems (FMS) are simple systems with low levels of automation that offer great flexibility through a skilled workforce working in teams.

(iii) Electronic data interchange (EDI) is primarily designed to allow the operating units in an organisation to communicate immediately and automatically with the sales and purchasing functions within the organisation.

A   (i) only

B   (i) and (ii) only

C   (i) and (iii) only

D   (ii) and (iii) only

44 *Definition 1*: 'A system that converts a production schedule into a listing of materials and components required to meet the schedule so that items are available when needed.'

Definition 2: 'An accounting system that focuses on ways by which the maximum return per unit of bottleneck activity can be achieved.'

Which of the following pairs of terms correctly matches definitions 1 and 2 above?

	Definition 1	Definition 2
A	Manufacturing resources planning (MRP2)	Backflush accounting
B	Material requirements planning (MRP1)	Throughput accounting
C	Material requirements planning (MRP1)	Theory of constraints
D	Supply chain management	Throughput accounting

45 A

46 A

47 C

48 Process 2 takes transfers from Process 1 and converts them to finished goods. Additional materials are added during the process. An abnormal loss occurred part way through the process in April. Output data for April are shown below:

	Kg	Equivalent units (kg)		
		From P1	Materials	Conversion
Transferred to finished goods	2,800	2,800	2,800	2,800
Normal loss	200			
Abnormal loss	100	100	100	50
Closing work-in-progress	700	700	700	150

The losses cannot be sold.

Costs incurred during April were:

Transfer from Process 1	$34,200
Materials added	$16,200
Conversion costs	$26,700

There was no opening work-in-progress at the beginning of the month.

Calculate the value of the abnormal loss that will be debited to the abnormal loss account.

(3 marks)

49 Which of the following definitions are correct?

(i) Just-in-time (JIT) systems are designed to produce or procure products or components as they are required for a customer or for use, rather than for inventory.

(ii) Flexible manufacturing systems (FMS) are integrated, computer-controlled production systems, capable of producing any of a range of parts and of switching quickly and economically between them.

(iii) Material requirements planning (MRP) systems are computer-based systems that integrate all aspects of a business so that the planning and scheduling of production ensures components are available when needed.

A (i) only

B (i) and (ii) only

C (i) and (iii) only

D (ii) and (iii) only

50 WTD Ltd produces a single product. The management currently uses marginal costing but is considering using absorption costing in the future.

The budgeted fixed production overheads for the period are $500,000. The budgeted output for the period is 2,000 units. There were 800 units of opening inventory at the beginning of the period and 500 units of closing inventory at the end of the period.

If absorption costing principles were applied, the profit for the period compared to the marginal costing profit would be:

A $75,000 higher.

B $75,000 lower.

C $125,000 higher.

D $125,000 lower.

PAPER P1 : MANAGEMENT ACCOUNTING – PERFORMANCE EVALUATION

51 JJ Ltd manufactures three products: W, X and Y. The products use a series of different machines but there is a common machine that is a bottleneck.

The standard selling price and standard cost per unit for each product for the forthcoming period are as follows:

	W $	X $	Y $
Selling price	200	150	150
Cost			
Direct materials	41	20	30
Labour	30	20	36
Overheads	60	40	50
Profit	69	70	34
Bottleneck machine – minutes per unit	9	10	7

40% of the overhead cost is classified as variable

Using a throughput accounting approach, what would be the ranking of the products for best use of the bottleneck? **(3 marks)**

52 X Ltd has two production departments, Assembly and Finishing, and two service departments, Stores and Maintenance.

Stores provides the following service to the production departments: 60% to Assembly and 40% to Finishing.

Maintenance provides the following service to the production and service departments: 40% to Assembly, 45% to Finishing and 15% to Stores.

The budgeted information for the year is as follows:

Budgeted fixed production overheads
- Assembly $100,000
- Finishing $150,000
- Stores $50,000
- Maintenance $40,000

Budgeted output 100,000 units

At the end of the year after apportioning the service department overheads, the total fixed production overheads debited to the Assembly department's fixed production overhead control account were $180,000.

The actual output achieved was 120,000 units.

Calculate the under-/over-absorption of fixed production overheads for the Assembly department. **(4 marks)**

SECTION A-TYPE QUESTIONS : SECTION 1

53 A company simultaneously produces three products (X, Y and Z) from a single process. X and Y are processed further before they can be sold; Z is a by-product that is sold immediately for $6 per unit without incurring any further costs. The sales prices of X and Y after further processing are $50 per unit and $60 per unit respectively.

Data for October are as follows:

	$
Joint production costs that produced 2,500 units of X, 3,500 units of Y and 3,000 units of Z	140,000
Further processing costs for 2,500 units of X	24,000
Further processing costs for 3,500 units of Y	46,000

Joint costs are apportioned using the final sales value method.

Calculate the total cost of the production of X for October. **(3 marks)**

54 **CW Ltd makes one product in a single process. The details of the process for period 2 were as follows:**

There were 800 units of opening work-in-progress valued as follows:

Material	$98,000
Labour	$46,000
Production overheads	$7,600

During the period 1,800 units were added to the process and the following costs were incurred:

Material	$387,800
Labour	$276,320
Production overheads	$149,280

There were 500 units of closing work-in-progress, which were 100% complete for material, 90% complete for labour and 40% complete for production overheads.

A normal loss equal to 10% of new material input during the period was expected. The actual loss amounted to 180 units. Each unit of loss was sold for $10 per unit.

CW Ltd uses weighted average costing.

Calculate the cost of the output for the period. **(4 marks)**

STANDARD COSTING

55 The materials price variance for the month of January was $2,000 (F) and the usage variance was $450 (F). The standard material usage per unit is 6 kg, and the standard material price is $3.00 per kg. 600 units were produced in the period and there was no change in inventory levels during the period.

Material purchases in the period were:

A 2,000 kg

B 2,933 kg

C 3,450 kg

D 3,600 kg

PAPER P1 : MANAGEMENT ACCOUNTING – PERFORMANCE EVALUATION

The following data relate to Questions 56 and 57.

X40 is one of many items produced by the manufacturing division. Its standard cost is based on estimated production of 10,000 units per month. The standard cost schedule for one unit of X40 shows that 2 hours of direct labour are required at $15 per labour hour. The variable overhead rate is $6 per direct labour hour. During April, 11,000 units were produced; 24,000 direct labour hours were worked and charged; $336,000 was spent on direct labour; and $180,000 was spent on variable overheads.

56 The direct labour rate variance for April is:

- A $20,000 Favourable
- B $22,000 Favourable
- C $24,000 Adverse
- D $24,000 Favourable

57 The variable overhead efficiency variance for April is:

- A $12,000 Adverse
- B $12,000 Favourable
- C $15,000 Adverse
- D $15,000 Favourable

58 The fixed overhead volume variance is defined as:

- A the difference between the budgeted value of the fixed overheads and the standard fixed overheads absorbed by actual production
- B the difference between the standard fixed overhead cost specified for the production achieved, and the actual fixed overhead cost incurred
- C the difference between budgeted and actual fixed overhead expenditure
- D the difference between the standard fixed overhead cost specified in the original budget and the same volume of fixed overheads, but at the actual prices incurred.

The following data relate to Questions 59 and 60.

PQ operated a standard costing system for its only product. Information concerning the overhead cost of the product is as follows:

		$ per unit
Variable overhead	(4 hours at $3 per hour)	12
Fixed overhead	(4 hours at $5 per hour)	20

Fixed overheads are absorbed on the basis of labour hours.

Fixed overhead costs are budgeted at $120,000 per annum arising at a constant rate during the year.

Activity in March is budgeted to be 15% of total activity for the year. Actual results for March were as follows:

Actual hours worked	1,970
Actual production	500 units
Fixed overhead costs	$9,800
Variable overhead costs	$5,900

SECTION A-TYPE QUESTIONS : **SECTION 1**

59 The fixed overhead expenditure variance for March was:

A $2,200 (F)

B $200 (F)

C $200 (A)

D $,200 (A)

60 The variable overhead efficiency variance for March was:

A £10 (F)

B £90 (F)

C £90 (A)

D £100 (F)

61 Y has set the current budget for operating costs for its delivery vehicles, using the formula described below. Analysis has shown that the relationship between miles driven and total monthly vehicle operating costs is described in the following formula:

$$y = \$800 + \$0.0002x^2$$

where

y is the total monthly operating cost of the vehicles, and

x is the number of miles driven each month

The budget for vehicle operating costs needs to be adjusted for expected inflation in vehicle operating costs of 3%, which is not included in the relationship shown above.

The delivery mileage for September was 4,100 miles, and the total actual vehicle operating costs for September were $5,000.

The total vehicle operating cost variance for September was closest to:

A $713 Adverse

B $737 Adverse

C $777 Adverse

D $838 Adverse

62 The CIMA official definition of the 'variable production overhead efficiency variance' is set out below with two blank sections.

'Measures the difference between the variable overhead cost budget flexed on _____ and the variable overhead cost absorbed by _____ .'

Which combination of phrases correctly completes the definition?

	Blank 1	Blank 2
A	actual labour hours	budgeted output
B	standard labour hours	budgeted output
C	actual labour hours	output produced
D	standard labour hours	output produced

PAPER P1 : MANAGEMENT ACCOUNTING – PERFORMANCE EVALUATION

63 P has the following budget and actual data:

Budget fixed overhead cost $170,000
Budget production (units)   42,500
Actual fixed overhead cost $182,000
Actual production (units)   40,000

The fixed overhead volume variance is:

A $7,500 (A)

B $10,000 (A)

C $10,000 (F)

D $7,500 (F)

64 R uses a standard costing system and has the following labour cost standard in relation to one of its products:

10 hours skilled labour at $9.50 per hour = $95.00

During March 20X9, 6,200 of these products were made which was 250 units less than budgeted. The labour cost incurred was $596,412 and the number of direct labour hours worked was 62,890.

The direct labour variances for the month were:

	Rate	Efficiency
A	$1,043 (F)	$8,900 (A)
B	$7,412 (F)	$8,455 (A)
C	$1,043 (F)	$8,455 (A)
D	$7,412 (F)	$8,900 (A)

65 L uses a standard costing system. The standard cost card for one of its products shows that the product should use 6 kgs of material P per finished unit, and that the standard price per kg is $6.75. L values its inventory of materials at standard prices.

During November 20X1, when the budgeted production level was 2,000 units, 2,192 units were made. The actual quantity of material P used was 13,050 kgs and material L inventories were reduced by 500 kgs. The cost of the material L which was purchased was $72,900.

The material price and usage variances for November 20X1 were:

	Price	Usage
A	15,185.50 (F)	450.00 (F)
B	11,812.50 (F)	688.50 (F)
C	15,187.50 (F)	450.00 (A)
D	11,812.50 (F)	688.50 (A)

The following data relate to Questions 66 and 67.

Trafalgar budgets to produce 10,000 units of product D12, each requiring 45 minutes of labour. Labour is charged at $20 per hour, and variable overheads at $15 per labour hour. During September, 11,000 units were produced. 8,000 hours of labour were paid at a total cost of $168,000. Variable overheads in September amounted to $132,000.

SECTION A-TYPE QUESTIONS : SECTION 1

66 What is the labour efficiency variance for September?

A $5,000 Adverse

B $5,000 Favourable

C $5,250 Favourable

D $10,000 Adverse

67 What is the variable overhead expenditure variance for September?

A $3,750 Favourable

B $,125 Favourable

C $12,000 Adverse

D $12,000 Favourable

68 QR uses a standard absorption costing system. The following details have been extracted from its budget for April 20X3:

Fixed production overhead cost $48,000

Production (units) 4,800

In April 20X3 the fixed production overhead cost was under-absorbed by $8,000 and the fixed production overhead expenditure variance was $2,000 adverse.

Calculate the actual number of units produced in April 20X3.

69 A standard marginal costing system:

(i) calculates fixed overhead variances using the budgeted absorption rate per unit

(ii) records adverse variances as debit entries in variance accounts within the ledger

(iii) values finished goods inventories at the standard variable cost of production.

Which of the above statements is/are correct?

A (i) and (iii) only

B (ii) only

C (ii) and (iii) only

D (i) and (ii) only

70 Sim plc uses a standard absorption costing system. Details for period 7 were as follows:

	Budget	Actual
Sales units	8,500	8,840
Selling price per unit	$25.00	$25.90
Profit per unit	$6.50	$7.20

(a) Calculate the sales price variance for period 7. **(1 mark)**

(b) Calculate the sales volume profit variance for period 7. **(1 mark)**

(c) Calculate the sales volume revenue variance for period 7. **(1 mark)**

(Total: 3 marks)

KAPLAN PUBLISHING

PAPER P1 : MANAGEMENT ACCOUNTING – PERFORMANCE EVALUATION

The following data relate to Questions 71 and 72.

Z sells PCs that it purchases through a regional distributor. An extract from its budget for the 4-week period ended 28 March 20X8 shows that it planned to sell 600 PCs at a unit price of $500, which would give a contribution to sales ratio of 25%.

Actual sales were 642 PCs at an average selling price of $465. The actual contribution to sales ratio averaged 20%.

71 The sales price variance (to the nearest $1) was:

    A $22,470   (F)

    B $1,470   (A)

    C $1,470   (F)

    D $22,470   (A)

72 The sales volume contribution variance (to the nearest $1) was:

    A $5,050   (F)

    B $5,150   (F)

    C $5,250   (F)

    D $5,350   (F)

The following data relate to Questions 73 and 74.

SW manufactures a product known as the TRD100 by mixing two materials. The standard material cost per unit of the TRD100 is as follows:

				$
Material X	12 litres	@	$2.50	30
Material Y	18 litres	@	$3.00	54

In October 20X3, the actual mix used was 984 litres of X and 1,230 litres of Y. The actual output was 72 units of TRD100.

73 Calculate the total material mix variance for October 20X3.   (3 marks)

74 Calculate the total material yield variance for October 20X3.   (3 marks)

The following data relate to Questions 75 and 76.

A cleaning material, X2, is manufactured by mixing three materials. Standard cost details of the product are as follows.

Cost per batch of 10 litres of X2

				$
Material C	6 litres	@	$3	18
Material D	3 litres	@	$1	3
Material E	1 litre	@	$5	5
	10			26

In the latest period, the actual mix used was 200 litres of C, 75 litres of D and 25 litres of E. The output achieved was 280 litres of cleaning material X2.

SECTION A-TYPE QUESTIONS : SECTION 1

75 Using the average valuation basis, calculate the material mix variance for each material and in total. **(4 marks)**

76 Calculate the total material yield variance.

77 A company has a process in which the standard mix for producing 9 litres of output is as follows:

	$
4.0 litres of D at $9 per litre	36.00
3.5 litres of E at $5 per litre	17.50
2.5 litres of F at $2 per litre	5.00
	58.50

A standard loss of 10% of inputs is expected to occur. The actual inputs for the latest period were:

	$
4,300 litres of D at $9.00 per litre	38,700
3,600 litres of E at $5.50 per litre	19,800
2,100 litres of F at $2.20 per litre	4,620
	63,120

Actual output for this period was 9,100 litres.

Calculate:

(a) the total materials mix variance **(2 marks)**

(b) the total materials yield variance. **(2 marks)**

(Total: 4 marks)

78 Which of the following events would help to explain an adverse material usage variance?

(i) The standard allowance for material wastage was set too high.

(ii) Material purchased was of a lower quality than standard.

(iii) Lower grade and less experienced employees were used than standard.

(iv) More material was purchased than budgeted for the period because output was higher than budgeted.

A (i), (ii) and (iii) only

B (ii), (iii) and (iv) only

C (ii) and (iii) only

D (ii) and (iv) only

79 Which of the following is the *most likely* to result in an adverse variable overhead efficiency variance?

A Higher bonus payments to employees than standard

B Less experienced employees were used than standard

C The use of more expensive, higher quality materials than standard

D Machine power costs per hour were higher than standard

80 D Limited manufactures and sells musical instruments, and uses a standard cost system. The budget for production and sale of one particular drum for April was 600 units at a selling price of $72 each. When the sales director reviewed the results for April in the light of the market conditions that had been experienced during the month, she believed that D Limited should have sold 600 units of this drum at a price of $82 each. The actual sales achieved were 600 units at $86 per unit.

Calculate the following variances for this particular drum for April:

(a) selling price planning variance (2 marks)

(b) selling price operating variance. (2 marks)

(Total: 4 marks)

The following data relate to Questions 81 to 83.

The following data relate to Product Z and its raw material content for September:

Budget
Output   11,000 units of Z
Standard materials content   3 kg per unit at $4.00 per kg

Actual
Output   10,000 units of Z
Materials purchased and used   32,000 kg at $4.80 per kg

It has now been agreed that the standard price for the raw material purchased in September should have been $5 per kg.

81 The materials planning price variance for September was:

   A $6,000 Adverse
   B $30,000 Adverse
   C $32,000 Adverse
   D $33,000 Adverse

82 The materials operational usage variance for September was:

   A $8,000 Adverse
   B $9,600 Adverse
   C $9,600 Favourable
   D $10,000 Adverse

83 The materials operational price variance for September was:

   A $6,000 Adverse
   B $6,400 Favourable
   C $30,000 Adverse
   D $32,000 Adverse

SECTION A-TYPE QUESTIONS : SECTION 1

84 A company operates a standard costing system and prepares monthly financial statements. All materials purchased during February were used during that month. After all transactions for February were posted, the general ledger contained the following balances:

	Debit $	Credit $
Finished goods control	27,450	
Materials price variance	2,400	
Materials usage variance		8,400
Labour rate variance	5,600	
Labour efficiency variance		3,140
Variable production overhead variance	2,680	
Fixed production overhead variance		3,192

The standard cost of the goods produced during February was $128,500.

The actual cost of the goods produced during February was:

A $96,998

B $124,448

C $132,552

D $160,002

The following data are given for sub-questions 85 and 86 below.

A company has a process in which three inputs are mixed together to produce Product S. The standard mix of inputs to produce 90 kg of Product S is shown below:

	$
50 kg of ingredient P at $75 per kg	3,750
30 kg of ingredient Q at $100 per kg	3,000
20 kg of ingredient R at $125 per kg	2,500
	9,250

During March 2,000 kg of ingredients were used to produce 1,910 kg of Product S. Details of the inputs are as follows:

	$
1,030 kg of ingredient P at $70 per kg	72,100
560 kg of ingredient Q at $106 per kg	59,360
410 kg of ingredient R at $135 per kg	55,350
	186,810

85 Calculate the materials mix variance for March.   (3 marks)

86 Calculate the materials yield variance for March.

PAPER P1 : MANAGEMENT ACCOUNTING – PERFORMANCE EVALUATION

The following data are given for sub-questions 87 and 88 below.

Q plc uses standard costing. The details for April were as follows:

Budgeted output	15,000	units
Budgeted labour hours	60,000	hours
Budgeted labour cost	$540,000	
Actual output	14,650	units
Actual labour hours paid	61,500	hours
Productive labour hours	56,000	hours
Actual labour cost	$522,750	

87 Calculate the idle time variance for April.

88 Calculate the labour efficiency variance for April.

The following data are given for sub-questions 89 to 90 below

A company uses standard absorption costing. The following information was recorded by the company for October:

	Budget	Actual
Output and sales (units)	8,700	8,200
Selling price per unit	£26	£31
Variable cost per unit	£10	£10
Total fixed overheads	$34,800	$37,000

89 The sales price variance for October was:

    A $38,500 Favourable

    B $41,000 Favourable

    C $41,000 Adverse

    D $65,600 Adverse

90 The sales volume profit variance for October was:

    A $6,000 Adverse

    B $6,000 Favourable

    C $8,000 Adverse

    D $8,000 Favourable

91 The fixed overhead volume variance for October was:

    A $2,000 Adverse

    B $2,200 Adverse

    C $2,200 Favourable

    D $4,200 Adverse

92

RJD Ltd operates a standard absorption costing system. The following fixed production overhead data are available for one month:

Budgeted output	200,000	units
Budgeted fixed production overhead	$1,000,000	
Actual fixed production overhead	$1,300,000	
Total fixed production overhead variance	$100,000	Adverse

The actual level of production was:

A 180,000 units.

B 240,000 units.

C 270,000 units.

D 280,000 units.

93

PP Ltd operates a standard absorption costing system. The following information has been extracted from the standard cost card for one of its products:

Budgeted production	1,500 units
Direct material cost: 7 kg × $4.10	$28.70 per unit

Actual results for the period were as follows:

Production	1,600 units
Direct material (purchased and used): 12,000 kg	$52,200

It has subsequently been noted that, owing to a change in economic conditions, the best price that the material could have been purchased for was $4.50 per kg during the period.

(a) Calculate the material price planning variance.

(b) Calculate the operational material usage variance.   **(4 marks)**

94

SS Ltd operates a standard marginal costing system. An extract from the standard cost card for the labour costs of one of its products is as follows:

Labour cost
5 hours × $12 $60

Actual results for the period were as follows:

Production	11,500 units
Labour rate variance	$45,000 adverse
Labour efficiency variance	$30,000 adverse

Calculate the actual rate paid per direct labour hour.   **(4 marks)**

PAPER P1 : MANAGEMENT ACCOUNTING – PERFORMANCE EVALUATION

BUDGETING

95 Which of the following can be identified as purposes of budgeting?

(i) Communication

(ii) Authorisation

(iii) Sales maximisation

(iv) Co-ordination

A (ii) and (iv) only

B (i) and (ii) only

C (i), (ii) and (iv) only

D All of them

The following information is to be used to answer Questions 96 and 97.

Extracts from B's master budget for the latest period are as follows:

Income statement	$000
Revenue	5,440
Gross profit	2,730
Profit from operations	900
Balance sheet	
Non-current assets	1,850
Inventory	825
Receivables	710
Bank	50
Current liabilities	780

You are required to calculate a number of key metrics for evaluation in the budgetary planning process.

---

96 (a) Calculate the operating profit margin for the budget period. (2 marks)

(b) Calculate the total net asset turnover for the period. (3 marks)

(Total: 5 marks)

97 (a) Calculate the budgeted current ratio. (2 marks)

(b) Calculate the budgeted quick (acid test) ratio. (2 marks)

(Total: 4 marks)

98 An incremental budgeting system is:

A a system which budgets only for the extra costs associated with a particular plan

B a system which budgets for the variable manufacturing costs only

C a system which prepares budgets only after the manager responsible has justified the continuation of the relevant activity

D a system which prepares budgets by adjusting the previous year's values by expected changes in volumes of activity and price/inflation effects.

SECTION A-TYPE QUESTIONS : SECTION 1

99 EFG uses an Activity Based Budgeting system. It manufactures three products, budgeted details of which are set out below:

	Product E	Product F	Product G
Budgeted annual production (units)	75,000	120,000	60,000
Batch size (units)	200	60	30
Machine set-ups per batch	5	3	9
Purchase orders per batch	4	2	2
Processing time per unit (minutes)	3	4	4

Three cost pools have been identified. Their budgeted costs for the year ending 30 September 20X3 are as follows:

Machine set-up costs	$180,000
Purchasing of materials	$95,000
Processing	$110,000

Calculate the budgeted machine set-up cost per unit of product F. **(3 marks)**

The following data relate to Questions 100 and 101.

A division of LMN operates a fleet of minibuses that carries people and packages for other divisions.

In the year ended 31 October 20X3, it carried 4,420 people and 30,500 kgs of packages. It incurred costs of $850,000.

The division has found that 60% of its total costs are variable, and that 50% of these vary with the number of people and the other 50% varies with the weight of the packages.

The company is now preparing its budget for the three months ending 31 January 20X4 using an incremental budgeting approach. In this period it expects:

- All prices to be 2% higher than the average paid in the year ended 31 October 20X3.
- Efficiency levels to be unchanged.
- Activity levels to be:
    - 1,150 people
    - 8,100 kgs of packages.

100 The budgeted people-related cost (to the nearest $100) for the three months ending 31 January 20X4 is:

   A $55,300

   B $6,400

   C $66,300

   D $67,700

101 The budgeted package-related cost (to the nearest $100) for the three months ending 31 January 20X4 is:

   A $56,400

   B $57,600

   C $67,800

   D $69,000

102 A purpose of a flexible budget is:

A to cap discretionary expenditure

B to produce a revised forecast by changing the original budget when actual costs are known

C to control resource efficiency

D to communicate target activity levels within an organisation by setting a budget in advance of the period to which it relates.

103 A fixed budget is:

A a budget for a single level of activity

B used when the mix of products is fixed in advance of the budget period

C a budget which ignores inflation

D an overhead cost budget.

104 The following details relate to product X in two accounting periods:

Number of units	500	800
	$/unit	$/unit
Direct materials	2.00	2.00
Direct labour	1.50	1.50
Production overhead	2.50	1.75
Other overhead	1.00	0.625
	7.00	5.875

The fixed cost per period and variable cost per unit are:

	Period fixed cost $	Variable cost/unit $
A	1,000	1.125
B	1,000	4.00
C	1,500	3.50
D	1,500	4.00

105 M prepared the following flexible budget for April:

Activity (% of capacity)	75%	85%	90%
Total costs	$33,500	$35,500	$36,500

Budgeted capacity for the month was 60,000 machine hours.

If the actual activity in April was 50,000 machine hours, the budget cost allowance for April (to the nearest $1,000) would have been:

A $18,000

B $20,000

C $35,000

D $38,000

106
The following data have been extracted from the budget working papers of WR:

Activity (machine hours)	Overhead cost $
10,000	13,468
12,000	14,162
16,000	15,549
18,000	16,242

In November 20X3, the actual activity was 13,780 machine hours and the actual overhead cost incurred was $14,521.

Calculate the total overhead expenditure variance for November 20X3. **(4 marks)**

107
The following cost per unit details have been extracted from a production overhead cost budget:

Output (units)	6,000	10,000
Production overhead ($/unit)	3.20	3.00

The budget cost allowance for production overhead for an activity level of 7,350 units is:

A $20,505

B $21,765

C $22,845

D $23,515

108
Which of the following statements are true?

(i)   A flexible budget can be used to control operational efficiency.

(ii) Incremental budgeting can be defined as a system of budgetary planning and control that measures the additional costs that are incurred when there are unplanned extra units of activity.

(iii) Rolling budgets review and, if necessary, revise the budget for the next quarter to ensure that budgets remain relevant for the remainder of the accounting period.

A   (i) and (ii) only

B   (ii) and (iii) only

C   (iii) only

D   (i) only

109
In the context of budget preparation the term 'goal congruence' is:

A   the alignment of budgets with objectives using feed-forward control

B   the setting of a budget which does not include budget bias

C   the alignment of corporate objectives with the personal objectives of a manager

D   the use of aspiration levels to set efficiency targets.

110 Which of the following definitions best describes 'Zero-Based Budgeting'?

A   A method of budgeting where an attempt is made to make the expenditure under each cost heading as close to zero as possible.

B   A method of budgeting whereby all activities are re-evaluated each time a budget is formulated.

C   A method of budgeting that recognises the difference between the behaviour of fixed and variable costs with respect to changes in output and the budget is designed to change appropriately with such fluctuations.

D   A method of budgeting where the sum of revenues and expenditures in each budget centre must equal zero.

111 Which of the following statements about imposed budgets are correct?

(i)   Imposed budgets are likely to set realistic targets because senior management have the best idea of what is achievable in each part of the business.

(ii) Imposed budgets can be less effective than budgets set on a participative basis, because it is difficult for an individual to be motivated to achieve targets set by someone else.

(iii) Imposed budgets are generally quicker to prepare and finalise than participative budgets.

A   (i) and (ii) only

B   (i) and (iii) only

C   (ii) and (iii) only

D   (iii) only

112 In the context of a balanced scorecard approach to the provision of management information, which of the following measures might be appropriate for monitoring the innovation and learning perspective?

(i)   Training days per employee

(ii) Percentage of revenue generated by new products and services

(iii) Labour turnover rate

A   (i) (ii) and (iii)

B   (i) and (iii) only

C   (ii) only

D   (ii) and (iii) only

SECTION A-TYPE QUESTIONS : SECTION 1

113 The overhead costs of RP have been found to be accurately represented by the formula:

y = $10,000 + $0.25x

where y is the monthly cost and x represents the activity level measured as the number of orders.

Monthly activity levels of orders may be estimated using a combined regression analysis and time series model:

a = 100,000 + 30b

where a represents the de-seasonalised monthly activity level and b represents the month number.

In month 240, the seasonal index value is 108.

Calculate the overhead cost for RP for month 240 to the nearest $1,000. **(3 marks)**

The following data relate to Questions 114 and 115.

H is forecasting its sales for next year using a combination of time series and regression analysis models. An analysis of past sales units has produced the following equation for the quarterly sales trend:

y = 26x + 8,850

where the value of x represents the quarterly accounting period and the value of y represents the quarterly sales trend in units. Quarter 1 of next year will have a value for x of 25.

The quarterly seasonal variations have been measured using the multiplicative (proportional) model and are:

Quarter 1   − 15%

Quarter 2   − 5%

Quarter 3   + 5%

Quarter 4   + 15%

Production is planned to occur at a constant rate throughout the year.

The company does not hold inventories at the end of any year.

---

114 The difference between the budgeted sales for quarter 1 and quarter 4 next year are:

A   78 units

B   2,850 units

C   2,862 units

D   2,940 units

115 The number of units to be produced in each quarter of next year will be nearest to:

A   9,454 units

B   9,493 units

C   9,532 units

D   9,543 units

116 Monthly sales of product R follow a linear trend of y = 9.72 + 5.816x, where y is the number of units sold and x is the number of the month. Monthly deviations from the trend follow an additive model.

The forecast number of units of product R to be sold in month 23, which has a seasonal factor of plus 6.5 is, to the nearest whole unit:

A   134
B   137
C   143
D   150

117 Nile is preparing its sales budget for 20X4. The sales manager estimates that sales will be 120,000 units if the Summer is rainy, and 80,000 units if the Summer is dry. The probability of a dry Summer is 0.4.

What is the expected value for sales volume for 20X4?

A   96,000 units
B   100,000 units
C   104,000 units
D   120,000 units

118 Copenhagen is an insurance company. Recently there has been concern that too many quotations have been sent to clients either late or containing errors.

The department concerned has responded that it is understaffed, and a high proportion of current staff has recently joined the firm. The performance of this department is to be carefully monitored.

Which ONE of the following non-financial performance indicators would NOT be an appropriate measure to monitor and improve the department's performance?

A   Percentage of quotations found to contain errors when checked
B   Percentage of quotations not issued within company policy of three working days
C   Percentage of department's quota of staff actually employed
D   Percentage of budgeted number of quotations actually issued

119 The CIMA definition of zero-based budgeting is set out below, with two blank sections.

'Zero-based budgeting: A method of budgeting which requires each cost element _____, as though the activities to which the budget relates _____.'

Which combination of two phrases correctly completes the definition?

	Blank 1	Blank 2
A	to be specifically justified	could be out-sourced to an external supplier
B	to be set at zero	could be out-sourced to an external supplier
C	to be specifically justified	were being undertaken for the first time
D	to be set at zero	were being undertaken for the first time

SECTION A-TYPE QUESTIONS : SECTION 1

The following data relate to Questions 120 and 121.

The summarised financial statements for P Limited, a potential major supplier, are shown below. Before a contract is signed, the financial performance of P Limited is to be reviewed.

Summary balance sheets for P Limited at year end

	20X3 $000	20X2 $000
Non-current assets	1,600	1,400
Inventories	300	280
Trade receivables	200	210
Cash	50	10
Trade payables	(280)	(290)
Long-term borrowings	(900)	(800)
Net assets	970	810
Share capital	600	600
Retained earnings	370	210
	970	810

Summary income statements for the years

	20X3 $000	20X2 $000
Sales	3,000	2,500
Cost of sales	1,600	1,300
Operating profit	600	450

120 Calculate the following financial statistics for P Limited for 20X3:

    (a) receivables days

    (b) payables days

    (c) inventory days. **(3 marks)**

121 Calculate the following financial statistics for P Limited for 20X3:

    (a) current ratio

    (b) acid test (quick ratio).

122 Which of the following statements are correct?

    (i) A fixed budget is a budget that considers all of an organisation's costs and revenues for a single level of activity.

    (ii) A flexible budget is a budget that is produced during the budget period to recognise the effects of any changes in prices and methods of operation that have occurred.

    (iii) Organisations can use budgets to communicate objectives to their managers.

A   (i) and (ii) only

B   (i) and (iii) only

C   (ii) and (iii) only

D   All of them

123 Which of the following best describes 'budgetary slack'?

A   The difference between what has been set as a budgetary objective and what has been achieved for the period.

B   The demotivating impact of a budgetary target that has been set too high.

C   The deliberate over-estimation of expenditure and/or under-estimation of revenues in the budgetary planning process.

D   Accumulated favourable variances reported against a specific item of budgeted expenditure.

124 A company is preparing its maintenance budget. The number of machine hours and maintenance costs for the past six months have been as follows:

Month	Machine hours	$
1	10,364	35,319
2	12,212	39,477
3	8,631	31,420
4	9,460	33,285
5	8,480	31,080
6	10,126	34,784

The budget cost allowance for an activity level of 9,340 machine hours, before any adjustment for price changes, is nearest to:

A $21,000

B $30,200

C $33,000

D $34,000

125 Z plc has found that it can estimate future sales using time series analysis and regression techniques. The following trend equation has been derived:

$$y = 25,000 + 6,500x$$

where

   y is the total sales units per quarter

   x is the time period reference number

Z has also derived the following set of seasonal variation index values for each quarter using a multiplicative (proportional) model:

Quarter 1	70
Quarter 2	90
Quarter 3	150
Quarter 4	90

Using the above model, calculate the forecast for sales units for the third quarter of year 7, assuming that the first quarter of year 1 is time period reference number 1.

126

A company is preparing its cash budget for February using the following data. One line in the cash budget is for purchases of a raw material, J. The opening inventory of J in January is expected to be 1,075 units. The price of J is expected to be $8 per unit. The company pays for purchases at the end of the month following delivery.

One unit of J is required in the production of each unit of Product 2, and J is only used in this product. Monthly sales of Product 2 are expected to be:

January	4,000 units
February	5,000 units
March	6,000 units

The opening inventory of Product 2 in January is expected to be 1,200 units.

The company implements the following inventory policies. At the end of each month the following amounts are held:

Raw materials: 25% of the requirement for the following month's production

Finished goods: 30% of the following month's sales

Calculate the value for purchases of J to be included in the cash budget for February.

(4 marks)

The following data relate to Questions 127 and 128.

K makes many products, one of which is Product Z. K is considering adopting an activity-based costing approach for setting its budget, in place of the current practice of absorbing overheads using direct labour hours. The main budget categories and cost driver details for the whole company for October are set out below, excluding direct material costs:

Budget category	$	Cost driver details
Direct labour	128,000	8,000 direct labout hours
Set-up costs	22,000	88 set-ups each month
Quality testing costs*	34,000	40 tests each month
Other overhead costs	32,000	Absorbed by direct labour hours

* A quality test is performed after every 75 units produced

The following data for Product Z is provided:

Direct materials	Budgeted cost of $21.50 per unit
Direct labour	Budgeted at 0.3 hours per unit
Batch size	30 units
Set-ups	2 set-ups per batch
Budgeted volume for October	150 units

127

Calculate the budgeted unit cost of Product Z for October assuming that a direct labour-based absorption method was used for all overheads.

128

Calculate the budgeted unit cost of Product Z for October using an activity-based costing approach.

(3 marks)

PAPER P1 : MANAGEMENT ACCOUNTING – PERFORMANCE EVALUATION

The following data relate to Questions 129 and 130.

T is a large pharmaceutical manufacturing company that is implementing a 'Kaplan and Norton style' Balanced Scorecard for its research and development division. The goals and measures for the 'customer perspective' and the 'financial perspective' have been set.

129 For each of the two perspectives given in the question data, state an appropriate performance measure.

130 List the other two perspectives in the Balanced Scorecard for T's research and development division, and state for each of the perspectives a relevant goal and performance measure.

(3 marks)

131 If the budgeted fixed costs increase, the gradient of the line plotted on the budgeted Profit/Volume (P/V) chart will:

A   increase

B   decrease

C   not change

D   become curvi-linear.

132 The following extract is taken from the production cost budget of L plc:

Output	2,000 units	3,500 units
Total cost	$12,000	$16,200

The budget cost allowance for an output of 4,000 units would be:

A $17,600

B $18,514

C $20,400

D $24,000

133 A company uses time series and regression techniques to forecast future sales. It has derived a seasonal variation index to use with the multiplicative (proportional) seasonal variation model. The index values for the first three quarters are as follows:

Quarter	Index value
Q1	80
Q2	80
Q3	110

The index value for the fourth quarter (Q4) is:

A   –270

B   –269

C   110

D   130

SECTION A-TYPE QUESTIONS : SECTION 1

134 The budgeted profit statement for a company, with all figures expressed as percentages of revenue, is as follows:

	%
Revenue	100
Variable costs	30
Fixed costs	22
Profit	48

After the formulation of the above budget it has now been realised that the sales volume will only be 60% of that originally forecast.

The revised profit, expressed as a percentage of the revised revenue will be:

A   20%

B   33.3%

C   60%

D   80%

135 The following details have been taken from the debtor collection records of W plc:

Invoices paid in the month after sale	60%
Invoices paid in the second month after sale	20%
Invoices paid in the third month after sale	15%
Bad debts	5%

Customers paying in the month after the sale are allowed a 10% discount.

Invoices for sales are issued on the last day of the month in which the sales are made.

The budgeted credit sales for the final five months of this year are:

Month	August	September	October	November	December
Credit sales	$80,000	$100,000	$120,000	$130,000	$160,000

Calculate the total amount budgeted to be received in December from credit sales.

136 D plc operates a retail business. Purchases are sold at cost plus 25%. The management team is preparing the cash budget and has gathered the following data:

1   The budgeted sales are as follows:

Month	$000
July	100
August	90
September	125
October	140

2   It is management policy to hold inventory at the end of each month which is sufficient to meet sales demand in the next half month. Sales are budgeted to occur evenly during each month.

3   Creditors are paid one month after the purchase has been made.

KAPLAN PUBLISHING   39

Calculate the entries for 'purchases' that will be shown in the cash budget for:

(i) August

(ii) September

(iii) October (3 marks)

137 **ZY is an airline operator. It is implementing a balanced scorecard to measure the success of its strategy to expand its operations. It has identified two perspectives and two associated objectives. They are:**

Perspective   *Objective*
Growth   Fly to new destinations
Internal capabilities   Reduce time between touch down and take off

(a) For the 'growth perspective' of ZY, recommend a performance measure and briefly justify your choice of the measure by explaining how it will reflect the success of the strategy.

(2 marks)

(b) For the 'internal capabilities perspective' of ZY, state data that you would gather and explain how this could be used to ensure the objective is met. **(2 marks)**

(Total: 4 marks)

138 **S plc produces and sells three products, X, Y and Z. It has contracts to supply products X and Y, which will utilise all of the specific materials that are available to make these two products during the next period. The revenue these contracts will generate and the contribution to sales (C/S) ratios of products X and Y are as follows:**

	Product X	*Product Y*
Revenue	$10 million	$20 million
C/S ratio	15%	10%

Product Z has a C/S ratio of 25%.

The total fixed costs of S plc are £5.5 million during the next period and management has budgeted to earn a profit of $1 million.

Calculate the revenue that needs to be generated by Product Z for S plc to achieve the budgeted profit. **(3 marks)**

139 **A master budget comprises the:**

A   budgeted income statement and budgeted cash flow only

B   budgeted income statement and budgeted balance sheet only

C   budgeted income statement and budgeted capital expenditure only

D   budgeted income statement, budgeted balance sheet and budgeted cash flow only

140 CJD Ltd manufactures plastic components for the car industry. The following budgeted information is available for three of its key plastic components:

	W $ per unit	X $ per unit	Y $ per unit
Selling price	200	183	175
Direct material	50	40	35
Direct labour	30	35	30
Units produced and sold	10,000	15,000	18,000

The total number of activities for each of the three products for the period is as follows:

Number of purchase requisitions	1,200	1,800	2,000
Number of set ups	240	260	300

Overhead costs have been analysed as follows:

Receiving/inspecting quality assurance	$1,400,000
Production scheduling/machine set up	$1,200,000

Calculate the budgeted profit per unit for each of the three products using activity-based budgeting. **(4 marks)**

CONTROL AND PERFORMANCE MEASUREMENT OF RESPONSIBILITY CENTRES

141 An organisation is divided into a number of divisions, each of which operates as a profit centre. Which of the following would be useful measures to monitor divisional performance?

(i) Contribution
(ii) Controllable profit
(iii) Return on investment
(iv) Residual income
(v) Economic value added

A (i) only
B (i) and (ii) only
C (iii), (iv) and (v) only
D All of them

142 One of the main reasons for adopting a decentralised organisation in preference to a centralised organisation structure is the:

A improved goal congruence between the divisional manager's goals and the goals of the organisation
B availability of less subjective measures of performance
C improved communication of information among the organisation's managers
D rapid response of management to environmental changes.

143 Green division is one of many divisions in the Colour group. At its year-end, the non-current assets invested in Green were $30 million, and the net current assets were $5 million.

Included in this total was a new item of plant that was delivered three days before the year end. This item cost $4 million and had been paid for by Colour, which had increased the amount of long-term debt owed by Green by this amount.

The profit earned in the year by Green was $6 million before the deduction of $1.4 million of interest payable to Colour. What is the most appropriate measure of ROI for the Green division?

A   13.1%

B   14.8%

C   17.1%

D   19.4%

144 A division of a company has capital employed of $2m and its return on capital is 12%. It is considering a new project requiring capital of $500,000 and is expected to yield profits of $90,000 per annum. The company's interest rate is 10%. If the new project is accepted, the residual income of the division will be:

A $40,000

B $80,000

C $30,000

D $330,000

145 Division M has produced the following results in the last financial year:

		$000
Net profit		360
Capital employed:	Non-current assets	1,500
	Net current assets	100

For evaluation purposes all divisional assets are valued at original cost. The division is considering a project which will increase annual net profit by $25,000, but will require average inventory levels to increase by $30,000 and non-current assets to increase by $100,000. There is an 18% capital charge on investments.

Given these circumstances, will the evaluation criteria of Return on Investment (ROI) and Residual Income (RI) motivate Division M management to accept this project?

	ROI	RI
A	Yes	Yes
B	Yes	No
C	No	Yes
D	No	No

SECTION A-TYPE QUESTIONS : SECTION 1

The following data relate to Questions 146 and 147.

Summary financial statements are given below for one division of a large divisionalised company.

Summary divisional financial statements for the year to 31 December

Balance sheet		Income statement	
	$000		$000
Non-current assets	1,500	Revenue	4,000
Current assets	600	Operating costs	3,600
	___		___
Total assets	2,100	Operating profit	400
	=====	Interest paid	70
			___
Divisional equity	1,000	Profit before tax	330
Long-term borrowings	700		=====
Current liabilities	400		
	___		
Total equity and liabilities	2,100		
	=====		

The cost of capital for the division is estimated at 12% each year.

Annual rate of interest on the long-term loans is 10%.

All decisions concerning the division's capital structure are taken by central management.

146 The divisional Return on Investment (ROI) for the year ended 31 December is:

    A   19.0%

    B   19.4%

    C   23.5%

    D   33.0%

147 The divisional Residual Income (RI) for the year ended 31 December is:

    A $160,000

    B $196,000

    C $230,000

    D $330,000

PAPER P1 : MANAGEMENT ACCOUNTING – PERFORMANCE EVALUATION

The following data relate to Questions 148 and 149.

A division has net assets of $420,000. The profit statement for the division for the latest period is as follows:

	$
Revenue	630,000
Variable costs	390,000
Contribution	240,000
Attributable fixed costs	180,000
Allocated central costs	25,000
Divisional profit	35,000

The divisional manager is considering investing in a machine costing $50,000. The machine would earn annual profits, after depreciation, of $5,500. The company's cost of capital is 10%.

148 (a) Calculate the division's controllable return on investment, without the new machine.

    (b) Calculate the division's controllable return on investment, with the new machine.

149 (a) Calculate the controllable residual income for the division, with and without the new machine. **(3 marks)**

    (b) Comment on the likely behavioural impact of the use of each performance measure. **(2 marks)**

(Total: 5 marks)

150 An investment centre has earned an accounting profit of $135,000, after charging historical cost depreciation of $22,000 and increasing the provision for doubtful debts by $8,000 to $12,000. If the non-current assets had been valued at replacement cost the depreciation charge would have been $41,000.

The net book value of the investment centre's net assets is $420,000 and the replacement cost is estimated to be $660,000.

The organisation's risk adjusted cost of capital is 14% but it has a large bank loan which incurs annual interest charges of 10%.

Ignoring taxation, the economic value added (EVA) for the investment centre is:

    A $29,920

    B $31,040

    C $31,600

    D $56,800

151 Division G has reported annual operating profits of $20.2 million. This was after charging $3 million for the full cost of launching a new product that is expected to last three years.

Division G has a risk adjusted cost of capital of 11% and is paying interest on a substantial bank loan at 8%. The historical cost of the assets in Division G, as shown on its balance sheet, is $60 million, and the replacement cost has been estimated at $84 million.

Ignore the effects of taxation.

What would be the EVA for Division G?

A $15.4 million

B $11.48 million

C $10.6 million

D $12.74 million

152 **B division has earned an accounting profit of $457,000 after charging the following costs:**

$120,000 cost of developing a new product that is expected to generate revenues for four years before it is superseded by newer products

$125,000 historical cost depreciation.

The net book value of the division's assets is $2.7million and the replacement cost of these assets is estimated to be $3.1million. If the non-current assets were valued at replacement cost, the depreciation charge would be $224,000.

The company's risk adjusted cost of capital is 11%.

Ignoring taxation, the economic value added (EVA) for B division is:

A $2,100

B $97,100

C $107,000

D $127,100

153 **Division Y has reported annual operating profits of $40.2 million. This was after charging $6 million for the full cost of launching a new product that is expected to last three years. Division Y has a risk adjusted cost of capital of 11% and is paying interest on a substantial bank loan at 8%. The historical cost of the assets in Division Y, as shown on its balance sheet, is $100 million, and the replacement cost has been estimated at $172 million.**

Ignore the effects of taxation.

The EVA® for Division Y is:

A $23.28 million

B $25.28 million

C $29.20 million

D $30.44 million

E $24.84 million

154 **ABC has two profit centres, Centre 1 and Centre 2. Centre 1 transfers one third of its output to Centre 2 and sells the remainder on the external market for $28 per unit. The transfers to Centre 2 are at a transfer price of cost plus 20%.**

Centre 2 incurs costs of $8 per unit in converting the transferred unit, which is then sold to external customers for $40 per unit.

Centre 1 costs are $20 per unit and the budgeted output for period 6 is 450 units. There is no budgeted change in inventories for either profit centre.

The budgeted results for Centre 1 and Centre 2 for period 6 will be:

	Centre 1	Centre 2
A	$1,800 profit	$2,400 profit
B	$3,000 profit	$1,200 profit
C	$3,000 profit	$4,800 profit
D	$3,900 profit	$2,400 profit

155 Which of the following statements about market-based transfer prices are correct?

(i) A profit centre buying the item is likely to be indifferent between buying externally and buying the item from within the business.

(ii) A transfer price at market value might not encourage profit centres buying the item to utilise spare capacity.

A (i) only

B (ii) only

C Both (i) and (ii)

D Neither (i) nor (ii)

The following data relate to Questions 156 and 157.

X plc, a manufacturing company, has two divisions: Division A and Division B. Division A produces one type of product, ProdX, which it transfers to Division B and also sells externally. Division B has been approached by another company which has offered to supply 2,500 units of ProdX for $35 each.

The following details for Division A are available:

	$
Sales revenue	
Sales to Division B @ $40 per unit	400,000
External sales @ $45 per unit	270,000
Less:	
Variable cost @ $22 per unit	352,000
Fixed costs	100,000
Profit	218,000

External sales of Prod X cannot be increased, and division B decides to buy from the other company.

156 Calculate the effect on the profit of division A.

157 Calculate the effect on the profit of company X.

SECTION A-TYPE QUESTIONS : SECTION 1

158 X and Y are two divisions of Newtyle. Division X manufactures one product, Alpha. Unit production cost and market price are as follows:

	$
Direct materials	6
Direct labour	4
Fixed overhead	1
	11
Prevailing market price	$16

Product Alpha is sold outside the company in a perfectly competitive market and also to Division Y. If sold outside the company, Alpha incurs variable selling costs of $2 per unit which are not incurred on internal transfers.

If the total demand for Alpha were more than sufficient for Division X to manufacture to capacity, at what price would the company prefer Division X to transfer Alpha to Division Y?

A $10
B $11
C $14
D $16

159 Division A transfers 100,000 units of a component to Division B each year. The market price of the component is $25 per unit.

Division A's variable cost is $15 per unit.

Division A's fixed costs are $500,000 each year.

What price per unit would be credited to Division A for each component that it transfers to Division B under marginal cost pricing and under two-part tariff pricing (where the Divisions have agreed that the fixed fee will be $200,000)?

	Marginal cost pricing	Two-part tariff pricing
A	$15	$15
B	$25	$15
C	$15	$25
D	$25	$25

160 Division S transfers 75,000 units of a component to Division T each year.

The market price of the component is £40.

Division S's variable cost is £28 per unit.

Division S's fixed costs are £380,000 each year.

What price would be credited to Division S for each component that it transfers to Division T under:

(i)   two-part tariff pricing (where the Divisions have agreed that the fixed fee will be £160,000)?

(ii) dual pricing (based on marginal cost and market price)?

KAPLAN PUBLISHING

	Two-part tariff pricing	Dual pricing
A	£12	£28
B	£12	£40
C	£28	£40
D	£33	£28

The following data relate to Questions 161 and 162.

CD Globes transferred 11,000 units of product N from its manufacturing division in Canada to its selling division in the UK during the year just ended.

The manufacturing cost of each unit of product N was $120 (75% of which was variable cost). The market price for each unit of product N in Canada was $300. The Canada division's profit after tax for its sales to the UK division for the year ended was $1,100,000.

The UK division incurred marketing and distribution costs of £40 for each unit of product N and sold the product for £250 a unit. The UK tax rate was 25%. (Exchange rate: £1 = $1.50)

161 If product N had been transferred at the Canadian market price, the tax rate in Canada must have been (to the nearest percentage point):

- A 32%
- B 36%
- C 40%
- D 44%

162 If the transfers had been made at variable cost, the UK division's profit after tax would have been:

- A £950,000
- B £987,500
- C £1,050,000
- D £1,237,500

163 CMW Ltd is a UK holding company with an overseas subsidiary. The directors of CMW Ltd wish to transfer profits from the UK to the overseas company.

They are considering changing the level of transfer prices charged on goods shipped from the overseas subsidiary to CMW Ltd and the size of the royalty payments paid by CMW Ltd to its subsidiary.

In order to transfer profit from CMW Ltd to the overseas subsidiary, the directors of CMW Ltd should:

- A increase both the transfer prices and royalty payments
- B increase the transfer prices but decrease royalty payments
- C decrease the transfer prices but increase royalty payments
- D decrease both the transfer prices and royalty payments.

SECTION A-TYPE QUESTIONS : SECTION 1

164 Division P produces plastic mouldings, all of which are used as components by Division Q. The cost schedule for one type of moulding – item 103 – is shown below.

Direct material cost per unit	$3.00
Direct labour cost per unit	$4.00
Variable overhead cost per unit	$2.00
Fixed production overhead costs each year	$120,000
Annual demand from Division Q is expected to be	20,000 units

Two methods of transfer pricing are being considered:

(i) full production cost plus 40%

(ii) a two-part tariff with a fixed fee of $200,000 each year.

The transfer price per unit of item 103 transferred to Division Q using both of the transfer pricing methods listed above is:

	(i) Full production cost plus 40%	(ii) Two-part tariff
A	$21.00	$9
B	$21.00	$15
C	$15.00	$19
D	$12.60	$9

The following data relate to Questions 165 and 166.

The KL Company provides legal and secretarial services to small businesses. KL has two divisions.

Secretarial Division

This division provides secretarial services to external clients and to the Legal Division. It charges all its clients, including the Legal Division, at a rate of $40 per hour. The marginal cost of one hour of secretarial services is $20.

Legal Division

The Legal Division provides legal services. One service, called L&S, involves a combination of legal and secretarial services. Each hour of L&S charged to clients involves one hour of legal services and one hour of secretarial services. The secretarial element of this service is purchased from the Secretarial Division. The likely demand for L&S at different prices is as follows:

Demand (hours)	Price per hour ($)
0	100
1,000	90
2,000	80
3,000	70
4,000	60
5,000	50

The marginal cost of one hour of legal services is $25.

165 Calculate the level of sales (hours) and total contribution of L&S that would maximise the profit from this service for the Legal Division. Assume the Legal Division pays the Secretarial Division at a rate of $40 per hour for secretarial services. **(3 marks)**

166 Calculate the level of sales (hours) and total contribution that would maximise the profit from L&S for the KL Company as a whole. **(3 marks)**

167 Division L has reported a net profit after tax of $8.6m for the year ended 30 April 2006. Included in the costs used to calculate this profit are the following items:

- interest payable of $2.3m;
- development costs of $6.3m for a new product that was launched in May 2005, and is expected to have a life of three years;
- advertising expenses of $1.6m that relate to the re-launch of a product in June 2006.

The net assets invested in Division L are $30m.

The cost of capital for Division L is 13% per year.

Calculate the Economic Value Added® for Division L for the year ended 30 April 2006.

(3 marks)

168 State four aims of a transfer pricing system. **(3 marks)**

The following data are given for sub-questions 169 and 170 below

The annual operating statement for a company is shown below:

	$000
Sales revenue	800
Less variable costs	390
Contribution	410
Less fixed costs	90
Less depreciation	20
Net income	300
Assets	$6.75m

The cost of capital is 13% per annum.

169 The return on investment (ROI) for the company is closest to:

A   4.44%

B   4.74%

C   5.77%

D   6.07%

170 The residual income (RI) for the company is closest to:

$000

A   (467)

B   (487)

C   (557)

D   (577)

171 A company has reported annual operating profits for the year of $89.2m after charging $9.6m for the full development costs of a new product that is expected to last for the current year and two further years. The cost of capital is 13% per annum. The balance sheet for the company shows fixed assets with a historical cost of $120m. A note to the balance sheet estimates that the replacement cost of these fixed assets at the beginning of the year is $168m. The assets have been depreciated at 20% per year.

The company has a working capital of $27.2m.

Ignore the effects of taxation.

The Economic Value Added® (EVA) of the company is closest to:

A $64.16m

B $70.56m

C $83.36m

D $100.96m

172 ZP plc operates two subsidiaries, X and Y. X is a component-manufacturing subsidiary and Y is an assembly and final product subsidiary. Both subsidiaries produce one type of output only. Subsidiary Y needs one component from subsidiary X for every unit of Product W produced. Subsidiary X transfers to Subsidiary Y all of the components needed to produce Product W. Subsidiary X also sells components on the external market.

The following budgeted information is available for each subsidiary:

	X	*Y*
Market price per component	$800	
Market price per unit of W		$1,200
Production costs per component	$600	
Assembly costs per unit of W		$400
Non production fixed costs	$1.5m	$1.3m
External demand	10,000 units	12,000 units
Capacity	22,000 units	
Taxation rates	25%	30%

The production cost per component is 60% variable. The fixed production costs are absorbed based on budgeted output.

X sets a transfer price at marginal cost plus 70%.

Calculate the post-tax profit generated by each subsidiary. **(4 marks)**

Section 2

SECTION B-TYPE QUESTIONS

COST ACCOUNTING SYSTEMS

173 MARGINAL COST PROFIT AND CASH FLOW

Briefly discuss the assertion that marginal costing profits are a better indicator of cash flow than absorption costing profits. **(5 marks)**

174 PROCESS COSTING

In the context of a process costing system, explain the difference between a normal loss and an abnormal loss and describe how their costing treatments differ. **(5 marks)**

175 THROUGHPUT ACCOUNTING

Explain why throughput accounting has been described as a form of 'super variable costing' and how the concept of contribution in throughput accounting differs from that in marginal costing. **(5 marks)**

176 THROUGHPUT ACCOUNTING RATIO

Explain the calculation of the throughput accounting ratio and the uses to which the ratio may be put. **(5 marks)**

177 IMPROVING THE THROUGHPUT ACCOUNTING RATIO

Management considers that the throughput accounting (TA) ratio for product C in relation to the labour-intensive packing process is unacceptably low. Explain three actions that could be considered to improve the TA ratio. **(5 marks)**

178 ABC COST DRIVERS

Explain the factors that should be considered when selecting cost drivers for an activity based costing system. **(5 marks)**

179 ABC AND PROFITABILITY

Explain the circumstances in which the use of activity based costing is likely to result in more meaningful information about product costs and profitability. **(5 marks)**

180 MANUFACTURING RESOURCE PLANNING

Identify the information produced by a Manufacturing Resource Planning (MRP II) system that would be of assistance in the budgetary planning process. **(5 marks)**

181 JUST-IN-TIME

Explain the conditions that are necessary for the successful implementation of a JIT manufacturing system. **(5 marks)**

182 TQM AND JIT

Give four reasons why the adoption of Total Quality Management (TQM) is particularly important within a Just-in-Time (JIT) production environment. **(5 marks)**

183 QUALITY COST

Explain how quality cost can be measured in a programme of Total Quality Management (TQM). **(5 marks)**

184 MARGINAL AND ABSORPTION COSTING (MAY 06 EXAM)

A manufacturing company uses a standard costing system. Extracts from the budget for April are shown below:

Sales	1,400	units
Production	2,000	units
	$	
Direct costs	15	per unit
Variable overhead	4	per unit

The budgeted fixed production overhead costs for April were $12,800.

The budgeted profit using marginal costing for April was $5,700.

(i) Calculate the budgeted profit for April using absorption costing. **(3 marks)**

(ii) Briefly explain two situations where marginal costing is more useful to management than absorption costing. **(2 marks)**

(Total: 5 marks)

185 MARGINAL COSTING AND THROUGHPUT ACCOUNTING (MAY 2006 EXAM)

Compare and contrast marginal costing and throughput accounting. **(5 marks)**

STANDARD COSTING

186 IDEAL STANDARDS

A company currently uses ideal standards when setting standard costs for direct materials and direct labour. Explain and briefly discuss the level of efficiency assumed in these standards, and suggest an alternative level that may be more useful for operational control.

(5 marks)

187 FIXED PRODUCTION OVERHEAD VOLUME VARIANCE

Explain the meaning of the fixed production overhead volume variance and discuss briefly its usefulness to management. **(5 marks)**

188 LABOUR VARIANCES (NOVEMBER 05 EXAM)

A management consulting company had budgeted the staff requirements for a particular job as follows:

	$
40 hours of senior consultant at $100 per hour	4,000
60 hours of junior consultant at $60 per hour	3,600
Budgeted staff cost for job	7,600

The actual hours recorded were:

	$
50 hours of senior consultant at $100 per hour	5,000
55 hours of junior consultant at $60 per hour	3,300
Actual staff cost for job	8,300

The junior consultant reported that for 10 hours of the 55 hours recorded there was no work that she could do.

Calculate the following variances:

- idle time variance
- labour mix variance
- labour efficiency variance. **(5 marks)**

189 CRITICISMS OF STANDARD COSTING

Discuss the criticisms of the applicability of standard costing in a modern manufacturing environment. **(5 marks)**

190 STANDARD COSTING AND THE NEW MANAGEMENT ACCOUNTING

A company has adopted TQM and JIT in its recently automated manufacturing plant. Explain how the company's standard costing system will need to be adapted in the new environment. **(5 marks)**

191 RITZER'S MCDONALDIZATION MODEL

Explain the four dimensions in Ritzer's McDonaldization model, as applied to standard costing for services. **(5 marks)**

192 DIAGNOSTIC RELATED GROUPS

Explain how the use of diagnostic related groups enables standard costing to be applied in the healthcare industry. **(5 marks)**

193 MIX AND YIELD VARIANCES

Explain the meaning of the materials mix and yield variances and discuss briefly any limitations in their usefulness. **(5 marks)**

194 LABOUR RATE VARIANCE

State FIVE possible causes of an adverse labour rate variance. **(5 marks)**

PAPER P1 : MANAGEMENT ACCOUNTING – PERFORMANCE EVALUATION

195 INVESTIGATION OF VARIANCES (NOVEMBER 05 EXAM)

An analysis of past output has shown that batches have a mean weight of 90 kg and that the weights conform to the normal distribution with a standard deviation of 10 kg. The company has a policy to investigate variances that fall outside the range that includes 95% of outcomes. In September one sample batch weighed 110 kg.

(a) Calculate whether the material usage variance for this batch should be investigated according to the company policy described above. **(3 marks)**

(b) Discuss two other important factors that should be taken into account when deciding whether to investigate this variance. **(2 marks)**

(Total: 5 marks)

196 INTERPRETING VARIANCES (1)

Describe the factors that determine whether or not a variance is significant. **(5 marks)**

197 INTERPRETING VARIANCES (2)

Explain the factors that should be considered before deciding to investigate a variance.

(5 marks)

198 CENTRALLY SET STANDARDS

Explain the advantages and disadvantages of imposing centrally set standard costs on site managers. **(5 marks)**

199 BENCHMARKING

Explain benchmarking and how it can be used to improve an organisation's performance.

(5 marks)

200 HOSPITAL CARE (MAY 06 EXAM)

The standard cost schedule for hospital care for a minor surgical procedure is shown below.

Standard cost of hospital care for a minor surgical procedure

Staff: patient ratio is 0.75:1

	$
Nursing costs: 2 days × 0.75 × $320 per day	480
Space and food costs: 2 days × $175 per day	350
Drugs and specific materials	115
Hospital overheads: 2 days × $110 per day	220
Total standard cost	**1,165**

The actual data for the hospital care for one patient having the minor surgical procedure showed that the patient stayed in hospital for three days. The cost of the drugs and specific materials for this patient was $320. There were 0.9 nurses per patient on duty during the time that the patient was in hospital. The daily rates for nursing pay, space and food, and hospital overheads were as expected.

Prepare a statement that reconciles the standard cost with the actual costs of hospital care for this patient. The statement should contain FIVE variances that will give useful information to the manager who is reviewing the cost of hospital care for minor surgical procedures.

(5 marks)

201 C PLC (MAY 06 EXAM)

C plc uses a just-in-time (JIT) purchasing and production process to manufacture Product P. Data for the output of Product P, and the material usage and material price variances for February, March and April are shown below:

Month	Output (units)	Material usage variance		Material price variance	
February	11,000	$15,970	Adverse	$12,300	Favourable
March	5,100	$5,950	Adverse	$4,500	Favourable
April	9,100	$8,400	Adverse	$6,200	Favourable

The standard material cost per unit of Product P is $12.

Prepare a sketch (not on graph paper) of a percentage variance chart for material usage and for material price for Product P for the three-month period. (*Note:* Your workings must show the co-ordinates of the points that would be plotted if the chart were drawn accurately.)

(5 marks)

202 MODERN BUSINESS ENVIRONMENT (MAY 06 EXAM)

Briefly discuss THREE reasons why standard costing may not be appropriate in a modern business environment. **(5 marks)**

BUDGETING

203 PURPOSE OF BUDGETS

Describe and briefly explain the main purposes of budgets. **(5 marks)**

204 CONTROLLABILITY

Define the 'controllability principle' and give arguments for and against its implementation in determining performance measures. **(5 marks)**

205 BUDGET SLACK

Explain why incremental budgeting might not be appropriate as a basis of budgeting if budget slack is to be minimised. **(5 marks)**

206 ZERO-BASED BUDGETING

Briefly describe zero-based budgeting, how it might be implemented in an organisation and the benefits that should result. **(5 marks)**

207 J LIMITED (NOVEMBER 05 EXAM)

J Limited has recently been taken over by a much larger company. For many years the budgets in J have been set by adding an inflation adjustment to the previous year's budget. The new owners of J are insisting on a 'zero-based' approach when the next budget is set, as they believe many of the indirect costs in J are much higher than in other companies under their control.

(a) Explain the main features of 'zero-based budgeting'. **(2 marks)**

(b) Discuss the problems that might arise when implementing this approach in J Limited. **(3 marks)**

(Total: 5 marks)

208 ZBB V ABB

Explain the differences and similarities between zero-based budgeting and activity-based budgeting. **(5 marks)**

209 INCREMENTAL BUDGETS V ZBB

Explain the differences between an incremental budgeting system and a zero-based budgeting system. **(5 marks)**

210 ROLLING BUDGET

Explain what is meant by a rolling budget and what advantages and disadvantages can be claimed for this type of budget compared with a periodic budgeting system. **(5 marks)**

211 'WHAT IF' ANALYSIS

Explain what is meant by 'what if' analysis, describe the action that management might take in response to the information provided and state any limitations of the analysis. **(5 marks)**

212 FEEDBACK AND FEEDFORWARD

Briefly outline the main features of 'feedback control' and the 'feedback loop' and explain how, in practice, the procedures of feedback control can be transformed into 'feedforward control'. **(5 marks)**

213 FIXED V FLEXIBLE BUDGETS

Explain the difference between fixed and flexible budgets and how each may be used to control production costs and non-production costs. **(5 marks)**

214 SERVICE-BASED ORGANISATIONS

Distinguish between the use of budgetary control and standard costing as a means of cost control in service-based organisations. Explain clearly the arguments in favour of using both of these methods simultaneously. **(5 marks)**

SECTION B-TYPE QUESTIONS : SECTION 2

215 MCDONALDIZATION AND BUDGETS (NOVEMBER 05 EXAM)

UV Limited is a catering company that provides meals for large events. It has a range of standard meals at fixed prices. It also provides meals to meet the exact requirements of a customer and prices for this service are negotiated individually with each customer.

Discuss how a 'McDonaldization' approach to service delivery would impact on budget preparation and control within UV Limited. **(5 marks)**

216 ST PLC (NOVEMBER 05 EXAM)

ST plc is a medium-sized engineering company using advanced technology. It has just implemented an integrated enterprise resource planning (ERP) system in place of an old manufacturing resource planning (MRP) system.

Discuss the changes that are likely to be seen after the implementation of the ERP system in:

(a) the budget-setting process; and

(b) the budgetary control process. **(5 marks)**

217 BEHAVIOURAL FACTORS

Explain the behavioural factors which should be considered when budgets are being used to assess management performance. **(5 marks)**

218 W LIMITED (NOVEMBER 05 EXAM)

W Limited has conducted a review of its budget-setting procedures. The review co-ordinator frequently heard the following comment from staff interviewed:

'It's impossible to make this system work because senior managers want budgets to be a challenging target whereas the finance department requires an accurate forecast.'

Discuss the issues raised in this comment, and advise the review co-ordinator on practical action that could be taken to alleviate the situation described. **(5 marks)**

219 PARTICIPATION IN BUDGET SETTING (1)

Briefly outline the advantages and disadvantages of allowing profit centre managers to participate actively in the setting of the budget for their units. **(5 marks)**

220 BALANCED SCORECARD (1)

For each perspective of the balanced scorecard, suggest one performance measure that could be used by a company that provides a passenger transport service, explaining the reason for monitoring each measure that you suggest. **(5 marks)**

221 BEYOND BUDGETING (1)

Some critics of traditional budgeting advocate techniques that are 'beyond budgeting'. Describe their criticisms of traditional budgeting and outline what they suggest should be the features of an appropriate system of planning and control. **(5 marks)**

222 TIME SERIES IN FORECASTING

Describe the strengths and weaknesses of using time series analysis to prepare forecasts.

(5 marks)

PAPER P1 : MANAGEMENT ACCOUNTING – PERFORMANCE EVALUATION

223 BALANCED SCORECARD (2) (MAY 05 EXAM)

A general insurance company is about to implement a Balanced Scorecard. You are required to:

(a) State the four perspectives of a Balanced Scorecard.

(b) Recommend one performance measure that would be appropriate for a general insurance company, for each of the four perspectives, and give a reason to support each measure. (You must recommend one measure only for each perspective.)

(5 marks)

224 PARTICIPATION IN BUDGET SETTING (2) (MAY 05 EXAM)

Briefly discuss THREE different circumstances where participation in setting budgets is likely to contribute to poor performance from managers. **(5 marks)**

225 BEYOND BUDGETING (2) (MAY 05 EXAM)

W Limited designs and sells computer games. There are many other firms in this industry. For the last five years the senior management has required detailed budgets to be produced for each year with slightly less detailed plans for the following two years. The managing director of W Limited has recently attended a seminar on budgeting and heard the 'Beyond Budgeting' arguments that have been advanced by Hope and Fraser, among others.

You are required to:

(a) briefly describe the 'Beyond Budgeting' approach; and **(2 marks)**

(b) advise the management of W Limited whether or not it should change its current budgeting system to a 'Beyond Budgeting' approach. **(3 marks)**

(Total: 5 marks)

226 X PLC (NOVEMBER 06 EXAM)

The following scenario is given for sub-questions (a) to (f).

X plc manufactures specialist insulating products that are used in both residential and commercial buildings. One of the products, Product W, is made using two different raw materials and two types of labour. The company operates a standard absorption costing system and is now preparing its budgets for the next four quarters. The following information has been identified for Product W:

Sales
Selling price $220 per unit

Sales demand
Quarter 1   2,250 units
Quarter 2   2,050 units
Quarter 3   1,650 units
Quarter 4   2,050 units
Quarter 5   1,250 units
Quarter 6   2,050 units

Costs
Materials
A   5 kgs per unit @ $4 per kg
B   3 kgs per unit @ $7 per kg

Labour
    Skilled   4 hours per unit @ $15 per hour
    Semi-skilled   6 hours per unit @ $9 per hour

Annual overheads $280,000
                                                              40% of these overheads are fixed and the remainder varies with total labour hours. Fixed overheads are absorbed on a unit basis.

Inventory holding policy
Closing inventory of finished goods   30% of the following quarter's sales demand
Closing inventory of materials   45% of the following quarter's materials usage

The management team is concerned that X plc has recently faced increasing competition in the marketplace for Product W. As a consequence there have been issues concerning the availability and costs of the specialised materials and employees needed to manufacture Product W, and there is concern that these might cause problems in the current budget-setting process.

(a)   Prepare the following budgets for each quarter for X plc:

        (i)   Production budget in units

        (ii)   Raw material purchases budget in kgs and value for Material B.

(5 marks)

(b)   X plc has just been informed that Material A may be in short supply during the year for which it is preparing budgets. Discuss the impact this will have on budget preparation and other areas of X plc.

(5 marks)

(c)   Assume that the budgeted production of Product W was 7,700 units and that the following actual results were incurred for labour and overheads in the year:

                 Actual production   7,250 units
                 Actual overheads
                     Variable $185,000
                     Fixed $105,000
                 Actual labour costs
                     Skilled – $16.25 per hour $568,750
                     Semi-skilled – $8 per hour $332,400

Prepare a flexible budget statement for X plc showing the total variances that have occurred for the above four costs only. **(5 marks)**

(d)   X plc currently uses incremental budgeting. Explain how Zero-Based Budgeting could overcome the problems that might be faced as a result of the continued use of the current system.

(5 marks)

(e)   Explain how rolling budgets are used and why they would be suitable for X plc.

(5 marks)

(f)   Briefly explain how linear regression analysis can be used to forecast sales and briefly discuss whether it would be a suitable method for X plc to use. **(5 marks)**

(Total: 30 marks)

CONTROL AND PERFORMANCE MEASUREMENT OF RESPONSIBILITY CENTRES

227 DECENTRALISATION

Describe the advantages and disadvantages that an organisation might experience if it adopts a decentralised structure. **(5 marks)**

228 RESIDUAL INCOME V ECONOMIC VALUE ADDED

Explain and discuss the similarities and differences between Residual Income and Economic Value Added as methods for assessing the performance of divisions. **(5 marks)**

229 TRANSFER PRICING (1)

Explain the criteria an effective system of transfer pricing should satisfy. **(5 marks)**

230 INTERNATIONAL TRANSFER PRICING

Discuss the problems that arise specifically when determining transfer prices where divisions are located in different countries. **(5 marks)**

231 MARGINAL COSTS AND TRANSFER PRICING

Discuss one context in which a transfer price based on marginal cost would be appropriate and describe any issues that may arise from such a transfer pricing policy. **(5 marks)**

232 EVA® (MAY 05 EXAM)

(a) Briefly explain the main features of Economic Value Added (EVA®) as it would be used to assess the performance of divisions. **(2 marks)**

(b) Briefly explain how the use of EVA® to assess divisional performance might affect the behaviour of divisional senior executives. **(3 marks)**

(Total: 5 marks)

The following information is to be used to answer Questions 233 and 234.

C plc is a large company that manufactures and sells wooden garden furniture. It has three divisions:

The *Wood Division (WD)* purchases logs and produces finished timber as planks or beams. Approximately two-thirds of its output is sold to the Products Division, with the remainder sold on the open market.

The *Products Division (PD)* manufactures wooden garden furniture. The policy of C plc is that the PD must buy all its timber from the WD and sell all its output to the Trading Division.

The *Trading Division (TD)* sells wooden garden furniture to garden centres, large supermarkets, and similar outlets. It only sells items purchased from PD.

The current position is that all three divisions are profit centres and C plc uses Return on Investment (ROI) measures as the primary means to assess divisional performance. Each division adopts a cost-plus pricing policy for external sales and for internal transfers between divisions. The senior management of C plc has stated that the divisions should consider themselves to be independent businesses as far as possible.

233 ORGANISATION STRUCTURE (MAY 05 EXAM)

For each division suggest, with reasons, the behavioural consequences that might arise as a result of the current policy for the structure and performance evaluation of the divisions.

(5 marks)

234 TRANSFER PRICING (2) (MAY 05 EXAM)

The senior management of C plc has requested a review of the cost-plus transfer pricing policy that is currently used.

Suggest with reasons, an appropriate transfer pricing policy that could be used for transfers *from PD to TD*, indicating any problems that may arise as a consequence of the policy you suggest.

(5 marks)

235 T PLC (MAY 06 EXAM)

T plc is a large insurance company. The Claims Department deals with claims from policy holders who have suffered a loss that is covered by their insurance policy. Policy holders could claim, for example, for damage to property or for household items stolen in a burglary. The Claims Department staff investigate each claim and determine what, if any, payment should be made to the claimant.

The manager of the Claims Department has decided to benchmark the performance of the department and has chosen two areas to benchmark:

- the detection of false claims;
- the speed of processing claims.

For each of the above two areas:

(i) state and justify a performance measure;

(ii) explain how relevant benchmarking data could be gathered.

(5 marks)

Section 3

SECTION C-TYPE QUESTIONS

COST ACCOUNTING SYSTEMS

236 HENSAU

Hensau has a single production process for which the following costs have been estimated for the period ending 31 December 20X1.

	$
Material receipt and inspection cost	15,600
Power cost	19,500
Material handling cost	13,650

Three products – X, Y and Z – are produced by workers, who perform a number of operations on material blanks using hand-held electrically powered drills. The workers have a wage rate of $4 per hour.

The following budgeted information has been obtained for the period ending 31 December 20X1.

	Product X	Product Y	Product Z
Production quantity (units)	2,000	1,500	800
Batches of material	10	5	16
Data per product unit			
Direct material (square metres)	4	6	3
Direct material ($)	5	3	6
Direct labour (minutes)	24	40	60
Number of power drill operations	6	3	2

Overhead costs for material receipt and inspection, process power and material handling are presently each absorbed by product units using rates per direct labour hour.

An activity-based costing investigation has revealed that the cost drivers for the overhead costs are as follows.

Material receipt and inspection	number of batches of material
Process power	number of power drill operations
Material handling	quantity of material (square metres) handled

Required:

Prepare a summary which shows the budgeted product cost per unit for each of the products X, Y and Z for the period ending 31 December 20X1, detailing the unit costs for each cost element:

(a) using the existing method for the absorption of overhead costs, and **(6 marks)**

(b) using an approach which recognises the cost drivers revealed in the activity-based costing investigation. **(14 marks)**

(c) Comment on the results of your calculations and evaluate the benefits to the business of using activity based costing. **(10 marks)**

(Total: 30 marks)

237 BRUNTI

The following budgeted information relates to Brunti for the forthcoming period:

	Products		
	XYI (000)	YZT (000)	ABW (000)
Sales and production (units)	50	40	30
	$	$	$
Selling price (per unit)	45	95	73
Prime cost (per unit)	32	84	65
	Hours	Hours	Hours
Machine department (machine hours per unit)	2	5	4
Assembly department (direct labour hours per unit)	7	3	2

Overheads allocated and apportioned to production departments were as follows:

Machine department $504,000

Assembly department $437,000

You ascertain that the above overheads could be re-analysed into 'cost pools' as follows:

Cost pool	$000	Cost driver	Quantity for the period
Machining services	357	Machine hours	420,000
Assembly services	318	Direct labour hours	530,000
Set-up costs	26	Set-ups	520
Order processing	156	Customer orders	32,000
Purchasing	84	Suppliers' orders	11,200
	941		

You have also been provided with the following estimates for the budget period:

	Products		
	XYI	YZT	ABW
Number of set-ups	120	200	200
Customer orders	8,000	8,000	16,000
Suppliers' orders	3,000	4,000	4,200

Required:

Prepare and present budgeted profit statements using:

(a) conventional absorption costing; and **(6 marks)**

(b) activity based costing. **(12 marks)**

(c) Comment on these results. **(6 marks)**

(d) Actual results for the period are now available as follows:

Cost pool	$000	Cost driver	Quantity for the period
Machining services	385	Machine hours	402,000
Assembly services	302	Direct labour hours	535,000
Set-up costs	30	Set-ups	560
Order processing	154	Customer orders	32,050
Purchasing	78	Suppliers' orders	11,150
	949		

	Products		
	XYI	YZT	ABW
Units produced	48,000	35,000	32,000
Number of set-ups	140	220	200
Customer orders	7,850	8,100	16,100
Suppliers' orders	2,950	4,100	4,100

Calculate the total over or under absorption of set-up costs, order processing costs and purchasing costs. **(6 marks)**

(Total: 30 marks)

238 TRIMAKE

Trimake makes three main products, using broadly the same production methods and equipment for each. A conventional product costing system is used at present, although an activity based costing (ABC) system is being considered. Details of the three products for a typical period are:

	Hours per unit		Materials	Volumes
	Labour hours	Machine hours	Per unit $	Units
Product X	½	1½	20	750
Product Y	1½	1	12	1,250
Product Z	1	3	25	7,000

Direct labour costs $6 per hour and production overheads are absorbed on a machine hour basis. The rate for the period is $28 per machine hour.

Required:

(a) Calculate the cost per unit for each product using conventional methods. **(5 marks)**

Further analysis shows that the total of production overheads can be divided as follows:

	%
Costs relating to set-ups	35
Costs relating to machinery	20
Costs relating to materials handling	15
Costs relating to inspection	30
Total production overhead	100

The following total activity volumes are associated with the product line for the period as a whole.

	Number of set-ups	Number of movements of materials	Number of inspections
Product X	75	12	150
Product Y	115	21	180
Product Z	480	87	670
	670	120	1,000

Required:

(b) Calculate the cost per unit for each product using ABC principles. **(12 marks)**

(c) Comment on the reasons for any differences in the costs in your answers to (a) and (b). **(7 marks)**

(d) Explain the reasons for the development of activity based costing. **(6 marks)**

(Total: 30 marks)

239 A PAINT MANUFACTURER

XYZ, a paint manufacturer, operates a process costing system. The following details relate to process 2 for the month of October 20X7:

Opening work-in-progress	5,000 litres fully complete as to transfers from process 1 and 40% complete as to labour and overhead, valued at $60,000.
Transfer from process 1	65,000 litres valued at cost of $578,500
Direct labour	$101,400
Variable overhead	$80,000
Fixed overhead	$40,000
Normal loss	5% of volume transferred from process 1, scrap value $2.00 per litre.
Actual output	30,000 litres of Paint X (a joint product)
	25,000 litres of Paint Y (a joint product)
	7,000 litres of by-product Z
Closing work-in-progress	6,000 litres fully complete as to transfers from process 1 and 60% complete as to labour and overhead.

The final selling prices of products X, Y and Z are:

Paint X	$15.00 per litre
Paint Y	$18.00 per litre
Product Z	$4.00 per litre

There are no further processing costs associated with either Paint X or the by-product, but Paint Y requires further processing at a cost of $1.50 per litre.

All three products incur packaging costs of $0.50 per litre before they can be sold.

Required:

(a) Prepare the process 2 account for the month of October 20X7 apportioning the common costs between the joint products, based upon their values at the point of separation.

(17 marks)

(b) Prepare the abnormal loss/gain account showing clearly the amount to be transferred to the income statement. **(3 marks)**

(c) Explain the similarities and differences between process accounting and throughput accounting. **(10 marks)**

(Total: 30 marks)

240 CHEMICAL PROCESSING (PILOT PAPER)

PQR is a chemical processing company. The company produces a range of solvents by passing materials through a series of processes. The company uses the First In First Out (FIFO) valuation method.

In Process 2, the output from Process 1 (XP1) is blended with two other materials (P2A and P2B) to form XP2. It is expected that 10% of any new input to Process 2 (that is, transfers from Process 1 plus Process 2 materials added) will be immediately lost and that this loss will have no resale value. It is also expected that in addition to the loss, 5% of any new input will form a by-product, Z, which can be sold without additional processing for $2 per litre.

Data from Process 2 for November was as follows:

Opening work-in-process

Process 2 had 1,200 litres of opening work-in-process. The value and degree of completion of this was as follows:

	$	Degree of completion %
XP1	1,560	100
P2A	1,540	100
P2B	750	100
Conversion costs	3,790	40
	7,640	

Input

During November, the inputs to Process 2 were:

		$
XP1	5,000 litres	15,679
P2A	1,200 litres	6,000
P2B	3,000 litres	4,500
Conversion costs		22,800

Closing work-in-process

At the end of November, the work-in-process was 1,450 litres. This was fully complete in respect of all materials, but only 30% complete for conversion costs.

Output

The output from Process 2 during November was:

Z	460 litres
XP2	7,850 litres

Required:

Prepare the Process 2 account for November 20X3. **(17 marks)**

Marks awarded for presentation. **(3 marks)**

(Total: 20 marks)

PAPER P1 : MANAGEMENT ACCOUNTING – PERFORMANCE EVALUATION

241 BIOTINCT (NOVEMBER 05 EXAM)

(a) M Pty produces 'Biotinct' in a lengthy distillation and cooling process. Base materials are introduced at the start of this process, and further chemicals are added when it is 80% complete. Each kilogram of base materials produces 1 kg of Biotinct.

Data for October are:

Opening work-in-process	40 kg of base materials, 25% processed	
Cost of opening work-in-process	Base materials	$1,550
	Processing	$720
Costs incurred in October	Base materials (80 kg)	$3,400
	Conversion costs	$6,864
	Further chemicals	$7,200
Closing work-in-process	50 kg of base materials, 90% processed	
Finished output	65 kg of Biotinct	

Under normal conditions there are no losses of base materials in this process. However, in October 5 kg of partially complete Biotinct were spoiled immediately after the further chemicals had been added. The 5 kg of spoiled Biotinct were not processed to finished goods stage and were sold for a total of $200.

Required:

Using the FIFO method, prepare the process account for October. **(12 marks)**

(b) One of the company's management accountants overheard the Managing Director arguing as follows: "These process accounts are complicated to produce, and often conceal the true position. As I see it, the value of partly processed Biotinct is zero.

In October we spent $17,464 and the output was 65 kg. So the average cost was $268.68 per kilogram, while the target cost is $170 ($40 for base materials, $70 for processing and $60 for further chemicals). These figures make me concerned about production efficiency."

Required:

Explain to the Managing Director any errors in the comment he made, and discuss whether the data from the process account indicate that there has been production inefficiency. **(8 marks)**

(Total: 20 marks)

242 PHARMACEUTICAL DRUGS (MAY 05 EXAM)

F plc supplies pharmaceutical drugs to drug stores. Although the company makes a satisfactory return, the directors are concerned that some orders are profitable and others are not. The management has decided to investigate a new budgeting system using activity-based costing principles to ensure that all orders they accept are making a profit.

Each customer order is charged as follows. Customers are charged the list price of the drugs ordered plus a charge for selling and distribution costs (overheads). A profit margin is also added, but that does not form part of this analysis.

Currently F plc uses a simple absorption rate to absorb these overheads. The rate is calculated based on the budgeted annual selling and distribution costs and the budgeted annual total list price of the drugs ordered.

An analysis of customers has revealed that many customers place frequent small orders with each order requesting a variety of drugs. The management of F plc has examined more carefully the nature of its selling and distribution costs, and the following data have been prepared for the budget for next year:

Total list price of drugs supplied	$8m	
Number of customer orders	8,000	
Selling and distribution costs	$000	Cost driver
Invoice processing	280	See Note 2
Packing	220	Size of package – see Note 3
Delivery	180	Number of deliveries – see Note 4
Other overheads	200	Number of orders
Total overheads	880	

Notes:

(1) Each order will be shipped in one package and will result in one delivery to the customer and one invoice (an order never results in more than one delivery).

(2) Each invoice has a different line for each drug ordered. There are 28,000 invoice lines each year. It is estimated that 25% of invoice processing costs are related to the number of invoices, and 75% are related to the number of invoice lines.

(3) Packing costs are $32 for a large package, and $25 for a small package.

(4) The delivery vehicles are always filled to capacity for each journey. The delivery vehicles can carry either 6 large packages or 12 small packages (or appropriate combinations of large and small packages). It is estimated that there will be 1,000 delivery journeys each year, and the total delivery mileage that is specific to particular customers is estimated at 350,000 miles each year. $40,000 of delivery costs are related to loading the delivery vehicles, and the remainder of these costs are related to specific delivery distance to customers.

The management has asked for two typical orders to be costed using next year's budget data, using the current method, and the proposed activity-based costing approach. Details of two typical orders are shown below:

	Order A	Order B
Lines on invoice	2	8
Package size	Small	Large
Specific delivery distance	8 miles	40 miles
List price of drugs supplied	$1,200	$900

Required:

(a) Calculate the charge for selling and distribution overheads for Order A and Order B using:

    (i) the current system; and **(5 marks)**

    (ii) the activity-based costing approach. **(15 marks)**

PAPER P1 : MANAGEMENT ACCOUNTING – PERFORMANCE EVALUATION

(b) Write a report to the management of F plc in which you:

    (i) assess the strengths and weaknesses of the proposed activity-based costing approach for F plc; and **(5 marks)**

    (ii) recommend actions that the management of F plc might consider in the light of the data produced using the activity-based costing approach. **(5 marks)**

(Total: 30 marks)

243 MN LTD

MN Ltd manufactures automated industrial trolleys, known as TRLs. Each TRL sells for $2,000 and the material cost per unit is $600. Labour and variable overheads are $5,500 and $8,000 per week respectively. Fixed production costs are $450,000 per annum and marketing and administrative costs are $265,000 per annum.

The trolleys are made on three different machines. Machine X makes the four frame panels required for each TRL. Its maximum output is 180 frame panels per week. Machine X is old and unreliable and it breaks down from time to time. It is estimated that, on average, between 15 and 20 hours of production are lost per month. Machine Y can manufacture parts for 52 TRLs per week and machine Z, which is old but reasonably reliable, can process and assemble 30 TRLs per week.

The company has recently introduced a just-in-time (JIT) system and it is company policy to hold little work-in-progress and no finished goods stock from week to week. The company operates a 40-hour week, 48 weeks a year (12 months × 4 weeks) but cannot meet demand.

The management of MN Ltd is wondering whether it should now install a full standard costing and variance analysis system. At present, standard costs are calculated only as part of the annual budgeting process. Management is concerned about implementing so many changes in a short space of time, but feels the system could be very useful.

(a) Explain the concept of throughput accounting. **(6 marks)**

(b) Identify the bottleneck resource for MN Ltd. **(6 marks)**

(c) Calculate the throughput accounting ratio for the key resource for an average hour next year. **(6 marks)**

(d) Explain the meaning and uses of the throughput accounting ratio. **(6 marks)**

(e) Explain how the concept of contribution in throughput accounting differs from that in marginal costing. **(6 marks)**

(Total: 30 marks)

STANDARD COSTING

244 RS

RS makes and sells a single product, J, with the following standard specification for materials:

	Quantity	Price per kg
	kg	$
Direct material R	10	30
Direct material S	6	45

It takes 30 direct labour hours to produce one unit of J with a standard direct labour cost of $5.50 per hour.

The annual sales/production budget is 1,200 units evenly spread throughout the year.

The budgeted production overhead, all fixed, is $252,000 and expenditure is expected to occur evenly over the year, which the company divides into 12 calendar months. Absorption is based on units produced.

For the month of October the following actual information is provided. The budgeted sales quantity for the month was sold at the standard selling price.

	$	$
Sales		120,000
Cost of sales		
Direct materials used	58,136	
Direct wages	17,325	
Fixed production overhead	22,000	
		97,461
Gross profit		22,539
Administration costs	6,000	
Selling and distribution costs	11,000	
		17,000
Net profit		$5,539

Costs of opening inventories, for each material, were at the same price per kilogram as the purchases made during the month but there had been changes in the materials inventory levels, as follows:

	1 October	30 October
	Kg	Kg
Material R	300	375
Material S	460	225

Material R purchases were 1,100 kg for $35,000.

Material S purchases were 345 kg for $15,180.

The number of direct labour hours worked was 3,300 and the total wages incurred $17,325.

Work-in-progress and finished goods inventories may be assumed to be the same at the beginning and end of October.

Required:

(a) Present a standard product cost for one unit of product J showing the standard selling price and standard gross profit per unit. **(4 marks)**

(b) Calculate appropriate variances for the materials, labour and fixed production overhead, noting that it is company policy to calculate material price variances *at time of issue to production.* Material mix and yield variances are not calculated.

(12 marks)

(c) Present a statement for management reconciling the budgeted gross profit with the actual gross profit. **(6 marks)**

(d) Suggest a possible cause for each of the labour variances you show under (b) above, stating whether you believe each variance was controllable or uncontrollable and, if controllable, the job title of the responsible official. **(8 marks)**

(Total: 30 marks)

245 DL HOSPITAL TRUST

You have been appointed as the management accountant of the DL Hospital Trust, a newly-formed organisation with specific responsibility for providing hospital services to its local community. The hospital trust is divided into a number of specialist units: one of these, unit H, specialises in the provision of a particular surgical operation.

Although the trust does not have profit maximisation as its objective, it is concerned to control its costs and to provide a value-for-money service. To achieve this, it engages teams of specialist staff on a sub-contract basis and pays them an hourly rate based upon the direct hours attributable to the surgical operation being carried out.

Surgical team fees (i.e. labour costs) are collected and attributed to each surgical operation, whereas overhead costs are collected and attributed to surgical operations using absorption rates. These absorption rates are based on the surgical team fees. For the year ended 31 December 20X3, these rates were:

Variable overhead	62.5% of surgical team fees; and
Fixed overhead	87.5% of surgical team fees.

Each surgical operation is expected to take ten hours to complete, and the total fees of the team for each operation are expected to be $2,000.

The budget for the year ended 31 December 20X3 indicated that a total of 20 such surgical operations were expected to be performed each month, and that the overhead costs were expected to accrue evenly throughout the year.

During November 20X3 there were 22 operations of this type completed. These took a total of 235 hours and the total surgical team fees amounted to $44,400.

Overhead costs incurred in unit H in November 20X3 amounted to:

Variable overhead	$28,650
Fixed overhead	$36,950

Required:

(a) Prepare a statement which reconciles the original budget cost and the actual cost for this type of operation within unit H for the month of November 20X3, showing the analysis of variances in as much detail as possible from the information given. **(18 marks)**

(b) Distinguish between the use of budgetary control and standard costing as a means of cost control in service-based organisations.

Explain clearly the arguments in favour of using BOTH of these methods simultaneously. **(6 marks)**

(c) The DL Hospital Trust has been preparing its budgets for 20X4, and the finance director has questioned the appropriateness of using surgical team fees as the basis of attributing overhead costs to operations.

Write a brief report to her explaining the arguments for and against the use of this method. **(6 marks)**

(Total: 30 marks)

SECTION C-TYPE QUESTIONS : SECTION 3

246 RBF TRANSPORT

RBF Transport, a haulage contractor, operates a standard costing system and has prepared the following report for April 20X0:

Operating statement

			$	$	$
Budgeted profit					8,000
Sales volume profit variance					880 (A)
					7,120
Selling price variance					3,560 (F)
					10,680
Cost variances			A	F	
Direct labour	-	rate		1,086	
	-	efficiency	240		
Fuel	-	price	420		
	-	usage	1,280		
Variable overhead	-	expenditure		280	
	-	efficiency	180		
Fixed overhead	-	expenditure		400	
	-	volume	1,760		
			3,880	1,766	2,114 (A)
Actual profit					8,566

The company uses delivery miles as its cost unit, and the following details have been taken from the budget working papers for April 20X0:

(1) Expected activity   200,000 delivery miles

(2) Charge to customers $0.30 per delivery mile

(3) Expected variable cost per delivery mile:

    Direct labour (0.02 hours) $0.08

    Fuel (0.1 litres) $0.04

    Variable overhead (0.02 hours) $0.06

The following additional information has been determined from the actual accounting records for April 20X0.

- Fixed overhead cost $15,600
- Fuel price $0.42 per litre
- Direct labour hours   3,620

Required:

(a) Calculate for April 20X0:

    (i) the actual number of delivery miles;

    (ii) the actual direct labour rate per hour;

    (iii) the actual number of litres of fuel consumed;

    (iv) the actual variable overhead expenditure. **(16 marks)**

(b) State TWO possible causes of the fuel usage variance. **(4 marks)**

(c) Prepare a report, addressed to the transport operations manager, explaining the different types of standard which may be set, and the importance of keeping standards meaningful and relevant. **(10 marks)**

(Total: 30 marks)

247 ABC

The following profit reconciliation statement has been prepared by the management accountant of ABC for March 20X5.

		Adv $	Fav $	$
Budgeted profit				30,000
Sales volume profit variance				5,250 (A)
Selling price variance				6,375 (F)
				31,125
Cost variances:				
Material:	price	1,985		
	usage		400	
Labour:	rate		9,800	
	efficiency	4,000		
Variable overhead:	expenditure		1,000	
	efficiency	1,500		
Fixed overhead:	expenditure		500	
	volume	24,500		
		31,985	11,700	
				20,285 (A)
Actual profit				10,840

The standard cost card for the company's only product is as follows:

		$
Materials	5 litres @ $0.20	1.00
Labour	4 hours @ $4.00	16.00
Variable overhead	4 hours @ $1.50	6.00
Fixed overhead	4 hours @ $3.50	14.00
		37.00
Standard profit		3.00
Standard selling price		40.00

The following information is also available:

(1) There was no change in the level of finished goods inventory during the month.

(2) Budgeted production and sales volumes for March 20X5 were equal.

(3) Inventories of materials, which are valued at standard price, decreased by 800 litres during the month.

(4) The actual labour rate was $0.28 lower than the standard hourly rate.

Required:

(a) Calculate the following:

    (i) the actual production/sales volume; **(4 marks)**

    (ii) the actual number of hours worked; **(4 marks)**

    (iii) the actual quantity of materials purchased; **(4 marks)**

    (iv) the actual variable overhead cost incurred; **(2 marks)**

    (v) the actual fixed overhead cost incurred. **(2 marks)**

(b) State TWO possible causes of the labour efficiency variance **(4 marks)**

(c) ABC Ltd uses a standard costing system whereas other organisations use a system of budgetary control. Explain the reasons why a system of budgetary control is often preferred to the use of standard costing in non-manufacturing environments.

(10 marks)

(Total: 30 marks)

248 ZED

ZED sells two products, the Alpha and the Beta. These are made from three different raw materials that are bought from local suppliers using a Just-in-Time (JIT) purchasing policy. Products Alpha and Beta are made to customer order using a JIT manufacturing policy. Overhead costs are absorbed using direct labour hours as appropriate.

The following information relates to October:

	Alpha	Beta
Budgeted production (units)	2,400	1,800

Standard selling price

The standard selling price is determined by adding a 100% mark-up to the standard variable costs of each product.

Standard variable costs per unit	Alpha	Beta
	$	$
Direct material X ($5 per metre)	10.00	12.50
Direct material Y ($8 per litre)	8.00	12.00
Direct material Z ($10 per kg)	5.00	10.00
Direct labour ($7 per hour)	14.00	10.50
Variable overhead costs	3.00	2.25

Actual data for October

Direct material X	10,150 metres	costing	$48,890
Direct material Y	5,290 litres	costing	$44,760
Direct material Z	2,790 kgs	costing	$29,850
Direct labour	9,140 hours paid	costing	$67,980
Direct labour	8,350 hours worked		
Variable overhead			$14,300
Fixed overhead			$72,000
Actual production	Alpha	3,000 units	
	Beta	1,500 units	

Sales variances

The following sales variances have been calculated:

	Absorption costing		Marginal costing	
	Alpha	Beta	Alpha	Beta
	$	$	$	$
Selling price	6,000 (A)	4,500 (F)	6,000 (A)	4,500 (F)
Sales volume	18,000 (F)	11,925 (A)	24,000 (F)	14,175 (A)

Required:

(a) Calculate the budgeted fixed overhead cost for October. **(6 marks)**

(b) Calculate the budgeted profit for October. **(2 marks)**

(c) Calculate the actual profit for October. **(4 marks)**

(d) Prepare a statement, using absorption costing principles, that reconciles the budgeted and actual profits for October, showing the variances in as much detail as possible. Do not calculate material mix and yield variances. **(15 marks)**

(e) Explain why it would be inappropriate to calculate material mix and yield variances in requirement (d) above. **(3 marks)**

(Total: 30 marks)

249 SALES/OVERHEAD VARIANCES

You have been provided with the following data for S for September 20X6:

Accounting method	Absorption	Marginal
Variances	$	$
Selling price	1,900 (A)	1,900 (A)
Sales volume margin/contribution	4,500 (A)	7,500 (A)
Fixed overhead expenditure	2,500 (F)	2,500 (F)
Fixed overhead volume	1,800 (A)	not applicable

During September 20X6 production and sales volumes were as follows:

	Sales	Production
Budget	10,000	10,000
Actual	9,500	

Required:

(a) Calculate:

   (i) the standard contribution per unit;

   (ii) the standard profit per unit;

   (iii) the actual fixed overhead cost total;

   (iv) the actual production volume. **(12 marks)**

(b) Using the information presented above, explain why different variances are calculated depending upon the choice of marginal or absorption costing. **(6 marks)**

(c) Explain the meaning of the fixed overhead volume variance and its usefulness to management. **(6 marks)**

(d) Fixed overhead absorption rates are often calculated using a single measure of activity. It is suggested that fixed overhead costs should be attributed to cost units using multiple measures of activity (Activity Based Costing).

   Explain Activity Based Costing and how it may provide useful information to managers.

   (Your answer should refer to both the setting of cost driver rates and subsequent overhead cost control.) **(6 marks)**

(Total: 30 marks)

250 FB

FB makes and sells a single product. The standard cost and revenue per unit are as follows:

		$
Selling price		400
Direct material A	5 kg at $25 per kg	125
Direct material B	3 kg at $22 per kg	66
Direct labour	3 hours at $10 per hour	30
Variable overheads	3 hours at $7 per hour	21
Standard contribution		158

The budgeted production and sales for the period in question were 10,000 units.

The mix of materials can be varied and therefore the material usage variance can be sub-divided into mix and yield variances.

For the period under review, the actual results were as follows:

Production and sales		9,000 units
		$
Sales revenue		4,455,000
Material cost	A – 35,000 kg	910,000
	B – 50,000 kg	1,050,000
Labour cost	30,000 hours	385,000
Variable overhead		230,000

The general market prices at the time of purchase for material A and material B were $21 per kg and $19 per kg respectively.

There were no opening or closing inventories during the period.

Required:

(a) Prepare a statement detailing the variances (including planning and operational, and mix and yield variances) which reconciles the budgeted contribution and the actual contribution. **(22 marks)**

(b) Discuss the results and usefulness to FB of the planning and operational, and mix and yield variances that you have calculated in your answer to part (a). **(8 marks)**

(Total: 30 marks)

251 SATELLITE NAVIGATION SYSTEMS (MAY 05 EXAM)

S Limited installs complex satellite navigation systems in cars, at a very large national depot. The standard cost of an installation is shown below. The budgeted volume is 1,000 units installed each month. The operations manager is responsible for three departments, namely: purchasing, fitting and quality control. S Limited purchases navigation systems and other equipment from different suppliers, and most items are imported. The fitting of different systems takes differing amounts of time, but the differences are not more than 25% from the average, so a standard labour time is applied.

Standard cost of installation of one navigation system

	$	Quantity	Price ($)
Materials	400	1 unit	400
Labour	320	20 hours	16
Variable overheads	140	20 hours	7
Fixed overheads	300	20 hours	15
Total standard cost	1,160		

The Operations Department has gathered the following information over the last few months. There are significant difficulties in retaining skilled staff. Many have left for similar but better paid jobs and as a result there is a high labour turnover. Exchange rates have moved and commentators have argued this will make exports cheaper, but S Limited has no exports and has not benefited. Some of the fitters have complained that one large batch of systems did not have the correct adapters and would not fit certain cars, but this was not apparent until fitting was attempted. Rent, rates, insurance and computing facilities have risen in price noticeably.

The financial results for September to December are shown below.

Operating statement for S Limited for September to December

	September $	October $	November $	December $	4 months $
Standard cost of actual output	1,276,000	1,276,000	1,102,000	1,044,000	4,698,000
Variances materials					
Price	5,505 F	3,354 F	9,520 A	10,340 A	11,001 A
Usage	400 A	7,200 A	800 A	16,000 A	24,400 A
Labour rate	4,200 A	5,500 A	23,100 A	24,000 A	56,800 A
Efficiency	16,000 F	0	32,000 A	32,000 A	48,000 A
Variable overheads					
Expenditure	7,000 A	2,000 A	2,000 F	0	7,000 A
Efficiency	7,000 F	0	14,000 A	14,000 A	21,000 A
Fixed overheads					
Expenditure	5,000 A	10,000 A	20,000 A	20,000 A	55,000 A
Volume	30,000 F	30,000 F	15,000 A	30,000 A	15,000 F
Actual costs	1,234,095	1,267,346	1,214,420	1,190,340	4,906,201

A = adverse variance   F = favourable variance

Required:

(a) Prepare a report to the operations manager of S Limited commenting on the performance of the company for the four months to 31 December. State probable causes for the key issues you have included in your report and state the further information that would be helpful in assessing the performance of the company.

(15 marks)

(b) Prepare a short report to the operations manager of S Limited suggesting ways that the budgeting system could be used to increase motivation and improve performance.

(5 marks)

(c) Prepare a percentage variance chart for material usage and material price for the four-month period. Explain how this could be used to decide whether or not to investigate the variances.

(10 marks)

(Total: 30 marks)

252 X LTD (NOVEMBER 06 EXAM)

X Ltd uses an automated manufacturing process to produce an industrial chemical, Product P.

X Ltd operates a standard marginal costing system. The standard cost data for Product P is as follows:

Standard cost per unit of Product P

Materials

A	10 kgs	@ $15 per kilo	$150
B	8 kgs	@ $8 per kilo	$64
C	5 kgs	@ $4 per kilo	$20
	23 kgs		

Total standard marginal cost $234

Budgeted fixed production overheads $350,000

In order to arrive at the budgeted selling price for Product P the company adds 80% mark-up to the standard marginal cost. The company budgeted to produce and sell 5,000 units of Product P in the period. There were no budgeted inventories of Product P.

The actual results for the period were as follows:

Actual production and sales		5,450 units
Actual sales price		$445 per unit
Material usage and cost		
A	43,000 kgs	$688,000
B	37,000 kgs	$277,500
C	23,500 kgs	$99,875
	103,500 kgs	
Fixed production overheads		$385,000

Required:

(a) Prepare an operating statement which reconciles the budgeted profit to the actual profit for the period. (The statement should include the material mix and material yield variances.) **(12 marks)**

(b) The Production Manager of X Ltd is new to the job and has very little experience of management information. Write a brief report to the Production Manager of X Ltd that:

  (i) interprets the material price, mix and yield variances;

  (ii) discusses the merits, or otherwise, of calculating the materials mix and yield variances for X Ltd. **(8 marks)**

(Total: 20 marks)

BUDGETING

253 PUBLIC SECTOR ORGANISATION

A public sector organisation is extending its budgetary control and responsibility accounting system to all departments. One such department concerned with public health and welfare is called 'Homecare'. The department consists of staff who visit elderly 'clients' in their homes to support them with their basic medical and welfare needs.

A monthly cost control report is to be sent to the department manager, a copy of which is also passed to a Director who controls a number of departments. In the system, which is still being refined, the budget was set by the Director and the manager had not been consulted over the budget or the use of the monthly control report.

Shown below is the first month's cost control report for the Homecare department.

Cost Control Report – Homecare Department
Month ending May 20X0

	Budget	Actual	(Overspend)/ Underspend
Visits	10,000	12,000	(2,000)
	$	$	$
Department expenses:			
Supervisory salary	2,000	2,125	(125)
Wages (Permanent staff)	2,700	2,400	300
Wages (Casual staff)	1,500	2,500	(1,000)
Office equipment depreciation	500	750	(250)
Repairs to equipment	200	20	180
Travel expenses	1,500	1,800	(300)
Consumables	4,000	6,000	(2,000)
Administration and telephone	1,000	1,200	(200)
Allocated administrative costs	2,000	3,000	(1,000)
	15,400	19,795	(4,395)

In addition to the manager and permanent members of staff, appropriately qualified casual staff are appointed on a week to week basis to cope with fluctuations in demand. Staff use their own transport, and travel expenses are reimbursed. There is a central administration overhead charge over all departments. Consumables consist of materials which are used by staff to care for clients. Administration and telephone are costs of keeping in touch with the staff who often operate from their own homes.

As a result of the report, the Director sent a memo to the manager of the Homecare department pointing out that the department must spend within its funding allocation and that any spending more than 5% above budget on any item would not be tolerated. The Director requested an immediate explanation for the serious overspend.

You work as the assistant to the Directorate Management Accountant. On seeing the way the budget system was developing, he made a note of points he would wish to discuss and develop further, but was called away before these could be completed.

SECTION C-TYPE QUESTIONS : SECTION 3

Required:

(a) Develop and explain the issues concerning the budgetary control and responsibility accounting system which are likely to be raised by the management accountant. You should refer to the way the budget was prepared, the implications of a 20% increase in the number of visits, the extent of controllability of costs, the implications of the funding allocation, social aspects and any other points you think appropriate. You may include numerical illustrations and comment on specific costs, but you are not required to reproduce the cost control report. **(22 marks)**

(b) Briefly explain Zero-Based Budgeting (ZBB), describe how (in a situation such as that above) it might be implemented, and how as a result it could improve the budget setting procedure. **(8 marks)**

(Total: 30 marks)

254 AHW

AHW is a food processing company that produces high-quality, part-cooked meals for the retail market. The five different types of meal that the company produces (Products A to E) are made by subjecting ingredients to a series of processing activities. The meals are different, and therefore need differing amounts of processing activities.

Budget and actual information for October 20X2 is shown below:

Budgeted data

	Product A	Product B	Product C	Product D	Product E
Number of batches	20	30	15	40	25
Processing activities per batch:					
Processing activity W	4	5	2	3	1
Processing activity X	3	2	5	1	4
Processing activity Y	3	3	2	4	2
Processing activity Z	4	6	8	2	3

Budgeted costs of processing activities:

	$000
Processing activity W	160
Processing activity X	130
Processing activity Y	80
Processing activity Z	200

All costs are expected to be variable in relation to the number of processing activities.

Actual data

Actual output during October 20X2 was as follows:

	Product A	Product B	Product C	Product D	Product E
Number of batches	18	33	16	35	28

Actual processing costs incurred during October 20X2 were:

	$000
Processing activity W	158
Processing activity X	139
Processing activity Y	73
Processing activity Z	206

Required:

(a) Prepare a budgetary control statement (to the nearest $000) that shows the original budget costs, flexible budget costs, the actual costs, and the total variances of each processing activity for October 20X2. **(15 marks)**

Your control statement has been issued to the Managers responsible for each processing activity and the Finance Director has asked each of them to explain the reasons for the variances shown in your statement. The Managers are not happy about this as they were not involved in setting the budgets and think that they should not be held responsible for achieving targets that were imposed upon them.

Required:

(b) Explain briefly the reasons why it might be preferable for Managers **not** to be involved in setting their own budgets. **(5 marks)**

(c) (i) Explain the difference between fixed and flexible budgets and how each may be used to control production costs and non-production costs (such as marketing costs) within AHW plc. **(4 marks)**

(ii) Give two examples of costs that are more appropriately controlled using a fixed budget, and explain why a flexible budget is less appropriate for the control of these costs. **(3 marks)**

Many organisations use linear regression analysis to predict costs at different activity levels. By analysing past data, a formula such as $y = ax + b$ is derived and used to predict future cost levels.

Required:

(d) Explain the meaning of the terms y, a, x and b in the above equation. **(3 marks)**

(Total: 30 marks)

255 ST

ST produces three types of processed foods for a leading food retailer. The company has three processing departments (Preparation, Cooking and Packaging). After recognising that the overheads incurred in these departments varied in relation to the activities performed, the company switched from a traditional absorption costing system to a budgetary control system that is based on activity based costing.

The foods are processed in batches. The budgeted output for April was as follows:

	Output
Food A	100 batches
Food B	30 batches
Food C	200 batches

The number of activities and processing hours budgeted to process a batch of foods in each of the departments are as follows:

	Food A Activities per batch:	Food B Activities per batch:	Food C Activities per batch:
Preparation	5	9	12
Cooking	2	1	4
Packaging	15	2	6
Processing time	10 hours	375 hours	80 hours

The budgeted departmental overhead costs for April were:

	Overheads $
Preparation	100,000
Cooking	350,000
Packaging	50,000

Required:

(a) For food A ONLY, calculate the budgeted overhead cost per batch:

  (i) using traditional absorption costing, based on a factory-wide absorption rate per processing hour; and

  (ii) using activity based costing. **(10 marks)**

(b) Comment briefly on the advantages of using an activity based costing approach to determining the cost of each type of processed food compared to traditional absorption costing approaches. You should make reference to your answers to requirement (a) where appropriate. **(6 marks)**

(c) The actual output for April was:

	Output
Food A	120 batches
Food B	45 batches
Food C	167 batches

Required:

Prepare a flexed budget for April using an activity based costing approach. Your statement must show the total budgeted overhead for each department and the total budgeted overhead absorbed by each food. **(14 marks)**

(Total: 30 marks)

256 PRODUCTS R, S AND T

X manufactures three products in a modern manufacturing plant, using cell operations.

Budgeted output for April was:

Product R	1,800 units in 36 batches
Product S	1,000 units in 10 batches
Product T	1,000 units in 40 batches

The product details are as follows:

	Product R	Product S	Product T
Standard labour hours per batch	25	30	12
Batch size (units)	50	100	25
Machine set-ups per batch	3	2	5
Power (kj) per batch	1.4	1.7	0.8
Purchase orders per batch	5	3	7
Machine hours per batch	10	7.5	12.5

During April the actual output was:

Product R	1,500 units in 30 batches
Product S	1,200 units in 12 batches
Product T	1,000 units in 40 batches

The following production overhead budgetary control statement has been prepared for April on the basis that the variable production overhead varies in relation to standard labour hours produced.

Production overhead budgetary control report April

	Original budget	Flexed budget	Actual	Variances
Output (standard hours produced)	1,800	1,710	1,710	
	$000	$000	$000	$000
Power	1,250	1,220	1,295	75 (A)
Stores	1,850	1,800	1,915	115 (A)
Maintenance	2,100	2,020	2,100	80 (A)
Machinery cleaning	800	760	870	110 (A)
Indirect labour	1,460	1,387	1,510	123 (A)
	7,460	7,187	7,690	503 (A)

After the above report had been produced, investigations revealed that every one of the individual costs could be classified as wholly variable in relation to the appropriate cost drivers.

Required:

(a) Explain the factors that should be considered when selecting a cost driver. **(6 marks)**

(b) (i) Calculate the budgeted cost per driver for each of the overhead costs. **(8 marks)**

    (ii) Prepare a production overhead budgetary control report for April using an activity based approach. **(10 marks)**

(c) Comment on the validity of an activity based approach to budgetary control for an organisation such as X plc. **(6 marks)**

(Total: 30 marks)

257 PMF

PMF is a long-established public transport operator that provides a commuter transit link between an airport and the centre of a large city.

The following data has been taken from the sales records of PMF for the last two years:

Quarter	Number of passengers carried	
	Year 1	Year 2
1	15,620	34,100
2	15,640	29,920
3	16,950	29,550
4	34,840	56,680

The trend equation for the number of passengers carried has been found to be

$$x = 10{,}000 + 4{,}200q$$

Where x = number of passengers carried per quarter
and q = time period (year 1 quarter 1: $q = 1$)
(year 1 quarter 2: $q = 2$)
(year 2 quarter 1: $q = 5$)

Based on data collected over the last two years, PMF has found that its quarterly costs have the following relationships with the number of passengers carried:

Cost item	Relationship
Premises costs	$y = 260{,}000$
Premises staff	$y = 65{,}000 + 0.5x$
Power	$y = 13{,}000 + 4x$
Transit staff	$y = 32{,}000 + 3x$
Other	$y = 9{,}100 + x$

where y = the cost per quarter ($),
and   x = number of passengers per quarter.

Required:

(a) Using the trend equation for the number of passengers carried and the multiplicative (proportional) time series model, determine the expected number of passengers to be carried in the third quarter of year 3. **(8 marks)**

(b) Explain why you think that the equation for the transit staff cost is in the form y = 32,000 + 3x. **(4 marks)**

(c) Using your answer to part (a) and the cost relationships equations, calculate for each cost item and in total, the costs expected to be incurred in the third quarter of year 3.

(4 marks)

(d) Explain why there may be differences between the actual data for the third quarter of year 3 and the values you have predicted. **(10 marks)**

(e) Explain the difference between the multiplicative and additive models for producing seasonally adjusted data and why the multiplicative model may be more appropriate for PMF. **(4 marks)**

(Total: 30 marks)

258 MARSHALL

Marshall operates a business that sells advanced photocopying machines and offers on-site servicing. There is a separate department that provides servicing. The standard cost for one service is shown below along with the operating statements for the Service Department for the six months to 30 September. Each service is very similar and involves the replacement of two sets of materials and parts.

Marshall budgets for 5,000 services per month.

Standard cost for one service

	$
Materials – 2 sets @ $20 per set	40
Labour – 3 hours @ $11 per hour	33
Variable overheads – 3 hours @ $5 per hour	15
Fixed overheads – 3 hours @ $8 per hour	24
Total standard cost	112

Operating statements for six months ending 30 September

Months	1	2	3	4	5	6	Total
Number of services per month	5,000	5,200	5,400	4,800	4,700	4,500	29,600
	$	$	$	$	$	$	$
Flexible budget costs	560,000	582,400	604,800	537,600	526,400	504,000	3,315,200
Less: Variances:							
Materials							
Price	5,150F	3,090F	1,100F	–2,040A	–5,700A	–2,700A	–1,100A
Usage	–6,000A	2,000F	–4,000A	–12,000A	–2,000A	0	–22,000A
Labour							
Rate	26,100F	25,725F	27,331F	18,600F	17,400F	15,515F	130,671F
Efficiency	5,500F	9,900F	12,100F	–12,100A	–4,400A	–11,000A	0
Variable overheads:							
Spending	–3,500A	–3,500A	–2,500A	–4,500A	500F	2,500F	–11,000A
Efficiency	2,500F	4,500F	5,500F	–5,500A	–2,000A	–5,000A	0
Fixed overheads:							
Expenditure	–3,000A	–5,000A	–5,000A	–15,000A	5,000F	5,000F	–18,000A
Volume	0	4,800F	9,600F	–4,800A	–7,200A	–12,000A	–9,600A
Actual costs	533,250	540,885	560,669	574,940	524,800	511,685	3,246,229

Note: 'A' = adverse variance; 'F' = favourable variance

Required:

(a) Prepare a summary financial statement showing the overall performance of the Service Department for the six months to 30 September 200X. **(14 marks)**

(b) Write a report to the Operations Director of Marshall commenting on the performance of the Service Department for the six months to 30 September 200X.

Suggest possible causes for the features you have included in your report and state the further information that would be helpful in assessing the performance of the department. **(16 marks)**

(Total: 30 marks)

259 KEY METRICS

The following statements have been extracted from a company's master budget for the forthcoming period.

Income statement for the year ended 30 April 20X6

	$000
Revenue	4,885
Cost of sales	4,315
Gross profit	570
Selling/distribution/administration costs	275
Profit	295

Balance sheet as at 30 April 20X6

	$000	$000
Non-current assets		1,280
Current assets		
Inventory	335	
Trade receivables	320	
Bank	145	
		800
		2,080
Capital and reserves		1,380
Non-current liabilities		370
Trade payables		280
Other short-term liabilities		50
		2,080

The directors intend to appraise the budget using the following key metrics.

		Target for relevant metric
(i)	Return on capital employed	19.0%
(ii)	Profit/sales ratio	6.0%
(iii)	Net asset turnover	3.2 times
(iv)	Non-current asset turnover	4.5 times
(v)	Current ratio	2.1 times
(vi)	Quick or acid test ratio	1.4 times

Required:

(a) Calculate the six key metrics and state whether or not they will be acceptable to the directors. **(12 marks)**

(b) For each key metric which would not be acceptable, suggest any actions that might be taken to help to achieve the company target. **(12 marks)**

(c) Explain the meaning of the term 'critical success factors' in a business giving examples of such factors. **(6 marks)**

(Total: 30 marks)

260 M PLC (MAY 06 EXAM)

M plc designs, manufactures and assembles furniture. The furniture is for home use and therefore varies considerably in size, complexity and value. One of the departments in the company is the Assembly Department. This department is labour intensive; the workers travel to various locations to assemble and fit the furniture using the packs of finished timbers that have been sent to them.

Budgets are set centrally and are given to the managers of the various departments who then have the responsibility of achieving their respective targets. Actual costs are compared against the budgets and the managers are then asked to comment on the budgetary control statement. The statement for April for the Assembly Department is shown below.

PAPER P1 : MANAGEMENT ACCOUNTING – PERFORMANCE EVALUATION

	Budget	Actual	Variance	
Assembly labour hours	6,400	7,140		
	$	$	$	
Assembly labour	51,970	58,227	6,257	Adverse
Furniture packs	224,000	205,000	19,000	Favourable
Other materials	23,040	24,100	1,060	Adverse
Overheads	62,060	112,340	50,280	Adverse
Total	361,070	399,667	38,597	Adverse

Note: The costs shown are for assembling and fitting the furniture (they do not include time spent travelling to jobs and the related costs). The hours worked by the manager are not included in the figure given for the assembly labour hours.

The manager of the Assembly Department is new to the job and has very little previous experience of working with budgets but he does have many years' experience as a supervisor in assembly departments. Based on that experience he was sure that the department had performed well. He has asked for your help in replying to a memo he has just received asking him to 'explain the serious overspending in his department'. He has sent you some additional information about the budget:

(1) The budgeted and actual assembly labour costs include the fixed salary of $2,050 for the manager of the Assembly Department. All of the other labour is paid for the hours they work.

(2) The cost of furniture packs and other materials is assumed by the central finance office of M plc to vary in proportion to the number of assembly labour hours worked.

(3) The budgeted overhead costs are made up of three elements: a fixed cost of $9,000 for services from central headquarters; a stepped fixed cost which changes when the assembly hours exceed 7,000 hours; and some variable overheads. The variable overheads are assumed to vary in proportion to the number of assembly labour hours. Working papers for the budget showed the impact on the overhead costs of differing amounts of assembly labour hours:

Assembly labour hours	5,000	7,500	10,000
Overhead costs	$54,500	$76,500	$90,000

The actual fixed costs for April were as budgeted.

Required:

(a) Prepare, using the additional information that the manager of the Assembly Department has given you, a budgetary control statement that would be more helpful to him. **(7 marks)**

(b) (i) Discuss the differences between **the format** of the statement that you have produced and that supplied by M plc. **(4 marks)**

  (ii) Discuss the assumption made by the central office of M plc that costs vary in proportion to assembly labour hours. **(3 marks)**

(c) Discuss whether M plc should change to a system of participative budgeting.

(6 marks)

(Total: 20 marks)

CONTROL AND PERFORMANCE MEASUREMENT OF RESPONSIBILITY CENTRES

261 KDS

KDS is an engineering company which is organised for management purposes in the form of several autonomous divisions. The performance of each division is currently measured by calculation of its return on capital employed (ROCE). KDS existing accounting policy is to calculate ROCE by dividing the net assets of each division at the end of the year into the operating profit generated by the division during the year. Cash is excluded from net assets since all divisions share a bank account controlled by KDS's head office. Depreciation is on a straight-line basis.

The divisional management teams are paid a performance-related bonus conditional upon achievement of a 15% ROCE target. On 20 December 20X5 the divisional managers were provided with performance forecasts for 20X5 which included the following:

Forecast	Net assets at 31 December 20X5 $	20X5 operating profit $	ROCE
Division K	4,400,000	649,000	14.75%
Division D	480,000	120,000	25.00%

Subsequently, the manager of Division K invited members of her management team to offer advice. The responses she received included the following:

From the divisional administrator:

'We can achieve our 20X5 target by deferring payment of a $90,000 trade debt payable on 20 December until 1 January. I should add that we will thereby immediately incur a $2,000 late payment penalty.'

From the works manager:

'We should replace a number of our oldest machine tools (which have nil book value) at a cost of $320,000. The new equipment will have a life of eight years and generate cost savings of $76,000 per year. The new equipment can be on site and operational by 31 December 20X5.'

From the financial controller:

'The existing method of performance appraisal is unfair. We should ask head office to adopt residual income (RI) as the key performance indicator, using the company's average 12% cost of money for a finance charge.'

Requirements:

(a) Compare and appraise the proposals of the divisional administrator and the works manager, having regard to the achievement of the ROCE performance target in 20X5 and to any longer term factors you think relevant. **(12 marks)**

(b) Explain the extent to which you agree or disagree with the financial controller's proposal. **(10 marks)**

(c) Explain how non-financial performance measures could be used to assess the performance of divisions K and D. **(8 marks)**

(Total: 30 marks)

PAPER P1 : MANAGEMENT ACCOUNTING – PERFORMANCE EVALUATION

262 Y AND Z (NOVEMBER 05 EXAM)

Y and Z are two divisions of a large company that operate in similar markets. The divisions are treated as investment centres and every month they each prepare an operating statement to be submitted to the parent company. Operating statements for these two divisions for October are shown below:

Operating statements for October

	Y $000	Z $000
Sales revenue	900	555
Less variable costs	345	312
Contribution	555	243
Less controllable fixed costs	95	42
(includes depreciation on divisional assets)		
Controllable income	460	201
Less apportioned central costs	338	180
Net income before tax	122	21
Total divisional net assets	$9.76m	$1.26m

The company currently has a target return on capital of 12% per annum. However, the company believes its cost of capital is likely to rise and is considering increasing the target return on capital. At present the performance of each division and the divisional management are assessed primarily on the basis of Return on Investment (ROI).

Required:

(a) Calculate the annualised Return on Investment (ROI) for divisions Y and Z, and discuss the relative performance of the two divisions using the ROI data and other information given above. **(9 marks)**

(b) Calculate the annualised Residual Income (RI) for divisions Y and Z, and explain the implications of this information for the evaluation of the divisions' performance. **(6 marks)**

(c) Briefly discuss the strengths and weaknesses of ROI and RI as methods of assessing the performance of divisions. Explain two further methods of assessment of divisional performance that could be used in addition to ROI or RI. **(5 marks)**

(Total: 20 marks)

263 CTD

CTD has two divisions – FD and TM. FD is an iron foundry division which produces mouldings that have a limited external market and are also transferred to TM division. TM division uses the mouldings to produce a piece of agricultural equipment called the "TX" which is sold externally. Each TX requires one moulding. Both divisions produce only one type of product.

The performance of each Divisional Manager is evaluated individually on the basis of the residual income (RI) of his or her division. The company's average annual 12% cost of capital is used to calculate the finance charges. If their own target residual income is achieved, each Divisional Manager is awarded a bonus equal to 5% of his or her residual income. All bonuses are paid out of Head Office profits.

The following budgeted information is available for the forthcoming year:

	TM division TX per unit $	FD division Moulding per unit $
External selling price	500	80
Variable production cost	366*	40
Fixed production overheads	60	20
Gross profit	74	20
Variable selling and distribution cost	25	4**
Fixed administration overhead	25	4
Net profit	24	12
Normal capacity (units)	15,000	20,000
Maximum production capacity (units)	15,000	25,000
Sales to external customers (units)	15,000	5,000
Capital employed	$1,500,000	$750,000
Target RI	$105,000	$85,000

* The variable production cost of TX includes the cost of an FD moulding.

** External sales only of the mouldings incur a variable selling and distribution cost of $4 per unit.

FD division currently transfers 15,000 mouldings to TM division at a transfer price equal to the total production cost plus 10%.

Fixed costs are absorbed on the basis of normal capacity.

Required:

(a) Calculate the bonus each Divisional Manager would receive under the current transfer pricing policy and discuss any implications that the current performance evaluation system may have for each division and for the company as a whole. **(10 marks)**

(b) Both Divisional Managers want to achieve their respective residual income targets. Based on the budgeted figures, calculate:

   (i) the **maximum** transfer price per unit that the Divisional Manager of TM division would pay;

   (ii) the **minimum** transfer price per unit that the Divisional Manager of FD division would accept. **(6 marks)**

(c) Write a report to the management of CTD that explains, and recommends, the transfer prices which FD division should set in order to maximise group profits. Your report should also:

   - consider the implications of actual external customer demand exceeding 5,000 units;

   - explain how alternative transfer pricing systems could overcome any possible conflict that may arise as a result of your recommended transfer prices.

(14 marks)

(Total: 30 marks)

264 DIVISION A

Division A, which is a part of the ACF Group, manufactures only one type of product, a Bit, which it sells to external customers and also to division C, another member of the group. ACF Group's policy is that divisions have the freedom to set transfer prices and choose their suppliers.

PAPER P1 : MANAGEMENT ACCOUNTING – PERFORMANCE EVALUATION

The ACF Group uses residual income (RI) to assess divisional performance and each year it sets each division a target RI. The group's cost of capital is 12% a year.

Division A

Budgeted information for the coming year is:

Maximum capacity	150,000 Bits
External sales	110,000 Bits
External selling price	$35 per Bit
Variable cost	$22 per Bit
Fixed costs	$1,080,000
Capital employed	$3,200,000
Target residual income	$180,000

Division C

Division C has found two other companies willing to supply Bits:

X could supply at $28 per Bit, but only for annual orders in excess of 50,000 Bits.
Z could supply at $33 per Bit for any quantity ordered.

Required:

(a) Division C provisionally requests a quotation for 60,000 Bits from division A for the coming year.

   (i) Calculate the transfer price per Bit that division A should quote in order to meet its residual income target. **(6 marks)**

   (ii) Calculate the two prices division A would have to quote to division C, if it became group policy to quote transfer prices based on opportunity costs. **(4 marks)**

(b) Evaluate and discuss the impact of the group's current and proposed policies on the profits of divisions A and C, and on group profit. Illustrate your answer with calculations. **(12 marks)**

(c) Assume that divisions A and C are based in different countries and consequently pay taxes at different rates: division A at 55% and division C at 25%. Division A has now quoted a transfer price of $30 per Bit for 60,000 Bits.

Calculate whether it is better for the group if division C purchases 60,000 Bits from division A or from supplier X. **(8 marks)**

(Total: 30 marks)

265 MOBILE PHONES

M has two divisions, X and Y. Division X is a chip manufacturer and Division Y assembles mobile phones. Division X currently manufactures many different types of chip, one of which is used in the manufacture of the mobile phones. Division X has no external market for the chips that are used in the mobile phones and currently sets the transfer price on the basis of total cost plus 20% mark-up.

The budgeted income statement for Division Y for next year shows the following results:

Mobile phone range	P $000	Q $000	R $000
Sales	10,000	9,500	11,750
Less: Total costs	7,200	11,700	9,250
Profit/(loss)	2,800	(2,200)	2,500
Fixed costs	2,000	5,400	5,875

The total costs shown above include the cost of the chips.

Division Y uses a traditional absorption costing system based on labour hours.

M operates a performance measurement system based on divisional profits. In order to increase profit for the forthcoming year, Division Y has asked permission to buy chips from an external supplier.

The accountant of M has recently attended a course on activity based costing (ABC) and has recommended that the divisions should implement an ABC system rather than continue to operate the traditional absorption costing system.

Required:

(a) A presenter at the conference stated that 'ABC provides information that is more relevant for decision making than traditional forms of costing'. Discuss this statement, using Division Y when appropriate to explain the issues you raise.

(8 marks)

(b) (i) Discuss the current transfer pricing system and explain alternative systems that might be more appropriate for the forthcoming year. **(12 marks)**

(ii) Explain the impact that the introduction of an ABC system could have on the transfer price and on divisional profits. **(5 marks)**

(Total: 25 marks)

266 FP (MAY 06 EXAM)

FP sells and repairs photocopiers. The company has operated for many years with two departments, the Sales Department and the Service Department, but the departments had no autonomy. The company is now thinking of restructuring so that the two departments will become profit centres.

The Sales Department

This department sells new photocopiers. The department sells 2,000 copiers per year. Included in the selling price is $60 for a one-year guarantee. All customers pay this fee. This means that, during the first year of ownership, if the photocopier needs to be repaired then the repair costs are not charged to the customer. On average 500 photocopiers per year need to be repaired under the guarantee. The repair work is carried out by the Service Department who, under the proposed changes, would charge the Sales Department for doing the repairs. It is estimated that on average the repairs will take 3 hours each and that the charge by the Service Department will be $136,500 for the 500 repairs.

The Service Department

This department has two sources of work – the work needed to satisfy the guarantees for the Sales Department and repair work for external customers. Customers are charged at full cost plus 40%.

PAPER P1 : MANAGEMENT ACCOUNTING – PERFORMANCE EVALUATION

The details of the budget for the next year for the Service Department revealed standard costs of:

Parts	at cost
Labour	$15 per hour
Variable overheads	$10 per labour hour
Fixed overheads	$22 per labour hour

The calculation of these standards is based on the estimated maximum market demand and includes the expected 500 repairs for the Sales Department. The average cost of the parts needed for a repair is $54. This means that the charge to the Sales Department for the repair work, including the 40% mark-up, will be $136,500.

Proposed change

It has now been suggested that FP should be structured so that the two departments become profit centres and that the managers of the Departments are given autonomy. The individual salaries of the managers would be linked to the profits of their respective departments.

Budgets have been produced for each department on the assumption that the Service Department will repair 500 photocopiers for the Sales Department and that the transfer price for this work will be calculated in the same way as the price charged to external customers.

However the manager of the Sales Department has now stated that he intends to have the repairs done by another company, RS, because it has offered to carry out the work for a fixed fee of $180 per repair and this is less than the price that the Sales Department would charge.

Required:

(a) Calculate the individual profits of the Sales Department and the Service Department, and of FP as a whole *from the guarantee scheme* if:

    (i) the repairs are carried out by the Service Department and are charged at full cost plus 40%;

    (ii) the repairs are carried out by the Service Department and are charged at marginal cost;

    (iii) the repairs are carried out by RS. **(8 marks)**

(b) (i) Explain, with reasons, why a 'full cost plus' transfer pricing model may *not* be appropriate for FP. **(3 marks)**

    (ii) Comment on other issues that the managers of FP should consider if they decide to allow RS to carry out the repairs. **(4 marks)**

(c) Briefly explain the advantages and disadvantages of structuring the departments as profit centres. **(5 marks)**

(Total: 20 marks)

267 ZZ GROUP (NOVEMBER 06 EXAM)

The ZZ Group has two divisions, X and Y. Each division produces only one type of product: X produces a component (C) and Y produces a finished product (FP). Each FP needs one C. It is the current policy of the group for C to be transferred to Division Y at the marginal cost of $10 per component and that Y must buy all the components it needs from X.

The markets for the component and the finished product are competitive and price sensitive. Component C is produced by many other companies but it is thought that the external demand for the next year could increase to 1,000 units more than the sales volume shown in the current budget for Division X.

Budgeted data, taken from the ZZ Group Internal Information System, for the divisions for the next year are as follows:

Division X

Income statement

Sales	$70,000
Cost of sales	
Variable costs	$50,000
Contribution	$20,000
Fixed costs (controllable)	$15,000
Profit	$5,000

Production/Sales (units)	5,000	(3,000 of which are transferred to Division Y)
External demand (units)	3,000	(Only 2,000 of which can be currently satisfied)
Capacity (units)	5,000	
External market price per unit	$20	

Balance sheet extract

Capital employed	$60,000

Other information

Cost of capital charge	10%

Division Y

Income statement

Sales	$270,000
Cost of sales	
Variable costs	$114,000
Contribution	$156,000
Fixed costs (controllable)	$100,000
Profit	$56,000

Production/Sales (units)	3,000
Capacity (units)	7,000
Market price per unit	$90

Balance sheet extract

Capital employed	$110,000

Other information

Cost of capital charge	10%

Four measures are used to evaluate the performance of the Divisional Managers. Based on the data above, the budgeted performance measures for the two divisions are as follows:

	Division X	Division Y
Residual income	($1,000)	$45,000
Return on capital employed	8.33%	50.91%
Operating profit margin	7.14%	20.74%
Asset turnover	1.17	2.46

Current policy

It is the current policy of the group for C to be transferred to Division Y at the marginal cost of $10 per component and that Y must buy all the components that it needs from X.

Proposed policy

ZZ Group is thinking of giving the Divisional Managers the freedom to set their own transfer price and to buy the components from external suppliers, but there are concerns about problems that could arise by granting such autonomy.

Required:

(a) If the transfer price of the component is set by the Manager of Division X at the current market price ($20 per component), recalculate the budgeted performance measures for each division. **(8 marks)**

(b) Discuss the changes to the performance measures of the divisions that would arise as a result of altering the transfer price to $20 per component. **(6 marks)**

(c) (i) Explain the problems that could arise for each of the Divisional Managers and for ZZ Group as a whole as a result of giving full autonomy to the Divisional Managers.

   (ii) Discuss how the problems you have explained could be resolved without resorting to a policy of imposed transfer prices. **(6 marks)**

(Total: 20 marks)

Section 4

ANSWERS TO SECTION A-TYPE QUESTIONS

COST ACCOUNTING SYSTEMS

1   B

	$
Marginal costing profit	45,000
Less: fixed cost included in opening inventory (28,000 – 16,000)	(12,000)
Plus: fixed cost included in closing inventory (36,400 – 20,800)	15,600
Absorption costing profit	48,600

Alternative approach

Increase in inventory using marginal costing	$4,800
Increase in inventory using absorption costing	$8,400
Difference = fixed overhead absorbed in inventory	$3,600

Inventory is increasing so absorption costing profit is higher than marginal costing profit by the amount of fixed overhead absorbed.

Absorption costing profit = $45,000 + $3,600 = $48,600

2   B

The opening inventory was 400 units and the closing inventory was 900 units, therefore inventory has increased.

If production is greater than sales then absorption costing will show the higher profit.

Difference in profit:

= Change in inventory × Fixed production cost per unit

= (900 – 400) × $29,500/5,000 units = $2,950

3   B

Difference in profits = Change in inventory × Fixed production costs per unit
= 750 units × $36
= $27,000

Absorption costing profits would be higher than marginal costing profits, because inventory increased and some fixed production costs would be carried forward to the next period with absorption costing.

4 D

No inventories of finished goods would be held, therefore complete jobs would represent immediate sales. The full absorption cost of completed jobs would be transferred from work in progress to cost of sales.

Job number	Opening balance €	Direct material €	Direct labour €		Absorbed overhead €	Total cost €
427	87	190	200	(× 150%)	300	777
430	-	188	420	(× 150%)	630	1,238
						2,015

5 C

	€
Overhead incurred	34,789
Overhead absorbed (4,744 × €7)	33,208
Under-absorbed overhead	1,581

The under-absorbed overhead is debited in the income statement and credited in the production overhead control account.

6 A

Statement of input/output

	Input	Output
Op WIP	600	
Normal loss		500
Op WIP completed		600
Units started and finished in month		13,900
Cl WIP		800

Statement of equivalent units

	Total units	Materials		Conversion cost	
Normal loss	500	0%	0	0%	0
Op WIP completed	600	20%	120	40%	240
Units started and finished in month	13,900	100%	13,900	100%	13,900
Cl WIP	800	70%	560	40%	320
			14,580		14,460

7 C

The abnormal gain units are valued at the normal production cost so that the cost of the good output is not affected by abnormal events. The cost of the abnormal gain is debited in the process account and credited in the abnormal gain account. This eliminates options A and B. The abnormal gain account is then debited with the scrap value 'forgone' as a result of the lower than expected level of scrap. The correct answer is therefore C.

8 D

The abnormal loss units are valued at full production cost so that abnormal events do not affect the cost of good production.

9 C

Statement of equivalent units

	Total units		Equivalent units		
			Materials		Conversion cost
Abnormal gain	160	100%	160	75%	120

Statement of evaluation

	Equivalent units	Cost per equivalent unit	Cost
		$	$
Abnormal gain			
Materials	160	9.40	1,504
Conversion cost	120	11.20	1,344
			2,848

The cost of the abnormal gain is $2,848, but the scrap value of the gain reduces that abnormal gain, so the transfer to income statement = $2,848 − (160 units × $2) = $2,528

10

FIFO and weighted average methods give very similar results under various circumstances including the following:

Where the conversion percentage is virtually constant between accounting periods.

Where the conversion costs in work-in-process at the end of the month are very small in relation to the total conversion costs during the month. This is likely to occur where the process time is short and the process is repeated many times in the month.

In general, where unit cost fluctuations are minimal between the months.

11

	Proxy value of output		Share of joint costs	
		$		$
P 3,600 litres × $4.60 per litre		16,560		
Q 4,100 litres × $6.75		27,675		
R 2,800 litres × $10.50 per litre − $19,600		9,800	$\dfrac{9,800}{54,035} \times 42,500$	7,708
		54,035		

R's share of joint costs is $7,708.

12 B

Statement of input/output

	Input kg	Output kg	
Opening WIP	10,000		
Raw materials	34,880		
Output			
Opening WIP completed		10,000	30,500 kg
Units made entirely within month		20,500 Bal	output
Normal loss		5,232	
Closing WIP		9,700	
Abnormal gain		(552) Bal	
	44,880	44,880	

Statement of equivalent units

	Total units	Raw ingredients		Conversion	
Opening WIP completed	10,000	10%	1,000	60%	6,000
Units made entirely within month	20,500	100%	20,500	100%	20,500
Normal loss	5,232	0%	–	0%	–
Closing WIP	9,700	85%	8,245	35%	3,395
Abnormal gain	(552)	100%	(552)	100%	(552)
			29,193		29,343

13

Statement of input/output

	Input	Output	
Op WIP	200		
Op WIP completed		200 ⎫	1,400 units
Units started and finished in month		1,200 ⎭	Transfer to next process
Cl WIP		200	
Abnormal loss		50	

If we had been using the weighted average method, we would have written down 1,400 units transferred to the next process, but under FIFO, the completed output is broken into two, i.e. op WIP completed and units made entirely in month.

Statement of equivalent units

	Total units	Materials		Conversion cost	
Op WIP completed	200	0%	0	75%	150
Units started and finished in month	1,200	100%	1,200	100%	1,200
Cl WIP	200	100%	200	50%	100
Abnormal loss	50	100%	50	100%	50
			1,450		1,500

14 Cost/kg = $\dfrac{\text{Total cost - scrap value of normal loss}}{\text{Expected output}}$

Cost/kg = $\dfrac{19,200 + 4,800}{2,400 - 240}$

Cost/kg = $11.1111/kg

Process a/c

	Kg	$		Kg	$
Inputs	2,400	19,200	Normal loss	240	0
Process costs		4,800	To Packing dept	2,060	22,889
			Abnormal loss	100	1,111
	2,400	24,000		2,400	24,000

Abnormal loss a/c

	Kg	$		Kg	$
Process 1	100	1,111	Scrap	100	400
			Income statement		711
		1,111			1,111

15 C

Return per minute = $\dfrac{\text{Selling price - material cost}}{\text{Time on bottleneck resource}}$

$= \dfrac{50 - 16}{8}$

= €4.25

Return per hour = €4.25 × 60 = €255

16 (a)

          Product S   Product T

Throughput of process X per day

13.5 hrs × $\dfrac{60}{5}$ = 162.00   13.5 hrs × $\dfrac{60}{7.5}$ = 108.00

(Production time: 15 – 1.5 = 13.5 hours)

Throughput of process Y per day

14 hrs × $\dfrac{60}{18}$ = 46.67   14 hrs × $\dfrac{60}{12}$ = 70.00

(Production time: 15 – 1 = 14 hours)

Process Y is the bottleneck process because it limits the production of both products to figures that are less than sales demand.

(b) Throughput contribution per hour of product S: $\dfrac{(\$95.00 - 20.00)}{18} \times 60 = \$250.00$

Throughput contribution per hour of product T: $\dfrac{(\$85.00 - 20.00)}{12} \times 60 = \$325.00$

The optimum production plan to maximise throughput contribution per day is to produce 70 units of product T.

17 A

This is the CIMA *Official Terminology* definition of a bottleneck. With a throughput accounting approach, the aim should be to reduce or remove bottlenecks, so as to increase throughput.

18 B

The throughput per factory hour = ($100 - $40)/3.75 hours = $16

Factory costs per factory hour = ($10 + $30)/3.75 hours = $10.67

Throughput accounting ratio = Throughput per factory hour/cost per factory hour = $16/$10.67 = 1.5

19

(a) Machine utilisation rates

		Product		
Required machine hours	A	B	C	Total
Machine 1	1,200	400	200	1,800
Machine 2	1,800	600	300	2,700
Machine 3	600	200	100	900

Utilisation rates:

Machine 1 (1,800/1,600) 112%
Machine 2 (2,700/1,600) 169%
Machine 3 (900/1,600) 56%

(b) Machine 2 is the bottleneck – it has the highest utilisation and this is greater than 100%.

20

(a) The Goldratt procedure is:

- Identify the system's bottleneck.
- Decide how to exploit or relieve the bottleneck.
- Sub-ordinate everything else to relieving the bottleneck.
- Elevate the system's bottlenecks.
- When one bottleneck is no longer a constraint, start procedure again (there will always be a new bottleneck).

(b) Optimal allocation would be on the basis of contribution from the bottleneck resource.

Ranking of contribution per product from machine 2 is:

Product	A	B	C
Contribution per unit	$12	$10	$6
Machine 2 hours	9	3	1.5
Contribution per machine hour	$1.33	$3.33	$4.00
Ranking	3rd	2nd	1st

Thus allocation on this ranking:

	Units		Hours
Product C	200	× 1.5	300
Product B	200	× 3	600
Product A	77.78$^{Bal\ 2}$	× 9	700$^{Bal\ 1}$
			1,600

21 B

The inventory will be valued at production cost, to be more precise at variable production cost.

$$\text{Cost per unit} = \frac{\$40,000 + \$12,600 + \$9,400}{2,000 \text{ units}} = \$31 \text{ per unit}$$

No. of units in closing inventory = 2,000 − 1,750 = 250 units.

Therefore value of closing inventory = 250 units × $31 = $7,750.

22 A

Under throughput accounting, finished goods will be valued at direct material cost.

$$\text{Cost per unit} = \frac{\$40,000}{2,000 \text{ units}} = \$20 \text{ per unit}$$

No. of units in closing inventory = 2,000 − 1,750 = 250 units.

Therefore value of closing inventory = 250 units × $20 = $5,000

23

	Z1	Z2
Maximum production		
Department 1	480 min/12 min = 40 units	480 min/16 min = 30 units
Department 2	840 min/20 min = 42 units	840 min/15 min = 56 units

Department 1 is the problem for both products. We can make 42 units of Z1 as far as Department 2 is concerned, but Department 1 is only able to process 40 units. Similarly for Z2, Department 2 can deal with 56 units, but Department 1 can only cope with 30. In both cases Department 1 is the bottleneck.

24

	Z1	Z2
	$	$
Selling price	50	65
Variable cost	26.80	30.40
Contribution	23.20	34.60
No. of bottleneck min per unit	12	16
Contribution per min	1.93	2.16
Priority	2nd	1st

The optimum plan is to concentrate on Z2. We will make the maximum, which is 30 units (from Question 31).

Contribution = 30 units × $34.60 per unit = $1,038.

25

	Z1	Z2
	$	$
Selling price	50	65
Direct material	10	15
Throughput	40	50
No. of bottleneck min per unit	12	16
Throughput per min	3.33	3.13
Priority	1st	2nd

The optimum plan is to concentrate on Z1. We will make the maximum, which is 40 units.

Throughput = 40 units × $40 per unit = $1,600.

26 (a) **Absorption costing**

Value of closing inventory = $(13,500 + 11,800 + 32,400) × 200/2,000 = $5,770

	$	$
Sales (1,800 × $45)		81,000
Cost of production	57,700	
Less closing inventory	5,770	
Cost of sales		51,930
Gross profit		29,070
Non-production overhead		21,900
Profit		7,170

(b) **Marginal costing**

Value of closing inventory = $(13,500 + 11,800) \times 200/2,000 = \$2,530$

	$	$
Sales		81,000
Variable cost of production	25,300	
Less closing inventory	2,530	
Cost of sales		22,770
Contribution		58,230
Fixed overhead		54,300
Profit		3,930

(c) **Throughput accounting**

Value of closing inventory = $\$13,500 \times 200/2,000 = \$1,350$

	$	$
Sales		81,000
Material costs	13,500	
Less closing inventory	1,350	
Cost of sales		12,150
Throughput		68,850
Operating expenses		66,100
Net profit		2,750

27 D

Unit, batch, product and facility all relate to levels of activity. Value added and non-value added relate to the type of activity.

28 B

Activity	Classification
(i)	Facility-sustaining
(ii)	Facility-sustaining
(iii)	Product-sustaining
(iv)	Product-sustaining
(v)	Facility-sustaining

29 A

$$\text{Cost driver rate} = \frac{\text{Budgeted cost of orders}}{\text{Budgeted number of orders}} = \frac{\$110{,}010}{2{,}895} = \$38 \text{ for each order}$$

	$
Cost recovered: 210 orders × $38	7,980
Actual costs incurred	7,650
Over-recovery of costs for four-week period	330

30 D

Statement (i) provides a definition of a cost driver. Cost drivers for long-term variable overhead costs will be the volume of a particular activity to which the cost driver relates, so Statement (ii) is correct. Statement (iii) is also correct. In traditional absorption costing, standard high-volume products receive a higher amount of overhead costs than with ABC. ABC allows for the unusually high costs of support activities for low-volume products (such as relatively higher set-up costs, order processing costs and so on).

31

(a)

Budgeted number of batches:
Product D (100,000/100)	=	1,000
Product R (100,000/50)	=	2,000
Product P (50,000/25)	=	2,000
		5,000

(b)

Budgeted machine set-ups:
Product D (1,000 × 3)	=	3,000
Product R (2,000 × 4)	=	8,000
Product P (2,000 × 6)	=	12,000
		23,000

(c)

Budgeted number of purchase orders:
Product D (1,000 × 2)	=	2,000
Product R (2,000 × 1)	=	2,000
Product P (2,000 × 1)	=	2,000
		6,000

(d)

Budgeted processing minutes:
Product D (100,000 × 2)	=	200,000	
Product R (100,000 × 3)	=	300,000	
Product P (50,000 × 3)	=	150,000	
		650,000	minutes

ns to section a-type questions : section 4

32 **Budgeted cost per set-up:**

$$= \frac{\$150{,}000}{23{,}000} = \$6.52 \qquad \text{Budgeted unit cost of R:} = \frac{\$6.52 \times 4}{50} = \$0.52$$

Budgeted cost per order:

$$= \frac{\$70{,}000}{6{,}000} = \$11.67 \qquad \text{Budgeted unit cost of R:} = \frac{\$11.67 \times 1}{50} = \$0.23$$

Budgeted processing cost per minute:

$$= \frac{\$80{,}000}{650{,}000} = \$0.12 \qquad \text{Budgeted unit cost of R} = \$0.12 \times 3 = \$0.36$$

Total budgeted unit cost of R is:

	$
Set-up costs =	0.52
Purchasing costs =	0.23
Processing costs =	0.36
Total cost =	1.11 per unit

33 Costs could be higher under ABC if:

- a product is produced in small batches
- there is production complexity not represented in direct labour hours.

Management may choose to increase batch sizes and/or increase selling prices in order to cover the extra product costs.

34 **D**

Statements A, B and C are incorrect. JIT makes an organisation more vulnerable to disruptions in the supply chain, because there are no buffer inventories as protection against a breakdown in supply. JIT is easier to implement when an organisation operates within a narrow geographical area, and close to its suppliers. (At Toyota, where JIT originated, manufacturing operations were initially carried out within a 50 kilometre radius.) With little or no inventories, the risk of inventory obsolescence should not exist.

Statement D is correct. When demand is difficult to predict, it becomes more difficult to operate a demand-driven operation.

35 **C**

Item (ii) is not an aspect of JIT. There will be more small production runs and so more time spent on machine set-up. Total machine set up time will therefore rise rather than decline if JIT is introduced. Producing only in response to demand, and organising work into work cells, with each cell producing an entire product or job (and so reducing material movements), are characteristic features of JIT.

36 **B**

Inventory levels should be close to zero in a JIT system. A close relationship with suppliers is essential since no buffer inventories are held.

37 D

Training should prevent future failure costs. Reworking costs are an internal failure cost.

38 C

	$
Cost of goods sold	100,000
Less material cost $45 × 1,000	45,000
Conversion cost allocated	55,000
Conversion cost incurred	60,000
Excess charged to cost of goods sold account	5,000
Total debit on cost of goods sold account $100,000 + $5,000 =	105,000

39 A

Instead of building up product costs sequentially from start to finish of production, backflush accounting calculates product costs retrospectively, at the end of each accounting period, when goods are completed or sold.

40 B

The trigger point is at the point of sales and thus the cost of goods sold account is debited with the cost of the finished goods sold, i.e. $1,700,000.

Included within the $1,700,000 is $840,000 for conversion costs allocated, but the conversion costs incurred were $890,000, so an extra $50,000 has to be debited to the cost of goods sold account.

41 A

	$000	$000
Sales revenue		820
Variable cost of sales		
Opening inventory	0	
Variable production costs	300	
	300	
Less closing inventory	45	
		255
		565
Variable selling costs		105
Contribution		460
Fixed costs		
Production	180	
Selling	110	
		290
Profit		170

ANSWERS TO SECTION A-TYPE QUESTIONS : SECTION 4

Working

The closing inventory is valued at cost. As it is a marginal costing system the inventory is valued at variable cost, i.e. $300,000/1,000 units = $300 per unit. The closing inventory is 150 units, therefore the closing inventory value is $300/unit × 150 units = $45,000.

42 D

Definition A is a definition of Optimised Production Technology. Definition B is a definition of Just in time.

43 A

Option (i) is true.

Option (ii) is false. Flexible manufacturing systems may not be simple and may have a substantial degree of automation.

Option (iii) is false. EDI is most often used to allow communication with outside businesses, with customers and suppliers.

44 B

Definition 1 is of an MRP1 system and definition 2 is of throughput accounting.

45 A

(i) is correct. An FMS is a highly automated, complex, computerised production system so (ii) is incorrect. JIT purchases inventory as required so (iii) is incorrect.

46 A

Finished output = OWIP + units started and finished

575 = 225 + ? so units started and finished = 350

	Total units	Material Z	Equivalent units Conversion cost
To complete opening WIP	225	45	45
Started and finished	350	350	350
Closing WIP	150	90	60
Total EU		**485**	**455**

47 C

Option A may lead to over-absorption but this will depend on the extent to which actual overhead costs differ from budget. Option B describes under-absorption. Option D refers to budgeted overheads, which are used to calculate the OAR but otherwise not used in the calculation of under-/over-absorption.

48

	Kg	From P1	Materials	Conversion
		\multicolumn{3}{c}{Equivalent units (kg)}	
Transferred to finished goods	2,800	2,800	2,800	2,800
Normal loss	200			
Abnormal loss	100	100	100	50
Closing work-in-progress	700	700	700	150
	3,800	3,600	3,600	3,000
Costs ($)		34,200	16,200	26,700
Cost per EU ($)		9.50	4.50	8.90

Abnormal loss = $(100 \times \$9.50) + (100 \times \$4.50) + (50 \times \$8.90) = \$1,845$

49 B

(i) and (ii) are the correct definitions. An MRP system is a computer system for production, planning, purchasing and inventory control. It does not integrate all aspects of a business.

50 B

OAR = $500,000/2,000 = $250 per unit

Inventory has fallen by 300 units in the period.

Absorption costing profit will be 300 × $250 = $75,000 lower than marginal costing profit as some fixed overhead from previous periods will be brought forward to be matched against sales in the period using absorption costing. In marginal costing only the fixed overhead incurred in the period will be included in the profit statement.

51

	W $	X $	Y $
Selling price	200	150	150
Direct materials	41	20	30
Throughput	159	130	120
Bottleneck machine			
– minutes per unit	9	10	7
Throughput per minute	17.67	13	17.14
Ranking	1st	3rd	2nd

52

$	Assembly	Finishing	Stores	Maintenance	Total
Budgeted overhead	100,000	150,000	50,000	40,000	340,000
Reapportion maintenance	16,000	18,000	6,000	(40,000)	-
			56,000		
Reapportion stores	33,600	22,400	(56,000)		-
Total overhead	149,600	190,400			340,000

OAR for assembly department = $149,600/100,000 = $1.496 per unit

	$
Overhead absorbed 120,000 × 1.496	179,520
Overhead incurred	180,000
Under-absorption	480

53 Total common cost for apportionment:

Joint costs	$140,000
Less by-product sales (3,000 × $6)	18,000
	$122,000

Product	Sales value	Share of common cost
X	2,500 × $50 = 125,000	45,522 (125,000/335,000 × $122,000)
Y	3,500 × $60 = 210,000	76,478 (210,000/335,000 × $122,000)
	335,000	122,000

Total cost of production for X:

	$
Joint cost	45,522
Further processing cost	24,000
	69,522

54 Normal loss = 10% × 1,800 = 180

Actual loss = 180 so there is no abnormal loss or gain

OWIP	800 units
Added material	1,800 units
Less normal loss	180 units
CWIP	500 units
Finished output	1,920 units

Equivalent units	Total	Material	Labour	Overhead
Finished goods	1,920	1,920	1,920	1,920
CWIP	500	500	450	200
Total	2,420	2,420	2,370	2,120
Total cost ($)				
OWIP		98,000	46,000	7,600
Current period		387,800	276,320	149,280
Less scrap value of normal loss		(1,800)		
		484,000	322,320	156,880
Cost per equivalent unit ($)	410	200	136	74

Cost of the output = 1,920 × $410 = $787,200

PAPER P1 : MANAGEMENT ACCOUNTING – PERFORMANCE EVALUATION

STANDARD COSTING

55 C

			$	
SQSP				
6 kg/unit × 600 units	×	$3/kg =	10,800	Usage
AQSP				$450 F
	×	$3/kg =		
AQAP				$2,000 F
	×	=		Price

This is a 'backwards' question. Given some information including the variances, we then have to work backwards to find some missing numbers – here, the number of kg purchased.

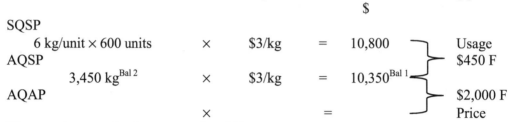

			$	
SQSP				
6 kg/unit × 600 units	×	$3/kg =	10,800	Usage
AQSP				$450 F
3,450 kg$^{Bal\ 2}$	×	$3/kg =	10,350$^{Bal\ 1}$	
AQAP				$2,000 F
	×	=		Price

The question can also be answered as follows:

	Kg	
600 units should use (× 6 kg)	3,600	
Usage variance in kg ($450(F)/3)	150	(F)
Therefore 600 units did use	3,450	

Given no change in stock levels, usage quantity = purchase quantity.

56 D

Direct labour variance

			$	
AHSR				
24,000 hrs	×	$15/hr =	360,000	
AHAR				$24,000 F
		=	336,000	Rate

57 A

Variable overhead variance

			$	
SHSR				
2 hrs/unit × 11,000 units	×	$6/hr =	132,000	Efficiency
AHSR				$12,000 A
24,000 hrs	×	$6/hr =	144,000	

ANSWERS TO SECTION A-TYPE QUESTIONS : SECTION 4

58 A

One way of calculating the fixed overhead volume variance is that it is the difference between the budgeted value of the fixed overheads and the standard fixed overheads absorbed by actual production, so the correct answer is A.

Option B does not represent any type of variance, although if the words 'variable overheads' had been used instead of 'fixed overheads', it would have been the definition of a variable overhead expenditure variance.

Option C is the definition of the fixed overhead expenditure variance.

Option D makes no sense at all.

59 B

	$
Budgeted fixed overhead expenditure ($120,000/12)	10,000
Actual expenditure	9,800
Fixed overhead expenditure variance	200 (F)

60 B

	Hours
500 units should take (× 4 hours)	2,000
did take	1,970
Efficiency variance in hours	30 (F)
× standard variable overhead rate per hour	× $3
Variable overhead efficiency variance	$90 (F)

61 A

	$
Expected cost = ($800 + $0.0002 × 4,100^2) × 1.03	4,287
Actual cost	5,000
	713A

62 C

This is the CIMA definition.

63 B

$$\text{Absorption rate} = \frac{\$170,000}{42,500} = \$4/\text{unit}$$

	Units	
Budgeted output	42,500	
Actual output	40,000	
Volume variance in units	2,500	(A)
Standard fixed overhead cost/unit	× $4	
Fixed overhead volume variance in $	$10,000	(A)

64 C

Labour variances

```
                                                          $
SHSR
    10 hrs/unit × 6,200 units   ×   $9.50/hr   =   589,000 ┐ Efficiency
AHSR                                                        ├ $8,455 A
    62,890 hrs                   ×   $9.50/hr   =   597,455 ┤
AHAR                                                        ├ $1,043 F
                                               =   596,412   Rate
```

The variances could also be calculated as follows:

Rate variance:

	$	
62,890 hours should cost (× $9.50)	597,455	
They did cost	596,412	
Labour rate variance	1,043	(F)

Efficiency variance:

	Hours	
6,200 units should take (× 10)	62,000	
They did take	62,890	
Efficiency variance in hours	890	(A)

Efficiency variance in $ = 890 hours (A) × $9.50 per hour = $8,455 Adverse.

65 B

Inventories are valued at standard prices, so the material price variance must be calculated by reference to the quantity purchased.

Price variance

	Kgs
Actual quantity used	13,050
Reduction in stock	500
Quantity purchased	12,550 kgs

Material variances

$$\begin{array}{l}
\text{SQSP} \\
\quad 6 \text{ kg/unit} \times 2{,}192 \text{ units} \quad \times \quad \$6.75/\text{kg} = 88{,}776 \\
\text{AQSP} \\
\quad 13{,}050 \text{ kg} \quad \times \quad \$6.75/\text{kg} = 88{,}087.50
\end{array} \Bigg\} \begin{array}{l} \text{Usage} \\ \$688.50 \text{ F} \end{array}$$

For a usage variance the quantity must be the quantity used.

$$\begin{array}{l}
\text{AQSP} \\
\quad 12{,}550 \text{ kg} \quad \times \quad \$6.75/\text{kg} = 84{,}712.50 \\
\text{AQAP} \\
\quad \hphantom{12{,}550 \text{ kg} \quad \times \quad \$6.75/\text{kg}} = 72{,}900
\end{array} \Bigg\} \begin{array}{l} \$11{,}812.50 \text{ A} \\ \text{Price} \end{array}$$

As the price variance is calculated at the time of *purchase* then the quantity must be the quantity *purchased* and we had to use the more complicated format than the usual 3-line format.

	$	
12,550 kgs should cost ($6.75/kg)	84,712.50	
They did cost	72,900.00	
Price variance	$11,812.50	(F)

Usage variance	kgs	
2,192 finished units should use (× 6)	13,152	
They did use	13,050	
Usage variance in kgs	102 kgs	(F)

Usage variance in $ = 102 kgs (F) × $6.75/kg (standard price) = $688.50 (F)

66 B

Labour variance

			$	
SHSR				
0.75 hrs/unit × 11,000 units ×	$20/hr	=	165,000	Efficiency
AHSR				$5,000 F
8,000 hrs ×	$20/hr	=	160,000	

The variance scould be calculated as follows:

	Hours	
11,000 units should take (× 0.75 hr)	8,250	
did take	8,000	
Efficiency variance in hours	250	Favourable
Standard rate per hour	× $20	
Efficiency variance in $	$5,000	Favourable

67 C

Variable overhead variance

			$	
AHSR				
8,000 hrs ×	$15/hr	=	120,000	
AHAR				$12,000 A
		=	132,000	Expenditure

The variance could also be calculated as follows:

	$	
8,000 hours should cost (×$15)	120,000	
did cost	132,000	
Expenditure variance	12,000	Adverse

68

Actual number of units produced = 4,200

	$
Budgeted overhead expenditure	48,000
Actual overhead expenditure ($48,000 + $2,000)	50,000
Overhead expenditure absorbed ($50,000 − $8,000)	42,000

Budgeted overhead per unit = $48,000/4,800 = $10

Actual output = $42,000/$10 = 4,200 units

69 C

Fixed overheads are not absorbed in a marginal costing system. Therefore statement (i) is incorrect.

Adverse variances are always recorded as debits in the relevant variance account. Therefore statement (ii) is correct.

Statement (iii) is correct because fixed overhead costs are not included in inventory values in a marginal costing system.

70 (a) Sales price variance = 8,840 units × ($25.90 − $25.00) = $7,956 (F)

(Favourable variance because the actual sales price was higher than the standard sales price).

(b) Sales volume profit variance = ($8,840 units − 8,500 units) × $6.50 profit per unit $2,210 (F)

(Favourable variance because the actual sales volume was higher than the budgeted sales volume.)

(c) Sales volume revenue variance measures the change in sales revenue caused by actual sales volume differing from that budgeted.

Sales volume revenue variance = (8,840 units − 8,500 units) × $25 standard selling price = $8,500 (F)

71 D

Sales price variance

	$	
Std selling price	500	
Actual selling price	465	
Sales price variance	35	(A)
× Actual no of units sold	× 642	
	22,470	

72 C

Sales volume contribution variance

	Units	
Budgeted quantity sold	600	
Actual quantity sold	642	
Sales volume variance in units	42	(F)
× Std contribution per unit (25% × $500)	× $125	
	$5,250	(F)

73

	Actual mix Litres	Standard mix Litres	Difference Litres		Price $	Variance $	
X	984	885.6	98.4	(A)	2.50	246.0	(A)
Y	1,230	1,328.4	98.4	(F)	3.00	295.2	(F)
Totals	2,214	2,214.0	nil			49.2	(F)

74

Expected output $= \dfrac{2,214}{30} = 73.8$ units

Actual output $= 72.0$ units

Shortfall $= 1.8$ units

1.8 units × $84/unit $= \$151.2$ (A)

An alternative would be only 73 complete units of output were expected, thus the shortfall would be 1 unit. The variance would be 1.0 × $84 per unit = $84 adverse.

75 Weighted average standard price per litre = $26/10 = $2.60

	Actual usage Litres		Standard mix Litres	Mix variance Litres		Rate $	Mix variance $	
Material C	200	(6/10)	180	20	(A)	(3 – 2.60)	8	(A)
Material D	75	(3/10)	90	15	(F)	(1 – 2.60)	24	(A)
Material E	25	(1/10)	30	5	(F)	(5 – 2.60)	12	(F)
	300		300	Nil			20	(A)

The variance for material C is adverse because actual usage was greater than standard, for a material costing more than the weighted average cost.

The variance for material D is adverse because actual usage was less than standard, for a material costing less than the weighted average cost.

The variance for material E is favourable because actual usage was less than standard, for a material costing more than the weighted average cost.

76

	Litres	
Standard usage for actual output of X2	280	
Actual usage	300	
Yield variance in litres	20	(A)
× weighted average standard price per litre	× $2.60	
Yield variance in $	$52	(A)

77 There are two methods of calculating mix and yield variances – one is the individual unit price method and the other is the weighted average price method. The two methods give different mix variances for individual materials, but give the same total mix variance. We are only asked for the total mix variance and so either method can be used. We have shown both methods. Most people would prefer the first.

ANSWERS TO SECTION A-TYPE QUESTIONS : SECTION 4

(a) **Individual material price method**

Mix variance

	Material D Litres	Material E Litres	Material F Litres	Total Litres
Actual input	4,300	3,600	2,100	10,000
Actual input in std proportions 4:3.5:2.5	4,000	3,500	2,500	⇐10,000
Difference in quantity	300 A	100 A	400 F	
× Std price	× $9	× $5	× $2	
Mix variance	$2,700 A	$500 A	$800 F	$2,400 A

Weighted average price method

Weighted average standard price per litre = $\dfrac{\$58.50}{4.0 + 3.5 + 2.5 \text{ litres}}$ = $5.85 per litre

Mix variance

	Material D Litres	Material E Litres	Material F Litres	Total Litres
Actual input	4,300	3,600	2,100	10,000
Actual input in std proportions 4:3.5:2.5	4,000	3,500	2,500	⇐ 10,000
Difference in quantity	300	100	− 400	
× Difference in price (weighted av.std price − Ind. Material std price)				
× (5.85 − 9)	× − 3.15			
× 5.85 − 5)		× 0.8		
× (5.85 − 2)			3.85	
Mix variance	$945 A	$85 I	$1,540 A	$2,400 A

(b) **Yield variance**

This is calculated in exactly the same way under both methods.

Std cost per litre of output = $\dfrac{\$58.50}{9 \text{ litres}}$ = $6.50/litre

	Litres
Std yield 10,000 × 90%	9,000
Actual yield	9,100
	100 F
× Std cost per litre of output	× 6.50
Yield variance	$650 F

KAPLAN PUBLISHING

78 C

Event (i) is more likely to result in a favourable usage variance therefore it is not correct. Event (ii) could cause an adverse usage variance since a lower quality material might lead to higher wastage and a higher level of quality control rejects. Event (iii) could cause an adverse usage variance because lower skilled employees might waste material and quality control rejects might again be higher. Event (iv) would not necessarily cause an adverse usage variance. The usage variance is based on the expected usage for the actual output, not on the budgeted usage for the budgeted output.

79 B

Less experienced employees are likely to take longer than standard to produce a given level of output. The result would be an adverse variable overhead efficiency variance. Option A is more likely to result in a favourable variable overhead efficiency variance because employees are likely to work faster than standard. Option C might also result in a favourable efficiency variance because higher quality material is likely to be easier to process, thus saving time against standard. Option D would result in an adverse variable overhead expenditure variance but would not directly affect the variable overhead efficiency variance.

80 (a) Selling price planning variance

	$
Original standard selling price	72
Revised standard selling price	82
	10 F
× No. of units sold	× 600
	6,000 F

(b) Selling price operating variance

	$
Revised standard selling price	82
Actual selling price	86
	4 F
× No. of units sold	× 600
	2,400 F

ANSWERS TO SECTION A-TYPE QUESTIONS : SECTION 4

81 Unfortunately there are different ways of calculating planning and operational variances and with the way that this question is written the correct answer could be B or D.

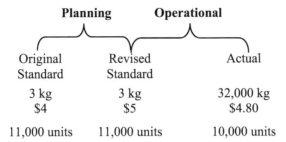

	Original Standard	Revised Standard	Actual
	3 kg	3 kg	32,000 kg
	$4	$5	$4.80
	11,000 units	11,000 units	10,000 units

One way is to calculate planning variances as the difference between the original standard and revised standard.

Planning price variance = ($4 – $5) × 3 kg × 11,000 units = $33,000 A

The correct answer is D using the first method.

Alternatively the variance could be calculated on the actual number of units:

Planning price variance = ($4 – $5) × 3 kg × 10,000 units = $30,000 A

The correct answer is B using the second method.

82 **D** (see below)

83 **B**

Material variance

				$	
SQSP					
	3 kg/unit × 10,000 units ×	$5/kg	=	150,000	Usage
AQSP					$10,000 A
	32,000 kg ×	$5/kg	=	160,000	
AQAP					$6,400 F
	32,000 kg ×	$4.80/kg	=	153,600	Price

The standards here are the revised standards.

84 **B**

The balance on finished goods control is not relevant as the question requires cost of goods produced (not sold).

	$	$
Standard cost of goods produced		128,500
Plus adverse variances:		
Materials price	2,400	
Labour rate	5,600	
Variable overheads	2,680	10,680
Less favourable variances:		
Material usage	8,400	
Labour efficiency	3,140	
Fixed overheads	3,192	(14,732)
Actual cost of goods produced		**124,448**

KAPLAN PUBLISHING

85 Mix variance = $500 Favourable

	Actual mix (kg)	Actual quantity/ Standard mix (kg)	Difference (kg)	Standard price (£)	Mix variance (£)
P	1,030	1,000	30A	75	2,250 A
Q	560	600	40F	100	4,000 F
R	410	400	10A	125	1,250 A
	2,000	2,000			500 F

86 Yield variance = $11,306 Favourable

2,000 kgs should produce 2,000/100 × 90	1,800 kg of output
did produce	1,910 kg of output
Difference	110 F
Value at standard cost per kg ($9,250/90)	$11,306 F

87

Idle hours = 61,500 − 56,000 = 5,500

Standard rate per hour = $540,000/60,000 = $9

Idle time variance = 5,500 × $9 = $49,500 Adverse

88

14,650 units should take	60,000/15,000 = 4 hours per unit	58,600 hours
Did take		56,000 hours
Difference		2,600 hours F
Value at standard rate per hour ($9)		$23,400 F

89 B

8,200 × ($31 − $26) = $41,000 F

90 A

OAR = $34,800/8,700 = $4 per unit

Standard profit per unit = $26 − $10 − $4 = $12

Volume variance = (8,700 − 8,200) × $12 = $6,000 A

91 A

(8,700 − 8,200) × $4 = $2,000 A

ANSWERS TO SECTION A-TYPE QUESTIONS : SECTION 4

92 **B**

OAR = $1,000,000/200,000 = $5 per unit

Overhead absorbed (Actual output × $5)	?
Less actual overhead	1,300,000
= Total fixed production overhead variance	100,000 A

Overhead absorbed is therefore $1,200,000

and actual output = $1,200,000/$5 = 240,000 units

93 (a) Material price planning variance

Original standard price	$4.10
Revised standard price	$4.50
	.40 A × 11,200 units = $4,480 A

(b) Operational material usage variance

1,600 units should use (× 7)	11,200 kg
did use	12,000 kg
	800 kg A

Valued at revised standard price ($4.50) $3,600 A

94

11,500 units should use 5 hours each	57,500 hours
Did use	?
Variance in hours	
Value at $12 per hour	
Labour efficiency variance	$30,000 A

Working backwards:

The variance in hours = $30,000/12 = 2,500 A

The actual hours used are 57,500 + 2,500 = 60,000

60,000 hours should cost (× $12)	720,000
Did cost	?
Labour rate variance	45,000 A

Working backwards:

The actual labour cost = $765,000

so the actual rate paid per hour = $765,000/60,000 = $12.75.

PAPER P1 : MANAGEMENT ACCOUNTING – PERFORMANCE EVALUATION

BUDGETING

95 C

The budget communicates to individual managers what is expected of them in the forthcoming budget period and how much expenditure they can incur in meeting their targets. Thus communication (i) is a purpose of budgeting. An agreed budget provides authorisation for individual managers to incur expenditure in undertaking the activities in their own budget centre. Therefore authorisation (ii) is a purpose of budgeting. Although an organisation might have an objective of maximising sales and might set a budget to enable them to achieve this objective, the maximisation of sales is not in itself a purpose of budgeting. Therefore (iii) is not correct. Individual budget targets are set within the framework of the plan for the organisation as a whole and in this way a budget provides a means of coordinating the efforts of everyone within the organisation. Therefore (iv) is correct.

96 (a) Operating profit margin = 900/5,440 × 100% = 16.5%

(b)

	$000	$000
Non-current assets		1,850
Current assets		
Inventory	825	
Receivables	710	
Bank	50	
		1,585
		3,435
Less current liabilities		(780)
		2,655

Net asset turnover = 5,440/2,655 = 2.05 times

97 (a) Current ratio = 1,585/780 = 2.03 times

(b) Acid test/quick ratio = (1,585-825)/780 = 0.97 times

98 D

An incremental budget starts with the current period's budget and 'builds' on this to produce the budget for the next period.

99

	E	F	G	Total
Budgeted number of batches to be produced:	75,000/200 = 375	120,000/60 = 2,000	60,000/30 = 2,000	
Machine set-ups per batch:	5	3	9	
Total machine set-ups	1,875	6,000	18,000	25,875

So budgeted cost per set-up: $180,000/25,875 = $6.96 per set-up

Therefore the budgeted machine set-up cost per unit of F produced is:

($6.96 × 3)/60 = $0.35 per unit or $6.96 × 6,000/120,000 = $0.35 per unit

ANSWERS TO SECTION A-TYPE QUESTIONS : **SECTION 4**

100 D

See workings below.

101 D

In the year ended October 20X3 total variable costs were $850,000 × 60% = $510,000. These can be analysed as follows:

	People	Packages (kg)	Total
Variable costs 50:50	$255,000	$255,000	$510,000
Units in year	4,420	30,500	-
Cost per unit	$57.69	$8.36	-
Adjusted cost (× 1.02)	$58.84	$8.53	-
Activity for period to 31 January 20X4	1,150	8,100	-
Total related costs	$67,666	$69,093	$136,759

102 C

A flexible budget helps to control resource efficiency by providing a realistic budget cost allowance for the actual level of activity achieved. Control action can therefore be more effective because the effects of any volume change have been removed from the comparison.

103 A

A fixed budget is a budget prepared for a planned single level of activity. It does not ignore inflation (option C is incorrect) and it includes direct costs as well as overhead costs (option D is incorrect). A fixed budget can be prepared for a single product as well as a mix of products (option B is incorrect).

104 D

Production overhead:

	Units		$
High	800	(× 1.75)	1,400
Low	500	(× 2.50)	1,250
	300		150

Variable cost = $150/300 = $0.50

Fixed cost = $1,400 − (800 × $0.50) = $1,000

Other overhead:

	Units		$
High	800	(× 0.625)	500
Low	500	(× 1.00)	500

This is a wholly fixed cost.

Variable cost per unit:

	$
Direct material	2.00
Direct labour	1.50
Variable production overhead	0.50
	4.00

Period fixed cost:

	$
Fixed production overhead	1,000
Other overhead	500
	1,500

105 C

	% Capacity	$
High	90	36,500
Low	75	33,500
Change	15	3,000

Variable cost per 1% capacity = $3,000/15 = $200

Fixed cost = $36,500 − (90 × $200) = $18,500

April activity = (50,000/60,000) × 100% = 83.33% of capacity.

Budget cost allowance for April	$
Fixed cost	18,500
Variable cost (83.33 × $200)	16,667
Total cost allowance	35,167

106 Use high/low method to separate fixed and variable budgeted overhead cost:

	Hours	$
High	18,000	16,242
Low	10,000	13,468
Difference	8,000	2,774

Variable cost per invoice processed

$$= \frac{\$2,774}{8,000} = \$0.34675$$

By substitution fixed cost

= $13,468 − (10,000 × $0.34675) = $10,000

Budget cost allowance	$
= $10,000 + (13,780 × $0.34675) =	14,778
Actual cost =	14,521
	257 (F)

ANSWERS TO SECTION A-TYPE QUESTIONS : SECTION 4

107 C

At output of 6,000 units, overhead = 6,000 × $3.20 = $19,200

At output of 10,000 units, overhead = 10,000 × $3.00 = $30,000

$$\therefore \text{Variable overhead / unit} = \frac{\$30,000 - \$19,200}{10,000 - 6,000} = \$2.70$$

Fixed overhead = $19,200 – (6,000 × $2.70) = $3,000

At activity of 7,350 units, budgeted production overhead = $3,000 + (7,350 × $2.70) = $22,845

108 D

A flexible budget controls operational efficiency by producing a realistic budget cost allowance for the actual level of activity achieved. This allows a more meaningful control comparison with the actual results. Statement (i) is therefore correct.

Incremental budgeting uses the current period's results as a base and adjusts this to allow for any known changes, including the cost increases caused by extra planned units of activity. Statement (ii) is therefore incorrect.

In a rolling budget system an extra quarter is added to the end of the budget when the most recent quarter has expired. The remaining budget might be updated at this point. Statement (iii) is therefore incorrect.

109 C

Where there is goal congruence, managers who are working to achieve their own personal goals will automatically also be working to achieve the organisation's goals. Although the use of aspiration levels to set targets (option D) is likely to help in the achievement of goal congruence, it is not of itself a definition of the term.

110 B

A zero based budgeting system begins each budget from scratch every time. All expenditure on the activity must be justified from zero and the method of carrying out each activity must be re-evaluated as if it were being carried out for the first time.

111 C

Statement (i) is incorrect. Managers at an operational level are more likely to know what is realistically achievable than a senior manager imposing budget targets from above. Statement (ii) is arguably correct: participation in budgeting could improve motivation. Statement (iii) is correct: imposed budgets should be much quicker to prepare, because less discussion time and negotiation time is required than with participative budget-setting.

112 A

Any of these measures could be suitable:

(i) Setting a performance target for training days per employee. In principle, the more training days an employee receives, the more knowledgeable and skilful he or she becomes.

(ii) A target for the percentage of total sales revenue earned from new products focuses on innovation. The higher the target percentage, the more innovative the organisation might be with new product development.

(iii) Labour turnover rate could be a suitable target. The rate at which staff leave and are replaced provides a measure of the loss of existing employee skills, and possibly also the recruitment of new staff with new ideas.

113 Orders = [100,000 + (30 × 240)] × 1.08 = 115,776

Overhead cost = $10,000 + (£0.25 × 115,776) = $38,944

Answer is $39,000

114 D

Quarter	Value of x		Trend units		Forecast sales units
1	25	y = (26×25) + 8,850	9,500	×85% =	8,075.0
2	26	y = (26×26) + 8,850	9,526	×95% =	9,049.7
3	27	y = (26×27) + 8,850	9,552	×105% =	10,029.6
4	28	y = (26×28) + 8,850	9,578	×115% =	11,014.7
					38,169.0

Difference between Q1 and Q4 budgeted sales = 11,014.7 – 8,075.0 = 2,939.7 units

115 D

Since no inventories are held, budgeted production will be equal to budgeted sales.

Budgeted production each quarter = 38,169/4 = 9,542.25 units

116 D

Trend	=	9.72 + (5.816 × 23)
	=	143.488
Seasonal factor	+	6.5
Forecast		149.988

To the nearest whole unit, the forecast number of units to be sold is 150.

117 C

Probability of rainy summer	=	1.0 – 0.4 = 0.6
Expected value of sales volume	=	(80,000 × 0.4) + (120,000 × 0.6)
	=	104,000 units

118 D

Measuring the budgeted number of quotations actually issued would be monitoring the output and activity of the department but it would not be helpful in improving the department's performance in terms of the accuracy or speed of quotations in the scenario described.

ANSWERS TO SECTION A-TYPE QUESTIONS : SECTION 4

119 C

The CIMA definition of zero-based budgeting is C.

120 (a) Receivables days $= \dfrac{\text{Receivables}}{\text{Sales}} \times 365$

$= \dfrac{200}{3,000} \times 365 = 24.3$ days

(b) Payables days $= \dfrac{\text{Payables}}{\text{Cost of Sales}} \times 365$

$= \dfrac{280}{1,600} \times 365 = 63.9$ days

(c) Inventory days $= \dfrac{\text{Inventories}}{\text{Cost of Sales}} \times 365$

$= \dfrac{300}{1,600} \times 365 = 68.4$ days

121 (a) Current ratio $= \dfrac{\text{Current assets}}{\text{Current liabilities}} = \dfrac{300 + 200 + 50}{280} = 1.96$

(b) Acid test ratio $= \dfrac{\text{Current assets - Inventories}}{\text{Current liabilities}} = \dfrac{200 + 50}{280} = 0.89$

122 B

Statement (i) is correct. A fixed budget is prepared for a single level of activity.

Statement (ii) is incorrect. A flexible budget is prepared during the budget period but it recognises only the effects of changes in the volume of activity.

Statement (iii) is correct. A major purpose of the budgetary planning exercise is to communicate an organisation's objectives to its managers.

123 C

Budgetary slack is also called budget bias. Budget holders may sometimes try to obtain a budget that is easier to achieve. They may do this either by bidding for expenditure in excess of what they actually need or, in the case of sales budgets, by deliberately setting easy revenue targets.

124 C

	Machine hours	$
High	12,212	39,477
Low	8,480	31,080
Change	3,732	8,397

Variable cost per machine hour	=	$8,397/3,732
	=	$2.25
Fixed cost = $39,477 − (12,212 × $2.25)	=	$12,000

KAPLAN PUBLISHING

Budget cost allowance for 9,340 machine hours:

	$
Fixed cost	12,000
Variable cost (9,340 × $2.25) =	21,015
	33,015

125 We have been given the trend equation. We need to plug in the value for x so that we can find y.

X is the time period reference number and for the first quarter of year 1 is 1. The time period reference number for the third quarter of year 7 is 27. (Just keep adding 1 to the time period reference number for each new quarter, thus quarter 2, year 1, x = 2; quarter 3, year 1, x = 3; quarter 4, year 1, x = 4; quarter 1, year 2, x = 5, etc.)

$$y = 25{,}000 + 6{,}500 \times 27 = 200{,}500 \text{ units}$$

This is the trend we now need to multiply by the seasonal variation for quarter 3:

Forecast = 200,500 × 150/100 = 300,750 units.

126

	January units	February units	March units
Production budget			
Sales	4,000	5,000	6,000
Add closing inventory	1,500	1,800	
	5,500	6,800	
Less opening inventory	1,200	1,500	
Production	4,300	5,300	
Materials budget			
Production (units)	4,300	5,300	
× No. of units of material per unit of product	× 1 unit	× 1 unit	
Usage quantity (units)	4,300	5,300	
Add closing inventory	1,325		
	5,625		
Less op inventory	1,075		
Purchase quantity (units)	4,550		
× purchase price	× $8		
Purchase cost (£)	36,400		

The purchase cost of materials in January is $36,400. This will be paid in February.

127

$$\text{OAR} = \frac{\text{Budgeted overheads}}{\text{Budgeted level of activity}}$$

$$= \frac{\$22,000 + \$34,000 + \$32,000}{8,000 \text{ hours}} = \$11 \text{ per direct labour hour}$$

$$\text{Labour rate} = \frac{\$128,000}{8,000 \text{ hours}} = \$16 \text{ per direct labour hour}$$

	$
Direct materials	21.50
Direct labour	4.80
Overheads	3.30
	29.60

128

	$
Direct material	21.50
Direct labour	4.80
Overheads	
Set-up costs	16.67
Quality testing costs	11.33
Other overhead costs	1.20
	55.50

$$\text{Set-up costs} = \frac{\$22,000}{88 \text{ set-ups}} = \$250 \text{ per set-up}$$

Charge to Product Z = $250 per set-up × 2 set-ups per batch ÷ 30 units per batch = $16.67

$$\text{Quality testing costs} = \frac{\$34,000}{40 \text{ tests}} = \$850 \text{ per test}$$

Tests are performed every 75 units, therefore charge per unit = $850/75 = $11.33

$$\text{Other overhead costs} = \frac{\$32,000}{8,000 \text{ hours}} = \$4 \text{ per direct labour hour}$$

Charge to product Z = $4 × 0.3 hours = $1.20

129 Customer perspective

Possible measure – Percentage of projects completed within budgeted time.

Financial perspective

Possible measure – Percentage of projects completed within budget.

130 Internal business process perspective

Relevant goal – To ensure that T has a continuous stream of new drugs to bring to the market.

Possible measure – Average time taken to bring a new drug to the market.

Learning and growth perspective

Relevant goal – To foster learning among the employees to encourage creativity and innovation.

Possible measure – Percentages of scores of 4 or 5 (out of 5) on training questionnaires.

131 C

The P/V line will move down as profit will be lower at all units of sales. The gradient represents the C/S ratio and this will be unchanged.

132 A

			Difference
Output	2,000 units	3,500 units	1,500 units
Total cost	$12,000	$16,200	$4,200

Variable cost per unit = 4,200/1,500 = $2.80

Fixed cost = 12,000 – (2,000 × 2.80) = $6,400 (*Note:* Alternatively you could have used the figures for 3,500 units.)

Therefore, the budget cost allowance for 4,000 units = $6,400 + (4,000 × 2.80) = $17,600.

133 D

The index values should add to 400 as there are four seasons.

80 + 80 + 110 + ? = 400

so ? = 130

134 B

Assuming the revenue was $100 will lead to the following revised figures:

	Original		*Revised*
Revenue	100	100 × 60%	60
Variable costs	30	30% × 60	18
Fixed costs	22	Unchanged	22
Profit	48		20

Revised profit = 20/60 × 100 = 33.3%

135

Month of sale	Cash receipts	
November	60% × 90%	70,200
October	20%	24,000
September	15%	15,000
Total		**$109,200**

136

Purchases are sold at cost plus 25% so cost of sales is 100/125= 0.8 × Sales

Closing inventory = 0.5 × Following month's cost of sales

Closing inventory = Opening inventory of the following month

Month	Sales	Cost of sales	Opening inventory	Closing inventory	Purchase	Paid
July	100	80	40	36	76	
August	90	72	36	50	86	**76**
September	125	100	50	56	106	**86**
October	140	112	56			**106**

137

(a) Fly to new destinations: Percentage of flights flying to new destinations. This will show the proportion of new destinations.

(b) Data to be gathered relates to ground time and includes time to refuel, time to unload and load baggage, cleaning and restocking. This will measure the success of achieving the objective.

138

$10m × 0.15 + $20m × 0.1 + ?m = $5.5m + $1m

$3.5m + ?m = $6.5m   so ? = $3m

Revenue needed to ensure a profit of $2m = 3/0.25 = $12m

139 D

This is the definition of a master budget.

140

				Total
Number of purchase requisitions	1,200	1,800	2,000	5,000
Number of set-ups	240	260	300	800

	W $	X $	Y $	Total $
Receiving/inspecting quality assurance (W1)	336,000	504,000	560,000	1,400,000
Production scheduling/machine set-up (W2)	360,000	390,000	450,000	1,200,000
Total overhead cost	696,000	894,000	1,010,000	2,600,000
Units produced and sold	10,000	15,000	18,000	
Overhead cost per unit	69.60	59.60	56.11	
Selling price	200	183	175	
Direct material	50	40	35	
Direct labour	30	35	30	
Overhead cost per unit	69.60	59.60	56.11	
Profit per unit	50.40	48.40	53.89	

Workings

(W1) $1,200/5,000 \times 1,400,000 = 336,000$

$1,800/5,000 \times 1,400,000 = 504,000$

$2,000/5,000 \times 1,400,000 = 560,000$

(W2) $240/800 \times 1,200,000 = 360,000$

$260/800 \times 1,200,000 = 390,000$

$300/800 \times 1,200,000 = 450,000$

CONTROL AND PERFORMANCE MEASUREMENT OF RESPONSIBILITY CENTRES

141 B

The manager of a profit centre can exercise control over revenues and controllable costs, but has no influence concerning the capital invested in the centre.

Contribution (i) would be a useful performance measure because a profit centre manager can exercise control over sales revenue and variable costs. Controllable profit (ii) would also be useful as long as any overhead costs charged in deriving the profit figure are controllable by the profit centre manager. Apportioned central costs would not be deducted when calculating controllable profit. Return on investment (iii), residual income (iv) and economic value added (v) would not be useful because they require a measure of the capital invested in the division.

142 D

Divisional managers will be more aware of changes in the environment in which their own part of the business operates. Thus a decentralised organisation can respond more rapidly to local environmental changes than can a centralised organisation.

A problem with decentralisation tends to be that managers will give priority to the performance of their own centre, even if an improvement in their own performance can cause a worse performance for the organisation overall. Goal congruence can be difficult to achieve in a decentralised organisation and option A is therefore incorrect.

The selection of non-subjective performance measures can be a problem in a decentralised organisation, therefore option B is incorrect.

Communication can be difficult in a decentralised organisation, especially if the various divisions are geographically widespread. Therefore option C is incorrect.

143 D

The most appropriate measure of ROI will include only assets available to earn profit during the year and will not include interest payable.

Thus ROI will be $6 million/($35 million – $4 million) = 19.4%

144 B

Original profit	=	$2,000,000 × 12%	=	$240,000
New profit	=	$240,000 + $90,000	=	$330,000
New capital employed	=	$2,000,000 + $500,000	=	$2,500,000
Residual income	=	$330,000 – (10% × $2,500,000)	=	$80,000

145 C

ROI before project	=	360/1,600	=	22.5%
ROI after project	=	385/(1,600 + 130)	=	22.3%

Therefore management would reject this project, if ROI is used as an evaluation criterion.

Residual value before project	=	360 – (1,600 × 0.18)	=	$72,000
Residual value after project	=	385 – (1,730 × 0.18)	=	$73,600

Therefore management would accept this project if residual income is used as an evaluation criterion.

146 C

$$ROI = \frac{\text{Profit before interest and tax}}{\text{Operations management capital employed}}$$

Profit before interest and tax is the reported profit of the division calculated by 'normal' accounting rules, based only on controllable figures.

The operations management capital employed is the capital employed for which the centre manager is responsible and accountable.

Capital employed can be calculated as equity + long-term debt or non-current assets + current assets – current liabilities.

$$ROI = \frac{400}{1,000 + 700} \text{ or } \frac{400}{1,500 + 600 - 400} = 23.5\%$$

147 B

	$000
Profit before interest and tax	400
Imputed interest	
12% × 1,700	204
	196

The imputed interest is the cost of capital × capital employed.

148

Controllable profit would be calculated before a charge is made for allocated central costs, over which the division manager cannot exercise control.

Controllable profit = $(35,000 + 25,000) = $60,000

(a) Controllable ROI = $60,000/$420,000 = 14.3%

(b) Controllable ROI = $(60,000 + 5,500)/(420,000 + 50,000)
    = 13.9%

149

(a)

	With machine $	Without machine $
Controllable profit	60,000	65,500
Interest charge	42,000	47,000
Residual income	18,000	18,500

(b) If the division manager's performance is based on the first year ROI, then the manager is likely to reject the purchase of the new machine.

However the new machine does generate a return which is greater than the cost of capital. This fact is revealed by the increase in the residual income. While this does not necessarily mean that the investment is worthwhile, the use of residual income as a performance measure would not discourage the manager from making the investment in the machine.

150 A

	$
Accounting profit	135,000
Less additional depreciation (41,000 – 22,000)	(19,000)
Add back increase in doubtful debt provision	8,000
NOPAT (ignoring tax)	124,000
Replacement cost of net assets	660,000
Add provision for doubtful debts	12,000
Economic value of capital employed	672,000
Cost of capital	× 14%
Capital charge	94,080
NOPAT	124,000
Capital charge	94,080
EVA	29,920

ANSWERS TO SECTION A-TYPE QUESTIONS : SECTION 4

151 D

	$ million
Operating profit	20.2
Add back launch costs	3.0
Less amortisation of launch costs	(1.0)
	22.2
Replacement cost of assets	84.0
Add increase in capitalised launch costs	2.0
	86.0
Cost of capital	× 11%
Capital charge	9.46

EVA = $(22.2 – 9.46) million = $12.74 million

152 B

		$
Accounting profit		457,000
Less additional depreciation	(224,000 – 125,000)	(99,000)
Add back development costs		120,000
Less amortised development cost	(120,000/4)	(30,000)
NOPAT (ignoring tax)		448,000
Replacement cost of assets		3,100,000
Add net increase in capitalised development costs	(120,000 – 30,000)	90,000
Economic value of capital employed		3,190,000
Cost of capital		× 11%
Capital charge		350,900
NOPAT		448,000
Capital charge		350,900
EVA		97,100

153 E

	$m
NOPAT	44.2
Capital charge	
11% × 176	19.36
EVA	24.84

NOPAT stands for net operating profit after tax.

EVA is similar to residual income. The difference is that, whereas residual income uses figures from the financial accounts, EVA adjusts those figures to give supposedly more relevant economic figures rather than just bookkeeping figures. The adjustments are as follows:

Calculation of NOPAT

	$m
Operating profit	40.2
Add back launch costs	6
Charging only 1 year's costs instead of the whole 3 years' worth	(2)
NOPAT	44.2

The capital charge is the weighted average cost of capital × the true economic value of the assets.

Calculation of economic value of assets

	$m
Replacement cost	172
Add back launch costs not yet charged	4
Economic value of assets	176

The correct answer as shown above is that the EVA is $24.84m. This was not one of the options given in the exam (option E has been added by us). Everyone who answered A, B, C or D was given the two marks. The examiner forgot to make the adjustment of $4m for the capitalisation of launch costs in the calculation of the economic value of the assets, and so calculated the EVA as 44.2m – 11% × 172m = $25.28m, Answer B.

154 B

	Centre 1		Centre 2	
	$		$	$
External sales (300 × $28)	8,400	(150 × $40)		6,000
Transfer sales (150 × $(20 + 20%))	3,600			-
	12,000			6,000
Transfer costs			3,600	
Own costs (450 × $20)	9,000	(150 × $8)	1,200	
				4,800
Profit	3,000			1,200

ANSWERS TO SECTION A-TYPE QUESTIONS : SECTION 4

155 C

Statement (i) is correct. The buying profit centre will incur the same cost when buying from within and outside the business, and so is likely to be indifferent about the source of supply.

Statement (ii) is correct. When there is spare capacity, a transfer price based on incremental cost rather than market price might encourage the buying profit centre to purchase internally in order to utilise spare capacity. A transfer price based on the full market price will not encourage the utilisation of spare capacity to make a marginal additional profit.

156

Division A will lose the contribution from internal transfers to Division B.

Contribution forgone = 2,500 × $(40 – 22)

= $45,000 reduction in profit

157

	$ per unit
Cost per unit from external supplier	35
Variable cost of internal manufacture saved	22
Incremental cost of external purchase	13

Reduction in profit of X = $13 × 2,500 units

= $32,500

158 C

The optimum transfer price is where:

Transfer price = marginal cost + opportunity cost

The opportunity cost is the contribution forgone from an external sale of alpha = $16
$(6 + 4 + 2) = $4
The optimum transfer price is therefore:
marginal cost $10 + opportunity cost $4 = $14 per unit

159 A

Marginal cost will be same as Variable cost, that is $15.

The two-part tariff transfer price per unit is marginal cost $15.

160 C

(i) *Two-part tariff system*: The price **per unit** credited to the supplying Division S would be the marginal cost of $28. The agreed fixed fee should be ignored when calculating the **unit** price.

(ii) *Dual price*: The price credited to the supplying Division S would be the market price $40. (The element of profit in this ($12) would be removed so that only $28 (the marginal cost) would be debited to Division T.)

161 D

	$
Market price of product N in Canada	300
Less: Total cost	120
Pre-tax profit	180
Post-tax profit per unit ($1,100,000/11,000 units)	100
Tax (balancing figure)	80

Tax as a percentage of pre-tax profit is $80/$180 × 100 = 44%.

162 D

	Per unit £	Per unit £
Market price in UK		250.0
Less: Transfer price at variable cost: $\frac{\$120 \times 0.75}{1.5}$	60.0	
UK marketing and distribution costs	40.0	100.0
		150.0
Less: Tax at 25%		(37.5)
		112.5

11,000 units at £112.50 = £1,237,500 profit after tax.

163 A

A higher transfer price will mean that CMW Ltd is charged more for goods transferred, thus decreasing UK profits and increasing the overseas profit.

Increased royalty payments paid by CMW Ltd will decrease UK profits and increase the overseas profit.

164 A

(i) The fixed overhead cost per unit is $120,000/20,000 units = $6 per unit

Full production cost = 3 + 4 + 2 + 6 =	$15
	× 140%
Transfer price	$21

(ii) The transfer price per unit is simply the variable cost = $9.

The fixed cost of $200,000 is paid as a lump sum, not per unit.

ANSWERS TO SECTION A-TYPE QUESTIONS : SECTION 4

165 We are trying to maximise the profit from the service from the Legal Division's point of view. As far as the Legal Division is concerned its variable costs are $65 ($25 + $40).

Hours sold	Price per hour	Variable cost per hour	Contribution per hour	Total contribution
0	100	65	35	0
1,000	90	65	25	25,000
2,000	80	65	15	30,000
3,000	70	65	5	15,000
4,000	60	65	(5)	(20,000)
5,000	50	65	(15)	(75,000)

The level of sales that would maximise the contribution for the Legal Division is 2,000 hours and its contribution would be $30,000.

166 We are trying to maximise the profit from the service from the group point of view. As far as the group is concerned the variable cost of the service is $45 ($20 + $25).

Hours sold	Price per hour	Variable cost per hour	Contribution per hour	Total contribution
0	100	45	55	0
1,000	90	45	45	45,000
2,000	80	45	35	70,000
3,000	70	45	25	75,000
4,000	60	45	15	60,000
5,000	50	45	5	25,000

The level of sales that would maximise the contribution for the whole company is 3,000 hours and the contribution would be $75,000.

This answer assumes that the Secretarial Division has spare capacity.

167

	$m	$m
Net profit after tax		8.6
Add		
Interest	2.3	
Development costs	6.3	
Advertising	1.6	10.2
		18.8
Less amortisation of development		2.1
		16.7
Capital	30	
Add back development costs not charged	4.2	
	34.2	
Capital charge 34.2 x 13%		4.45
EVA		**12.25**

KAPLAN PUBLISHING

168 The aims of a transfer pricing system are:

- to ensure an optimal allocation of resources;
- to promote goal congruence;
- to motivate divisional managers;
- to allow for performance measurement;
- to promote autonomy.

169 A

ROI = Net income/Net assets = 300,000/6,750,000 × 100% = 4.44%

170 D

$300,000 – 13% × $6,750,000 = ($577,000)

171 A

EVA = NOPAT – Economic value of assets × Cost of capital

NOPAT	$m
Operating profit	89.2
Add back development costs	+9.6
Less amortisation of development costs	–3.2
Add back accounting depreciation	+24
Less economic depreciation	–33.6
	86
Economic value of assets	$m
Replacement cost of assets	168
Less economic depreciation	–33.6
Add net increase in development costs	+6.4
Add working capital	+27.2
	168

EVA = 86 – 13% × 168 = $64.16m

172 The variable cost of the component = $600 × 0.6 = $360

Transfer price = $360 × 1.7 = $612

$000	X	Y
Sales: External (W1)	8,000	14,400
Internal (W2)	7,344	
	15,344	14,400
Variable cost (W3)	(7,920)	(12,144)
Fixed production cost (W4)	(5,280)	
Fixed non-production cost	(1,500)	(1,300)
Profit before tax	644	956
Tax	(161)	(286.8)
Profit after tax	483	669.2

Workings

(W1) $800 × 10,000 = $8,000,000

$1,200 × 12,000 = $14,400,000

(W2) 12,000 × $612 = $7,344,000

(W3) $360 × 22,000 = $7,920,000

Variable cost for product W = $400 + $612 = $1,012 per unit

$1,012 × 12,000 = $12,144,000

(W4) $240 × 22,000 = $5,280,000

Section 5

ANSWERS TO SECTION B-TYPE QUESTIONS

COST ACCOUNTING SYSTEMS

173 MARGINAL COST PROFIT AND CASH FLOW

Marginal costing systems differ from absorption costing systems in the way that they treat fixed production overheads. In a marginal costing system the fixed production overheads are charged against the sales revenue in the period that they are incurred.

In contrast an absorption costing system will attribute some of the fixed production overheads to any units held in inventory and thus some fixed production overheads will be carried forward in inventory to future periods. These overheads will not be charged in calculating the profit in the month they are incurred, but in the month when the inventory is sold i.e. the charging of the fixed overheads against profit does not reflect the actual cash flow.

Thus marginal costing profits will provide a better indication of cash flow than will absorption costing profits, since more of the costs actually incurred will be charged against the sales revenue for the period. However there will still be a discrepancy between marginal costing profits and cash flow because of factors such as credit sales and purchases and the treatment of capital expenditure in profit calculations.

174 PROCESS COSTING

A normal loss is the expected level of loss that should arise in a process for a given level of input or activity. If the actual loss exceeds the normal loss then the difference is called an abnormal loss.

Both types of losses are credited in the process account but the difference in their costing treatment lies in the way that they are valued.

The cost of producing the normal loss units is absorbed by the good units produced. The normal loss units do not therefore absorb any of the process costs. They are valued at their scrap value, if any. This amount is credited in the process account and debited to the scrap inventory account or normal loss account.

The occurrence of an abnormal loss must not affect the cost of the good units produced. Therefore the abnormal loss units absorb a full share of the process costs and are valued at the same rate as good production. This amount is credited in the process account and debited in the abnormal loss account. The scrap value of the abnormal loss is not credited in the process account but instead it is credited in the abnormal loss account. Thus the scrap value of the abnormal event does not affect the cost of the good production.

In this way the net cost of the abnormal loss is highlighted in the abnormal loss account for management attention. The net balance on this account is then debited in the profit and loss account.

175 THROUGHPUT ACCOUNTING

Throughput accounting has been described as a form of 'super variable costing' because the concept of throughput has similarities to the concept of contribution. However there is a major difference in the definition of contribution in the two systems or, more specifically, in what is described as a variable cost.

The traditional marginal costing approach assumes that direct labour is a variable cost. Although this may have been true in the past when labour was typically paid a piece rate, this is no longer the case. In the short term, throughput accounting treats labour as a fixed cost.

Marginal costing also tends to emphasise cost behaviour, especially overheads, and usually attempts to separate these into fixed and variable components. As with labour costs, throughput accounting treats all production overhead as fixed in the short term and aggregates these with labour into what is referred to as 'total factory cost'. Consequently, in throughput accounting the only cost that is treated as variable is the direct material cost.

Furthermore, throughput accounting uses the total of direct materials purchased in the period in the calculation of throughput, rather than the cost of material actually used, as is the case with marginal costing.

176 THROUGHPUT ACCOUNTING RATIO

The throughput accounting (TA) ratio is calculated as follows:

$$\text{TA ratio} = \frac{\text{throughput per hour of bottleneck resource}}{\text{operating expenses per hour of bottleneck resource}}$$

A bottleneck resource sets a limit to the throughput through the system. It can take the form of a shortage of machine hours, or a shortage of labour hours, and so on.

Throughput is calculated as the selling price less the material cost of a product.

Effectively the ratio measures the rate at which money is generated compared with the rate at which it is spent. The ratio implies that only products with a TA ratio greater than 1 should be produced and that these products can be ranked in terms of profitability by their TA ratio. To maximise throughput in the short term, the products(s) with the highest TA ratio should be produced.

177 IMPROVING THE THROUGHPUT ACCOUNTING RATIO

$$\text{TA ratio} = \frac{\text{throughput per hour of bottleneck resource}}{\text{operating expenses per hour of bottleneck resource}}$$

Three actions that could be considered to improve the TA ratio are as follows:

(i) Increase the selling price of the product. This would improve the throughput per hour in the packing process, i.e. the numerator in the calculation and the TA ratio would increase.

(ii) Reduce the operating expenses in the packing process. This would reduce the denominator in the ratio calculation.

(iii) Improve the productivity of the employees engaged in the packing process, thus reducing the time taken to pack each unit of product C. Throughput per packing hour would increase, but the operating expenses per packing hour would remain unchanged. Therefore the TA ratio would increase.

178 ABC COST DRIVERS

The cost driver for a particular activity is the factor that causes a change in the cost of the activity. For the cost driver to be useful there must be an identifiable relationship between the cost and the cost driver, i.e. changes in the number of cost drivers must cause corresponding changes in the total cost incurred on the activity.

Another major consideration is the ease of accurately recording the number of cost drivers incurred. If the process of recording the cost drivers is very complex and time-consuming then the cost of the recording system might outweigh the benefits derived from the information obtained.

It is possible to identify three types of cost driver:

Transaction drivers

Here, the cost of an activity is affected by the number of times a particular action is undertaken. Examples would include number of set-ups, number of power drill operations, number of batches of material received, number of purchase orders, etc.

Duration drivers

In this case, the cost of the activity is not so much affected by the number of times the action is undertaken as by the length of time that it takes to perform the action, e.g. set-up costs may not be related to the number of set-ups so much as to the set-up time, because some products involve more complicated and time consuming set-ups than others.

Intensity drivers

In this case, efforts would be directed at determining what resources were used in the making of a product or service, e.g. rather than charging all purchase orders with the same cost per order, we might determine that overseas orders involve more work than home orders and apply a weighting to the overseas orders to reflect the extra work.

179 ABC AND PROFITABILITY

Activity based costing (ABC) could provide more meaningful information about product costs and profitability in the following circumstances.

(i) Where indirect costs are high relative to direct costs. The cost of direct materials, for example, can usually be attributed to cost units relatively easily. The attribution of overhead costs tends to be more problematic. Traditionally, overhead costs have been attributed to cost units by fairly arbitrary methods such as absorption costing on the basis of direct labour hours. The introduction of new technology has typically resulted in a reduction in labour cost and an increase in overhead cost and labour hours may no longer be an appropriate absorption basis. An ABC approach should lead to more accurate costings of products and departments by considering the processes that actually cause overhead costs to be incurred.

(ii) Where products or services are complex. By identifying the activities that consume resources and the cost drivers for each activity, the costs incurred can be traced more accurately to products and services according to the number of cost drivers that they generate.

(iii) Where some products or services are produced in large numbers but others are produced in small numbers. Products and services incur overhead costs because of the activities that go into producing them. These activities are not necessarily related to the volumes that are produced. An ABC system recognises that direct labour hours and machine hours are not the drivers of cost in many modern business environments.

(iv) Where products or services are tailored to customer specifications. An ABC system is more likely to trace accurately the costs incurred on each specific customer order. The result will be more accurate cost determination which will help in decisions such as pricing.

180 MANUFACTURING RESOURCE PLANNING

MRP II systems provide integration between the production planning, inventory control and purchasing systems and the accounting system. The accounting function has access to bills of materials and production schedules through the common database. The system also holds data on material and labour prices.

The system is therefore able to produce the following information to assist in the budgetary planning process:

(i) A production budget from the master production schedule

(ii) A material purchases budget

(iii) Some input to the cash budget

(iv) A standard cost for each product

(v) Updated standard costs, when changes are made to product specifications.

181 JUST-IN-TIME

A number of conditions are necessary for the successful implementation of a JIT manufacturing system.

(i) Accurate production scheduling. In order to avoid the build-up of finished inventory, it is important that production is undertaken only in accordance with demand. Each stage of production needs to be responsive to the next process in line, and produce in accordance with their requirements. This requires very careful, constant monitoring, which means that the information systems must be accurate and properly applied.

(ii) Staff training and empowerment. Being flexible and responsive to the 'internal customer' as above is something that may not come naturally to all staff members. Therefore some training in team working might be necessary. Workers should feel empowered to behave in the way that is most desirable. This may also mean a need for incentives such as flexible hours or perhaps longer holidays in return for working longer shifts. Furthermore, many employees will need to be multi-skilled so that they can move between different parts of the production process as demand requires.

(iii) Plant and equipment must be regularly inspected and maintained. The JIT system cannot afford any downtime due to unreliable machinery.

(iv) Long-term relationships with suppliers. Relationships with suppliers should be based on their reliability and the quality of their supply. Price will often become a secondary consideration. Since no buffer inventories are held there is no room for a breakdown in supply or the delivery of sub-standard items. Suppliers must be willing to work with the organisation to find ways of improving the quality of the product and the process. It is likely that fewer suppliers would be used in a JIT environment.

(v) Quality control. Since no buffer inventories are held there would be a requirement for 100% quality at all stages in the production process.

ANSWERS TO SECTION B-TYPE QUESTIONS : SECTION 5

182 TQM AND JIT

The aim of TQM (Total Quality Management) is that all goods and services produced can be relied upon to meet their specifications at all times. These specifications will include technical features and timing. The importance of TQM in a JIT environment includes the following:

- JIT requires very precise planning that is only possible when goods can be relied upon.

- JIT requires very low, or no, inventories to be held; thus there must be total reliability that goods will perform to specification, as there will be no alternative inventory if goods or services fail.

- Where JIT is operated with a Kanban system for inventory replacement, the inventory re-order point is decided on the basis that all inventory is usable and that replacement items will be delivered in the specified and very short time period.

- The consequences of poor quality are magnified in a JIT system and could cause considerable hold-ups in a process.

183 QUALITY COST

There are different philosophies about the cost of quality. Many businesses engineer quality into their processes while others set up systems to provide quality assurance.

The typical characteristics of quality cost are sometimes cited as follows:

Prevention cost

This would consist perhaps of the cost of the salaries of a quality control unit that carries out the sampling process to detect quality failures and prevents them from getting to the customer.

Inspection/appraisal cost

This would include the cost of investigation into quality failures as well as the cost of consumable items used to carry out routine examinations.

Internal failure cost

This would cover the cost of scrapped items, reworking any defective output or undertaking any re-engineering process to improve quality.

External failure cost

This would cover the cost of warranties, free replacements, repairs and other efforts to repair the loss of customer goodwill.

184 MARGINAL AND ABSORPTION COSTING

(i) OAR = $12,800/2,000 = $6.40 per unit

Inventory is budgeted to increase and therefore absorption costing profit will be higher than marginal costing profit.

Absorption costing profit = 5,700 + (600 × $6.40) = $9,540

(ii) Marginal costing is useful for:

- decision making because variable and fixed costs are separated. Often fixed costs are not relevant to a decision and so can be ignored;

- flexible budgeting as costs must be identified as fixed or variable to calculate the flexed budget allowance.

185 MARGINAL COSTING AND THROUGHPUT ACCOUNTING

The underlying methodology is the same except that throughput accounting (TA) assumes that direct materials are the only 'variable' cost and that labour is a fixed cost.

TA is based on the ideas of the 'Theory of Constraints' and seeks to maximise profits by maximising throughput by identifying and, where possible, removing bottlenecks.

Maximising throughput on a bottleneck is similar to the marginal costing (MC) idea of maximising contribution per unit of scarce resource.

TA controls production costs through a series of ratios that focus on throughput per bottleneck resource.

MC is used in many aspects of decision making such as pricing and breakeven analysis.

STANDARD COSTING

186 IDEAL STANDARDS

An ideal standard assumes that ideal operating conditions exist. No allowance is made for material wastage, labour waiting time, machine stoppages or other similar inefficiencies.

Ideal standards can be useful for highlighting the cost of performance below 100 per cent efficiency but most reported variances will be adverse. The motivational impact of continual adverse variances can be negative. Workers may feel that the targets are unfair and can never be reached and thus may be deterred from even trying to achieve them.

An alternative standard could be an attainable standard. This assumes a tough but fair and achievable level of efficiency. In theory this should have a better motivational impact. Workers should feel that the targets can be achieved and are more likely to attempt to achieve those targets.

The attainable standard should also provide a better basis for operational control since the actual performance will be compared against a realistic achievable standard, rather than against an unachievable standard. The reported variances are likely to be more meaningful from a point of view of cost control.

187 FIXED PRODUCTION OVERHEAD VOLUME VARIANCE

The fixed production overhead volume variance is reported in a standard absorption costing system. It arises due to the use of a predetermined overhead absorption rate based on budgeted costs and activity levels.

The standard absorption rate is designed so that, if the actual costs and activity levels are exactly the same as budgeted, then there will be no fixed production overhead variances. In practice of course this is rarely the case and any difference between the actual and budgeted production volume results in a fixed production overhead volume variance.

The fixed production overhead volume variance is the difference in output volume multiplied by the absorption rate per unit of output. It represents the under- or over-absorbed fixed production overhead due to a change in production volume from the budgeted level. If the volume of output is higher than budgeted, the variance is favourable (over-absorbed overhead). If the volume of output is lower than budgeted, the variance is adverse (under-absorbed overhead).

If the variance is adverse, then it is necessary to investigate why output was lower than budgeted. This is not necessarily a bad thing, if output were deliberately reduced because sales volume was lower than expected. In this case the cause of the sales shortfall would need to be investigated, rather than questioning the shortfall in production. If production had proceeded as budgeted, then this would have reduced the volume variance but this would not necessarily be the correct action for the organisation as a whole, if as a result the units remained unsold in inventory.

Similarly, if the variance is favourable this is not necessarily a good thing. If the output were sold, then the increase in production was worthwhile. However, simply increasing output in order to produce a favourable overhead volume variance would not be the correct action, if the extra units cannot be sold.

In conclusion it is not the fixed production overhead volume variance itself which provides useful information for management but the reason why the production volume differed from that budgeted and the consequential effects of that volume difference.

188 LABOUR VARIANCES

Labour variance – senior consultant

				$	
SHSR					
40 hours	×	$100/hr	=	4,000	Efficiency
AHSR					$1,000 A
50 hours	×	$100/hr	=	5,000	

Labour variance – junior consultant

				$	
SHSR					
60 hours	×	$60/hr	=	3,600	Efficiency
AHSR					$900 F
45 hours	×	$60/hr	=	2,700	

The efficiency variance looks at whether people **work** fast or slow and looks at hours **worked**.

The total efficiency variance was thus $1,000 A + $900 F = $100 A.

Idle time variance

The idle time variance is the difference between the actual hours worked and the actual hours paid for, then multiplied by the standard labour rate per hour.

Idle time variance = 10 hours × $60 per hour = $600 A

Mix variance

	Senior consultant hrs	Junior consultant hrs	Total hrs
Actual hours	50	45	95
Actual hours in std proportions			⇓
4:6	38	57	⇐ 95
Difference in hours	12 A	12 F	
× Std rate	× 100	× 60	
Mix variance	$1,200 A	$720 F	$480 A

The mix and yield variances are sub-divisions of the efficiency variance and thus focus on hours worked.

The mix variance was calculated using the individual unit prices; the weighted average method could also have been used.

189 CRITICISMS OF STANDARD COSTING

A number of criticisms have been suggested concerning the applicability of standard costing in a modern manufacturing environment.

(i) Setting standards can be said to create a climate whereby their achievement and maintenance is the ultimate goal. This is inconsistent with the philosophy of continuous improvement in the modern manufacturing environment.

(ii) There is an increasing trend away from mass production towards customised and non-standard products. This leads to a greater variability in operating conditions, where constant standards are less useful.

(iii) There is an increasing use of benchmarking as a means of establishing best practice and standards, by the use of both internal and external information. This will take account of the practices of other organisations in comparison with the organisation's own practices. The use of internally determined standards, based upon an organisation's own costs and procedures, may give too narrow a basis for measurement of the organisation's performance in a competitive environment.

(iv) Direct labour variances are less relevant as production is increasingly automated.

(v) The move towards strictly monitored input systems, such as JIT, decreases the variability in input costs, thus rendering variance analysis unnecessary.

190 STANDARD COSTING AND THE NEW MANAGEMENT ACCOUNTING

The company's standard costing system will need to be adapted in a number of ways in the new environment.

(i) *Cost reduction v cost control*

TQM enforces a management policy of continuous improvement and hence is focused on cost reduction. However, traditional standard costing is concerned with cost control where performance standards often remain constant for the life cycle of a product. In order to use standard costing successfully in a TQM environment it would be necessary to continually review and tighten the standards each period.

(ii) *Management responsibility*

Under standard costing individual responsibility for reported variances is encouraged. With TQM and JIT it is necessary to focus on group responsibility for performance. For standard costing to work in a TQM and JIT environment it would be necessary for each team of employees to bear group responsibility for variances.

(iii) *Demand based manufacturing*

JIT manufacturing only allows production to occur if the demand for the final product exists. In contrast, standard costing can encourage managers to produce for inventory. For example a favourable fixed overhead volume variance will result if output is increased, regardless of whether a demand exists. The standard costing variances reported would need to be adapted to reflect the demand based manufacturing of JIT.

(iv) *Direct material variances*

Both TQM and JIT encourage long-term relationships with suppliers, who are expected to deliver on time at the right quality. In return for the high level of service demanded, a fair price will be agreed. Thus material price and material usage variances will no longer be necessary.

(v) *Direct labour efficiency variance*

It will be important to ensure that workers do not focus on faster production, in order to minimise the efficiency variance, at the expense of the quality of output.

(vi) *Historical versus future information*

Standard costing is concerned with reviewing actual costs after the period has ended. JIT and TQM both focus on how improvements can be made in the future. Management will need to develop strategies to achieve better results in the future.

191 RITZER'S MCDONALDIZATION MODEL

The four dimensions to the McDonaldization model described by Ritzer are efficiency, calculability, control and predictability.

(i) *Efficiency*

The optimum means must be chosen to achieve a given end, so that consumers are able to get the service they want more rapidly and with less effort.

(ii) *Calculability*

Each service unit must be identical and the input must be measurable. Non-human technologies should be used as much as possible in order to standardise operations and the service output.

(iii) *Control*

There should be effective control over both employees and customers. Again, the use of non-human technologies in the provision of the service assists in the achievement of control.

(iv) *Predictability*

Customers and employees should know exactly what service will be provided, wherever in the world it is being provided. Predictability helps the service to be standardised so that standard costing can be used as a means of control.

192 DIAGNOSTIC RELATED GROUPS

Diagnostic related groups (DRGs) are a means of classifying patients according to certain characteristics such as their age, diagnosis and required treatment. Once a patient is classified into a certain group it is possible to determine a standard cost for their treatment and care. The standard cost will be based upon estimates of the standard consumption of hospital resources required and the expected length of stay.

This standard then provides a control measure against which the actual cost of the patient's treatment and care can be monitored. Therefore control by comparison can be achieved in the same way that product standard costs are used for control purposes.

The system was originally developed in the USA where the DRG classification provides a basis for determining the maximum payment that will be received by the hospital from a medical insurance company. This provides a direct incentive for hospital management to keep costs below the maximum payment that will be received from the insurance company.

193 MIX AND YIELD VARIANCES

When two or more materials are mixed together it may be possible to analyse further any recorded materials usage variance. The further analysis would subdivide the total usage variance into its component parts of materials mix variance and materials yield variance.

The materials mix variance is the change in standard cost caused by mixing the materials in a different proportion to standard. For example, if proportionately more of a cheaper material is used in the mix then a favourable mix variance will result.

The materials yield variance is the change in standard cost caused by using a different amount of material in total than the standard expected for the output achieved.

There are a number of limitations in the usefulness of material mix and yield variances.

(i) Mix and yield variances can only provide useful control information where the mix of materials is within the control of management, and where the information about total yield is more useful than usage variances for the individual materials calculated separately.

(ii) It is often found that the mix and yield variances are interdependent, and that one variance cannot be assessed without also considering the other. For example an adverse yield variance might be explained by the fact that the mix had a larger than expected proportion of cheaper material (favourable mix variance).

(iii) If management is able to achieve a cheaper mix of materials without affecting the yield then the standard becomes obsolete. The cheaper mix should become the new standard mix.

(iv) Control measures to achieve a favourable mix variance are likely to affect the quality of the output. Analysing mix and yield variances for control purposes does not take account of quality issues.

194 LABOUR RATE VARIANCE

Possible causes of an adverse labour rate variance include the following:

(i) The standard labour rate per hour may have been set too low.

(ii) Employees may have been of a higher grade than standard, with a consequent increase in the hourly rate paid.

(iii) There may have been an unexpected increase in the prevailing market rate of pay for employees with appropriate skills.

(iv) Where bonuses are included as a part of direct labour costs, increased bonus payments may have been made, above the standard level expected.

(v) There may have been a change in the composition of the work force, which resulted in an increase in the average rate of pay.

195 INVESTIGATION OF VARIANCES

(a) From the normal distribution tables, 95% of outcomes lie within 1.96 standard deviations of the mean.

1.96 standard deviations × 10 kg = 19.6 kg

90 kg ± 19.6 kg = a range between 70.4 kg and 109.6 kg

The actual weight of the sample batch was 110 kg, which falls outside the 95% control limits and the variance should thus be investigated.

(b) Four factors are listed below. Only two were asked for.

The cost of investigating the variance and correcting it

If the financial value of the variance is minor and/or the cost of investigating and correcting the variance is substantial, then the variance should not be investigated. The benefit from the control action must exceed the cost of the investigation.

The trend of the variance

If the variance is below 1.96 standard deviations, but has been showing a worsening of performance for a number of months, then it may be decided to investigate the variance now rather than wait for it to actually hit the control limit.

The controllability of the variance

If the variance cannot be controlled (cannot be fixed), then there may be no point in incurring the cost of investigating it.

The reliability of the standards

If the standard is not set on a reliable basis in the first place, then any variance from the standard is also unreliable and any variances falling outside the 95% control limits might not actually need investigating, or indeed some variances falling within the 95% limits should be investigated.

196 INTERPRETING VARIANCES (1)

A variance is significant if its size is material relative to the standard value of the cost or revenue to which it relates, or if it has implications for the activities of the business. If significant variances are those that require investigation, it is only worthwhile investigating a variance if the anticipated benefits of the investigation have a value greater than the expected costs.

Therefore the size of the variance is the crucial factor in determining its significance. The size of a variance can be measured in terms of its absolute monetary value, or as a percentage of its corresponding standard value.

The nature of the variance must also be considered. If it fluctuates from being adverse to favourable and back again, it is not as significant as a variance that always has the same sign. Therefore it is important to consider both the individual period variance and its trend over a number of periods.

Control limits might be set of, say, plus or minus 5% of standard cost. If a variance, or the cumulative total of a variance over a number of periods, exceeds this control limit then it would be identified as significant.

197 INTERPRETING VARIANCES (2)

The factors that should be considered before deciding to investigate a variance include the following:

(i) The size of the variance, both in absolute terms and as a percentage of the standard cost.

(ii) The trend in the variance. If the variance fluctuates from adverse to favourable and back again then over a period of time the trend in the variance might be insignificant and the cause is thus not worthy of investigation.

(iii) The cost of conducting an investigation should be balanced against the likely benefit to be derived from the investigation.

(iv) The likelihood of the variance being controllable. For example, certain price variances may be due to movements in external market prices which are outside the control of the organisation's management.

(v) The interrelationship of variances. An adverse material usage variance might be directly related to a favourable materials price variance due to lower quality material being purchased, leading to high wastage.

(vi) The type of standard that was set. For example an ideal standard is likely to result in adverse efficiency variances and a price standard that was set as an average for a period might produce favourable variances early in the period, followed by adverse variances later in the period.

198 CENTRALLY SET STANDARDS

The advantage of centrally imposed standard costs are as follows:

(i) Managers cannot build slack or bias into their standards in order to make them easy to achieve and thus make themselves look good.

(ii) By having the standards imposed by senior managers, i.e. someone outside the department, a more objective, fresher perspective may be gained.

(iii) It ensures that all sites will use the same standard and thus will be judged on the same basis.

(iv) The senior managers are aware of the strategic objectives of the business and can use the standards to influence the site managers to act in accordance with the group objectives.

(v) It is less time consuming if senior managers set the standards rather than letting the site managers set them and then having to discuss their suitability.

(vi) Managers may not possess the technical skill necessary to set their own standards.

The disadvantages of centrally imposed standard costs are as follows:

(i) The morale of the management is adversely affected. Site managers feel that their opinion is not listened to, that their opinion is of no value.

(ii) Managers are less likely to accept the standards and strive to achieve the targets than if they had some say in setting the standard. There will be some resistance to the standard. If the managers had had some say in setting the standard, then failure to achieve the target that they themselves had set would have been seen as a personal failure as well as an organisational failure. This motivational benefit is lost.

(iii) The lower level managers will have a more detailed knowledge of their particular site than senior managers and thus would have been able to produce more realistic and appropriate standards.

(iv) It may not be appropriate to use the same standard for different sites and local conditions should be taken into consideration, e.g. should the standard wage rate be used throughout the country? Should the standard for energy be the same, or can some sites use a cheaper energy supplier?

(v) Setting standards is time consuming and if the local managers set their own standards then this would free up senior managers' time and allow them to make the strategic decisions rather than the operational level detail of setting standards.

199 BENCHMARKING

Benchmarking is the practice of identifying an external organisation whose performance can be used as a comparator or benchmark for the organisation's own performance. The principle is that, by a close analysis of and comparison with other practices and processes, changes and adjustments can be made to those processes that will improve overall performance.

Four main types of benchmarking can be identified.

- *Internal benchmarking* involves comparisons with another department or division within the same company.

- *Competitive benchmarking* involves comparisons with the most successful competitors in the same field.

- *Functional benchmarking* is carried out by comparing the performance of a business function, for example the finance department, with the performance of the finance function in an organisation of similar size but which is not a direct competitor.

- *Strategic benchmarking* is a form of competitive benchmarking aimed at reaching decisions for strategic action and organisational change.

Benchmarking might help to improve overall performance by:

- providing managers with a warning about the need for change;
- enabling learning from others in order to improve performance;
- gaining a competitive edge (in the private sector);
- improving services (in the public sector).

200 HOSPITAL CARE

	$	$
Standard cost for 2-day procedure		1,165
Length of stay variances		
Nursing costs: 1 day × 0.75 × $320 per day	240 A	
Space and food costs: 1 day × $175 per day	175 A	
Hospital overheads	110 A	525 A
Standard cost for 3-day stay		1,690
Drug and specific cost variances		205 A
Nursing staffing variance: 3 days × $320 × (0.9 – 0.75)		144 A
Actual cost		2,039

201 C PLC

		Feb	March	April
1	Std material cost of output ($)	132,000	61,200	109,200
2	Usage variance ($)	15,970	5,950	8,400
3	Std cost of actual purchases ($)	147,970	67,150	117,600
4	Price variance ($)	12,300	4,500	6,200
	Usage % variance (2/1)	12.1%	9.7%	7.7%
	Price % variance (4/3)	8.3%	6.7%	5.3%

Percentage variance chart for February to April

202 MODERN BUSINESS ENVIRONMENT

Standard costing may not be appropriate in a modern business environment because:

- it is most appropriate for large volumes of similar products. In the modern environment products tend to be customised and produced in smaller batches;

- it is normally based on attainable working conditions. The modern environment emphasises continuous improvement and zero defects;

- it focuses on maximising the utilisation of capacity and minimising cost. In the modern environment breaks in production may be preferred to match production to demand and higher quality higher price inputs may be preferred such as highly skilled staff.

BUDGETING

203 PURPOSE OF BUDGETS

The main purposes of budgets include the following:

Planning

The budgeting process compels planning. It forces managers to consider the future rather than simply react to day-to-day operating pressures.

Control

The budget provides the plan against which actual results can be monitored. Management's attention can be directed to any major differences between planned and actual performance.

Co-ordination

The budgeting process helps co-ordinate the different parts of the business, because individual budgets are set within the framework of the plan for the organisation as a whole.

Communication

Budgets are also used as a communication device. Once budget holders have their budget available they know what is expected of them and the limitations to their expenditure in the forthcoming period.

Motivation

Budgets can motivate individuals to work to achieve the organisation's objectives.

Evaluation

The budget provides the basis for judging a manager's performance in relation to the budget.

Authorisation

The budget acts as an authorisation for budget managers to incur the expenditure and obtain the resources permitted by their budget.

Resource allocation

The budgetary planning process should ensure that available resources are allocated between the various budgets in the most effective way.

204 CONTROLLABILITY

Controllability is defined by Horngren, Bhimani et al as 'the degree of influence that a specific manager has over costs, revenues or other items in question'. Controllability refers to a specific manager – a superior may be able to control a cost, and for a period of time – all costs are controllable in the long run. The controllability principle is that managers should only be held responsible for costs that they have direct control over. So, for example, divisional managers would not be held responsible for the allocation of central costs to their department if they have no control over the incurrence or magnitude of these costs. Under this principle, it would be held that dysfunctional consequences would arise if managers were held accountable for costs over which they have no control.

An alternative view argues that there are considerable advantages to be gained in holding managers responsible for costs even when they do not have any direct control over them. For example, it stops managers treating some costs as 'free goods' and thus stops them overusing these goods and services. Further, holding managers responsible for items outside their control may encourage them to become more involved with such issues and, as a result, the total cost may be reduced or the goods or services may be provided more efficiently.

There is no clear evidence as to which of these views will produce the best performance from a division or a division manager.

205 BUDGET SLACK

Incremental budgeting is a system of budgeting that starts with the current year's budget and 'builds' on this to produce the budget for next year. There is no attempt at questioning the activities undertaken or the costs incurred in undertaking them. Most often the values are simply adjusted for inflation and for any known changes in the activity level for the next period.

Incremental budgeting is hence a rather unquestioning approach which allows budget holders and/or budget preparers to build in budget slack so that they will not be criticised but will rather be praised simply for achieving an unchallenging budget.

Unnecessary expenditure or budget slack is perpetuated in the budget and there is a continuing incentive to spend the budget, even if it is not required, otherwise the budget holder might not be allocated the same resources in the budget for the next period.

206 ZERO-BASED BUDGETING

Zero-Based Budgeting (ZBB) is an approach to budgeting which, instead of building on the previous year's budget as a base, requires justification of all expenditure from scratch. This technique would not suit expenditure planning in all areas, for example in the line departments of a manufacturing company, because here there will be clear relationships of input and output which are defined by standard values. In less clearly defined areas such as service departments or not for profit businesses ZBB might have some value if it is applied selectively.

ZBB would involve describing all of the organisation's activities in a series of decision packages. The decision package for each activity describes the activity, analyses its costs and benefits and identifies alternative methods of achieving the same purpose. The packages can then be evaluated and ranked: what is essential, what is highly desirable, what is desirable and so on. The available resources would then be allocated according to the packages selected. Once the budget is set the packages are adopted up to the spending level indicated, which represents the cut-off point.

ZBB may not be easy to install because it could be expensive in time and effort to analyse all expenditure and difficult to establish priorities for the activities or decision packages. However a number of benefits may be derived from the system.

It is possible that economies and increased efficiency could result if departments were to justify all expenditure, not just the incremental expenditure. It is argued that if expenditure were examined on a cost/benefit basis, a more rational allocation of resources would take place. Such an approach would force managers to make plans and prioritise their activities before committing themselves to the budget. It should achieve a more structured involvement of departmental management and should improve the quality of decisions and management information, enabling such questions to be asked as: Should this be done? At what quality/quantity? Should it be done in this way? What should it cost?

207 J LIMITED

(i) With zero-based budgeting (ZBB), nothing is taken for granted. The budget is started from scratch. This can be contrasted with incremental budgeting where the starting point is last year's budget or actual results and then possibly a percentage is added on to account for inflation, or any expected changes in the level of activity. With ZBB each manager sets out what he or she wishes to accomplish over the forthcoming period.

For each activity that they wish to undertake, they look at alternative methods of achieving the objective, and look at providing the service at different levels.

Each activity is put into what is known as a decision package and the costs and benefits are estimated. The activity will only go ahead if the benefits exceed the costs. Also, once all the packages have been evaluated, they can be ranked against each other and the company resources can be allocated to the best packages.

ZBB is usually used in service organisations and is particularly common in local government, where ZBB acts as a control to improve efficiency in the absence of competitive markets.

ZBB can be used to decide whether an activity is better carried out internally or whether it should be sub-contracted/outsourced.

(ii) A ZBB approach will definitely be more expensive and will be more time-consuming. The benefit from a better budget must exceed the extra cost.

The managers of J Limited may not have the skill or inclination to undertake the more time-consuming, laborious ZBB exercise. The staff may have to be persuaded as to the value of the exercise. This may be expensive in terms of senior management's time as they have to coax the staff of J Limited into taking on the culture change necessary for implementing a ZBB approach.

The ZBB exercise may need to be implemented with the aid of external consultants. This will, of course, be expensive and will also make things more complicated as now the consultants will have to be managed.

ZBB involves 're-inventing the wheel', where each year worthwhile activities are evaluated from scratch to see whether the benefit exceeds the cost.

208 ZBB v ABB

Zero-based budgeting (ZBB) is a form of budget preparation whereby activities of the organisation are analysed 'from scratch', as it were, or from zero. This includes an analysis of whether the activity should be performed, why it is performed, how it is performed and when it is performed. It is only once this analysis has taken place that the costs of performing it can be fully justified, using cost-benefit analysis.

Activity-based budgeting (ABB) is a form of budget preparation that focuses on the activities of the organisation and their importance to the organisation. All costs are related to these activities, which are divided into primary and secondary activities. The latter roughly equate with non-value adding activities, the object being that if secondary activities cannot be said to support value adding activities effectively then whether the activity should be done at all is in question.

Both forms of budgeting require that managers challenge the status quo and focus very carefully on what is being done and why, with the aim of justifying those activities. In practice ZBB, as it is a detailed and rather onerous approach, tends to be used on those activities of the organisation where it can be more difficult to relate outputs to inputs, such as advertising, research and human resource departments. ABB, on the other hand, looks at all the organisation's activities, primary (value adding) and secondary (non-value adding).

Furthermore ZBB is focused on the concept of responsibility accounting and not on a model of business processes. ABB is regarded as a more rigorous approach to cost control through the understanding of the underlying systems and activities as opposed to an arbitrary allocation of cost responsibility.

209 INCREMENTAL BUDGETS v ZBB

The basis of an incremental budget is the previous period's budget or actual results. These figures are then adjusted by a predetermined percentage for inflation and for known changes in the level of activity. An incremental budget is a very simple budget to prepare but it does not promote a questioning attitude. Unnecessary expenditure built into the budget is perpetuated and activities are undertaken simply because they were undertaken in the previous period.

A zero-based budget begins from zero. Nothing is taken for granted. Each budget holder sets out what they wish to accomplish. For each activity that they want to undertake the budget holder estimates the costs to be incurred and the benefits that will be derived. The activity will only be undertaken if the estimated benefits exceed the cost.

Furthermore, once all proposed activities have been evaluated, they can be ranked against each other and the organisation's resources are then directed to the most worthwhile activities. In addition, different ways of achieving the objective of each activity are considered, rather than simply continuing with the same tasks and expenditures as in the previous period.

210 ROLLING BUDGET

A rolling budget is a continuously updated budget whereby a further period's budget is added at the end of the budget when the earliest period has expired. The remainder of the budget might also be updated at this point. For example if rolling budgets are prepared quarterly, four quarter's rolling budgets will be available at any one time. As each quarter comes to an end, a new quarter is added at the end of the budget, to replace the current quarter just ending.

Advantages of this approach are as follows:

- Managers always have available a full year's plan. This will emphasise a longer term approach to planning.
- Managers will be constantly planning for the future and considering the validity of these plans.
- When conditions are subject to change, actual performance is compared with a more realistic target than if the budget were prepared on a fixed basis only once a year.
- Uncertainty is reduced in the planning process.

Disadvantages of a rolling budget system are as follows:

- Preparing new budgets on a regular basis can be time consuming.
- It can be difficult to communicate frequent budget changes.

211 'WHAT IF' ANALYSIS

'What if' analysis is used in the context of budgetary planning. A budgetary plan is based on a large number of forecasts and assumptions about the future. For example in preparing the sales budget for the forthcoming period forecasts will be made concerning variables such as the selling price of the products or services and the sales volume that will be achieved at this price. These forecasts are likely to be inaccurate, to a greater or lesser degree.

'What if' analysis investigates what the budgeted results would be if certain variables in the budget were different from forecast. The variable is altered by a given amount to investigate what the budgeted outcome would be if the variable were to change by that amount.

For example a 'what if' analysis might be carried out to ask the question: 'What if sales volume is 5 % lower than budgeted?' or 'What if sales volume is 5% higher than budgeted?'. The analysis would calculate the impact on the budgetary plans, including the effect each time on the master profit and loss account and balance sheet.

This would enable managers to see the potential impact of changes in forecast variables. They can then consider what measures should be taken, if any, to avoid exposure to unfavourable results or to capitalise on opportunities to achieve more favourable results.

Limitations of the analysis include the following:

- The amount by which the variables is adjusted is subjective.
- The analysis does not indicate the probability of the calculated outcome arising.

212 FEEDBACK AND FEEDFORWARD

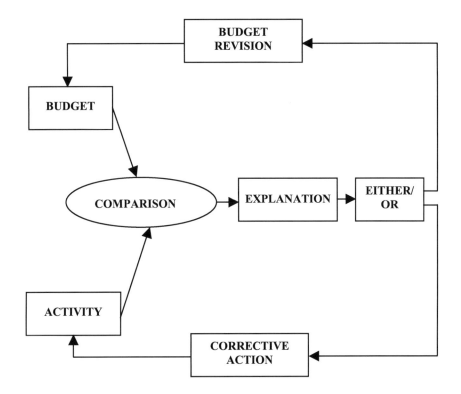

The classic control loop, shown above for a budgeting context, controls by setting an *ex ante* target (budget), measuring *ex post* performance (activity), making a comparison, seeking explanation for any significant variation and then taking one or both of two possible actions. Either action is taken to ensure that activity in future periods is in line with target, or in exceptional circumstances, the target is changed to conform with changes that have occurred since the target was set.

A major criticism of this approach is that it is reactive and backward looking. In other words, action is triggered by a report of variations from the set target or budget. One counter to this argument is the notion of 'feed forward' control. The same procedures take place as in feedback control outlined above. However, it is argued that the fact that a comparison and explanation will take place in the future affects behaviour and thus managers act to ensure that when the comparison takes place, the actual performance will be in line with the set target. This results in control being forward looking and proactive.

213 FIXED v FLEXIBLE BUDGETS

A fixed budget is typically set at the beginning of the budget period, based on a single level of activity for planning purposes.

A flexible budget recognises the different behaviour patterns of each cost and revenue in the budget. It is designed to be flexed, usually at the end of the control period, to provide realistic cost and revenue allowances for the actual level of activity achieved during the period. Thus a flexible budget is more useful for the purposes of cost control in situations where activity levels are likely to change.

Flexible budgets are particularly useful for monitoring costs which are affected by changes in activity levels. Production costs will typically feature in this category of cost, where variable costs and step-fixed costs are more common.

Fixed budgets are more useful for monitoring costs which are not affected by the level of activity, particularly non-production costs such as administration and marketing costs. Within a reasonable range these costs are less likely to be affected by changes in the level of activity and a fixed budget may be suitable for cost control in this situation.

214 SERVICE-BASED ORGANISATIONS

Budgetary control is based on controlling total costs by comparison of a budget total with the actual total expenditure. In contrast, standard costing is based on controlling unit costs.

In service organisations it is common for activities to be varied and consequently it may be difficult to determine a standard measure of activity and thus to determine a unit standard cost. It may also be difficult to identify costs with particular activities.

The disadvantage of using only budgetary control is that while it limits expenditure it does not provide a basis for monitoring the efficiency of expenditure.

In contrast standard costing provides a basis for monitoring such efficiency without limiting expenditure.

If possible therefore both budgetary control and standard costing should be used, though the latter may not be appropriate for some of a service organisation's activities.

215 MCDONALDIZATION AND BUDGETS

The concept of McDonaldization comes from the successes of the fast food company. The term was defined by George Ritzer (1996) as 'the process by which the principles of the fast-food restaurant are coming to dominate more and more sectors of American society, as well as the rest of the world'. Ritzer identified four dimensions to McDonaldization which are critical to the success of the model:

(1) Efficiency

(2) Calculability

(3) Control

(4) Predictability.

Management should be able to set accurate budgets for what it takes, in terms of materials and time, to provide standard items to customers and it should be very cheap to provide that information.

Owing to the supposed lack of variation the actual costs should be very close to the budgeted costs and thus any variances will be an indication of good or bad operational performance.

For UV Limited the provision of standard meals for large events does conform to the characteristics of McDonaldization and it should be very possible to flex the budgeted costs in accordance with the number of meals provided in order to predict costs accurately and then set prices which will guarantee a profit. These prices could then be used for a published price list.

UV Limited also provides meals to meet the exact requirements of a customer and prices are negotiated individually with each customer. This type of service does not have the characteristics of McDonaldization and the budgeting for this type of service will have to be different.

ANSWERS TO SECTION B-TYPE QUESTIONS : SECTION 5

216 ST PLC

(a) An enterprise resource system is a powerful computer system that integrates information from all parts of the organisation. It is an extension of the MRP philosophy, but provides more integration between different parts of the organisation. The implementation of the ERP system can affect the budget-setting process for ST plc in the following ways:

- The ERP system integrates the entire business and the financial effects of changing the operational plans can be quickly calculated, reducing the time taken for the budget-setting process.

- Once the operational plans have been created they can be easily amended, thus sensitivity analysis is facilitated and also budgets can be flexed more accurately.

- It has been argued by some that the budget-setting process almost disappears, because an effective ERP system will produce the budget figures as a natural consequence of the planning process.

(b) An ERP system causes more significant changes in terms of the budgetary control process.

- The actual data can be entered into the system and compared with the budget and all sorts of management reports/budgetary control statements can be produced within a very small timescale, leading to improved control and more rapid responses.

- The role of the accountant is reduced as much of the output from the system is produced automatically and can be delivered to the operational managers without the intervention of the management accountant.

- Less resources are needed to operate the budgetary control system (on the other hand the ERP system may require a considerable amount of resources to implement).

217 BEHAVIOURAL FACTORS

Two main behavioural factors should be considered when budgets are being used to assess management performance: the tendency to concentrate on achieving good performance on those factors that are measured and the behavioural effect of the style of performance evaluation.

Focus on measurable budget targets

The emphasis on achievement of budget targets can be increased, but also the potential for dysfunctional behaviour, if the budget is used to evaluate management performance. This evaluation is frequently associated with specific rewards such as remuneration increases or improved promotion prospects. In such cases it is likely that individuals will concentrate on those items which are measured and rewarded neglecting aspects on which no measurement exists. This may result in some aspects of the job receiving inadequate attention because they are not covered by goals or targets due to the complexity of the situation or the difficulty of measurement.

Managerial style

The use of budgets in evaluation and control is also influenced by the way they are used by the superior. Different management styles of budget use have been observed, for example:

Budget constrained	–	placing considerable emphasis on meeting short term budget targets
Profit conscious	–	where a balanced view is taken between budget targets, long-term goals and general effectiveness
Non-accounting	–	where accounting data is seen as relatively unimportant in the evaluation of subordinates

The style is suggested to influence, in some cases, the superior/subordinate relationship, the degree of stress and tension involved and the likelihood of budget attainment. The style adopted and its implications are affected by the environment in which management is taking place. For example, the degree of interdependency between areas of responsibility, the uncertainty of the environment and the extent to which individuals feel they influence results are all factors to consider in relation to the management style adopted and its outcomes.

218 W LIMITED

It is usually considered that, in order to get the best performance from managers and workers that they should be set tough but achievable targets. If managers/workers are set targets which are too easy, then they will work just hard enough to achieve the target, but no more. If the targets are set at a level which seems unachievable to the managers/workers, then they will give up on the target and take life fairly easily. Why work hard and get an adverse variance?

But, it should be borne in mind that, if a deliberately ambitious or over-ambitious target is set, then there is a good chance that the target may not be achieved. The workers/managers should not be criticised too harshly as this will breed resentment and lead to non-acceptance of the budget in future or cheating on the part of the staff to ensure that one particular target is met, possibly at the expense of other important areas.

Budgets have many purposes, one of which is motivation. Theory suggests that budgets should be set on a tough but fair basis to encourage the staff. Another purpose is control. If the actual performance is worse than budgeted this might not indicate poor performance, but simply that the workers did not achieve the deliberately tough standard. Their performance may have been good, just not as good as the tough standard.

A further purpose is planning. When using the budget to plan ahead managers will want to know what they really think is going to happen, rather than taking what they really think is going to happen and then adding on 5% perhaps for motivational reasons.

It is difficult if not impossible to prepare a budget which fulfils all the contrasting objectives. The majority of companies will produce one budget which is used for planning, control and evaluation and some then prepare another budget which can be used for motivation.

219 PARTICIPATION IN BUDGET SETTING (1)

Some of the main advantages of participation in the setting of budgets include:

- Acceptance and commitment – where managers have taken part in the setting of the budget they are more likely to accept the resulting targets as relevant.

- Us v Them attitudes can be reduced when targets and budgets are set with participation, not simply imposed. If managers are involved in the budget setting process more knowledge is made available since the managers have considerable detailed knowledge of day to day operations.

- Better communication is achieved through participation, in particular communication is both upwards and downwards within the organisation.
- It is also generally accepted from research findings that participation will lead to:
  - increased job satisfaction;
  - decreased job-related tension;
  - improved job attitudes.

However, there are potential disadvantages to participation, including:

- Under some circumstances, participation may lead to setting less difficult targets – the creation of 'budget slack'.
- Some personality types have been shown to react much better to an imposed budget, for example, 'externals under a locus of control' personality indicator.
- Increased need for training for non-financial managers – though this could also be argued as an advantage.
- The whole process may be more time-consuming.

220 BALANCED SCORECARD (1)

The four perspectives of the balanced scorecard approach to setting performance targets are customer perspective, internal business perspective, innovation and learning perspective and financial perspective.

Customer perspective

Performance measure:	Percentage of services arriving on time
Reason for monitoring:	On-time service is important to the customer

Internal business perspective

Performance measure:	Percentage of time for which vehicles unavailable due to breakdown, maintenance, etc
Reason for monitoring:	Maximising vehicle availability is important for achievement of service targets

Innovation and learning perspective

Performance measure:	Training days per employee
Reason for monitoring:	Need to keep employees updated with safety regulations, first aid and emergency procedures, etc

Financial perspective

Performance measure:	Operating profit per month
Reason for monitoring:	Achievement of budgetary profit target

Note: Other performance measures for each perspective would be equally acceptable.

221 BEYOND BUDGETING (1)

The criticisms of traditional budgeting include the following:

- Budgets are a commitment which act as a constraint on doing anything different. In a rapidly changing business environment the budgets are usually based on out of date assumptions.

- Traditional budgets are seen as a mechanism for top-down control by senior management, but instead organisations should be empowering front-line managers.

- Traditional budgets restrict flexibility because individuals feel they are committed to achieving the budget targets. This is a deterrent to continual improvement and so is inconsistent with TQM.

- Budgeting reinforces the barriers between departments, instead of encouraging an organisation-wide sharing of knowledge.

- Budgets are internally focused, bureaucratic and time consuming to prepare.

The features of a more appropriate system of planning and control might be as follows:

- Managers should prepare rolling plans, usually on a quarterly basis. Forecasts would then be more up to date in a changing environment and they can be revised more frequently, without censure, if necessary. However the purpose of these plans is for cash forecasting, not for cost control.

- Instead of a comparison of actual with budget, performance measures should be based on:

    - achieving strategic milestones rather than detailed short-term targets;

    - using relative measures of performance, for example by comparing actual results against a benchmark, in particular using external comparisons to avoid being too inward looking;

    - an emphasis on maximising value, rather than on minimising costs.

222 TIME SERIES IN FORECASTING

The strengths of time series analysis as a basis for forecasting are that:

- forecasts are based on clearly understood assumptions;

- trend lines can be reviewed after each successive time period to assess the reliability of the forecasts;

- forecasting accuracy can be improved with experience.

The limitations of the technique stem from the following assumptions that are made in its application. These assumptions may not be valid:

- that past events are a reliable guide to what will happen in the future;

- that there is a straight line trend;

- that seasonal variations are constant, either in absolute values if the additive model is used, or as a proportion of the trend line value in a multiplicative model.

223 BALANCED SCORECARD (2)

Examiner's comments

Common errors

- Not generating measures in all four perspectives.
- Suggesting unusual, implausible or unclear measures.
- Not providing reasons for the measures suggested.

We have given two examples for each perspective for illustration purposes. Only one was asked for.

Financial perspective

(1) Meeting a key financial target such as EVA®. Economic Value Added is regarded by some as one of the best overall measures of performance.

(2) Sales growth. Insurance companies are concerned with market share and would like to see strong sales growth.

Customer perspective

(1) Customer retention. This is the proportion of customers who renew their policies from one year to the next. If the proportion is high, then it would imply that the insurance company is keeping its customers happy; if low, it would seem that the company is doing something wrong.

(2) Number of complaints. This measure could be used for just about any organisation. A high level of complaints would indicate where the company's customers are not pleased with the service that they are receiving.

Learning and growth perspective or innovation and learning perspective

(1) Labour turnover. Labour measures come within this perspective. A high labour turnover would indicate that the workforce is not happy, which may then lead to problems with their performance. It also means that those workers who leave will have to be replaced and that their replacements will need training, leading to extra cost and possibly initially poor performance.

(2) The number of new types of policies issued each year. This would be a good indication of innovation.

Internal business process perspective

(1) The percentage of policies issued or claims processed with the target time. This is an indication of how well the company performs its core functions.

(2) Unit cost. The cost per policy issued, or per claim processed, would be an indication of how well the business is performing its internal functions. Care must be taken that if the cost is reducing so then the service to the customer is not getting worse.

224 PARTICIPATION IN BUDGET SETTING (2)

Examiner's comments

Common errors

- Failing to read the question carefully and thus not dealing with 'participation' or 'poor performance' but instead producing a much broader answer in relation to budgets.

If managers set their own budgets, they may build in budgetary slack. They may make the budgets easy to achieve and thus their actual performance will be poorer as the targets are so easy to achieve. If the managers set too easy a target in terms of a cost and it looks like they are going to underspend, they may indulge in some unnecessary expenditure in order to avoid highlighting the overstating of the budget, and in order to prevent their budget being cut next year.

Involving the managers in the preparation of the budget can bring benefits, but it is more time consuming and expensive. Involving the junior managers can be useful where they have expert knowledge, for instance where they have knowledge, of the local market, unlike the senior managers who are removed from the 'work surface'. However, where the junior managers have no special advantage in terms of knowledge then their participation may simply involve extra time and money with no great benefit.

The junior managers may not have the skill or desire to participate in the budgeting process, and if forced to participate, they may produce poor budgets which are not useful.

225 BEYOND BUDGETING (2)

Examiner's comments

Common errors

- Not relating answers clearly to the scenario provided.
- Offering little reasoned advice.

Some quotes just for fun:

The budget is a tool of repression rather than innovation.

Bob Lutz, ex-Chief Operating Officer, Chrysler

Budgeting is an unnecessary evil.

Dr Jan Wallander, Honorary President, Svenska Handelsbanken

The budget is the bane of corporate America

Jack Welch, ex-CEO, General Electric

(a) The main idea behind 'Beyond Budgeting' is that many companies spend considerable amounts on the budgeting process and that the benefits that they receive do not justify the expenditure.

In today's world with rapid technological change, global competition and global markets it is very difficult to make forecasts with any degree of accuracy. The problem is that once the budget has been set it is then used as a straitjacket, with managers being constrained by the (unrealistic) budget.

(b) W Limited has many competitors and operates in a market which is subject to considerable uncertainty. It is doubtful whether W's can produce budgets which are reliable in the first year, and extremely unlikely that the budgets are accurate for the second and third years. If W's 1-year predictions are accurate then budgets will serve a useful purpose, but the longer term budgets would provide little benefit.

The computer game market is highly dynamic and beyond budgeting supporters would argue that traditional budgetary control will not be useful, and indeed may well be damaging, as W Limited will be constrained by the budget which will limit the ability of the company to react to the market. If W Limited adopts a beyond budgeting approach it will still need to exercise control, but the forms of control will need to be more flexible, and may include non-financial factors.

Even if W Limited adopts a beyond budgeting approach, it will still need some sort of financial control, including a cash budget, a capital expenditure budget and a forecast of the profit. Many companies, instead of completely rejecting the budgeting process, produce budgets which have less detail and, which focus on the overall profit rather than on the line-by-line detail.

226 X PLC

(a) **Tutorial note:**

The budget for the next four quarters is required. However, closing stock values are determined by the following quarter's sales demand and material usage, so the budget for Q5 will also be prepared.

Units	Q1	Q2	Q3	Q4	Q5
Sales demand	2,250	2,050	1,650	2,050	1,250
Add closing inventory (W1)	615	495	615	375	616
Less opening inventory (W2)	(675)	(615)	(495)	(615)	(375)
Production budget	2,190	1,930	1,770	1,810	1,490
Raw material usage (× 3kg)	6,570	5,790	5,310	5,430	4,470
Closing inventory (W3)	2,605.5	2,389.5	2,443.5	2,011.5	
Opening inventory (W4)	(2,956.5)	(2,605.5)	(2,389.5)	(2,443.5)	
Purchases budget for B in kgs	6,219	5,574	5,364	4,998	
Purchases budget for B in $	43,533	39,018	37,548	34,986	

Total purchases budget for material B for Quarters 1–4 = $155,085

Workings

(W1) Q1 0.3 × 2,050

(W2) The opening inventory for any quarter is the same as the closing inventory of the previous quarter. The opening inventory for Q1 is 0.3 × 2,250 = 675

(W3) Q1 0.45 × 5,790

(W4) The opening inventory for any quarter is the same as the closing inventory of the previous quarter. The opening inventory for Q1 is 0.45 × 6,570 = 2,956.5

(b) If Material A is in short supply then this becomes the principal budget factor. This will affect budget preparation because the first step in the budgetary process will be to determine the optimum mix of products according to their contribution per kg of Material A. The optimum production plan can then be determined and the sales budget can be derived from the production plan. It may be necessary to revise the policy for holding inventory whilst Material A is in short supply.

Once the production plan has been determined then Material B, labour and overhead budgets can be derived. The limit on the level of production may mean that there is spare capacity in the factory and the fixed overhead absorption rate will increase. This will increase the cost per unit of products and lower profitability. In addition lower production levels may mean that there are spare labour resources. This could mean that output of products which do not use Material A could be increased.

In the long term, if the supply of Material A continues to be limited, X plc may wish to seek alternative sources of supply, change product design or produce alternative products.

(c)

	Fixed budget	Flexed budget	Actual costs	Variance
Units	7,700	7,250		
Labour		$	$	$
Skilled	4 × $15 per unit	435,000	568,750	133,750 A
Semi-skilled	6 × $9 per unit	391,500	332,400	59,100 F
Variable overhead		158,182 (W1)	185,000	26,818 A
Fixed overhead		112,000	105,000	7,000 F

Working

(W1) $280,000 × 0.6 = $168,000

Each product is budgeted to use 10 labour hours in total, so 77,000 hours in the original budget and the flexible budget allowance is 7,250 × 10 × $168,000/77,000 = $158,182.

(d) Incremental budgeting is a method of budgeting that starts with the current year's budget and adjusts this for known changes. The main problems associated with it are that:

- it can lead to inaccurate allocation of resources;
- managers may build in slack to make achieving targets easier.

Zero-Based Budgeting is a method of budgeting that requires all costs to be specifically justified by the benefits expected. Costs are built up from a zero base and ranked against other activities competing for limited resources. This should eliminate slack and lead to an optimal allocation of resources.

(e) A rolling budget is a budget that is continuously updated by adding a further accounting period when the earliest accounting period is over. In this way there is always a budget for a full year available and the budget is updated each period. Rolling budgets are particularly suitable when there is an uncertain environment, as is the case with X plc, as the budget target can be kept up to date. As there are concerns about the availability of specialised materials and employees, production may have to be changed from original budget throughout the year. A rolling budget approach will mean that X plc can recalculate optimal production plans each quarter with accurate information relating to resource availability.

(f) Linear regression analysis can be used to forecast sales when it can be assumed that there is a linear relationship between sales and time. Sales data can be plotted on a scattergraph and a line of best fit fitted by eye for forecasting purposes. Regression analysis is a statistical technique that calculates the line of best fit using formulae given for a and b in the straight line equation:

$y = a + bx$

where y = sales and x = time

Once the formula has been established, this can be used to forecast sales at any future time.

It can be seen that sales of Product W do not appear to have a linear trend over time. Linear regression analysis will therefore not be a suitable method for X plc to use for forecasting.

ANSWERS TO SECTION B-TYPE QUESTIONS : SECTION 5

CONTROL AND PERFORMANCE MEASUREMENT OF RESPONSIBILITY CENTRES

227 DECENTRALISATION

Advantages of a decentralised organisation structure include:

- Managers of the separate responsibility centres have the authority to use their initiative and make their own decisions. This can have a positive motivational impact.

- Senior managers will be free to concentrate on strategic issues while divisional managers oversee more short-term operational tasks and decisions.

- Head office bureaucracy will be reduced.

- The organisation is likely to be more flexible and able to respond more rapidly to changes in local conditions.

- Decision making will be improved because of the availability of local knowledge and proximity to the customer.

- Divisionalised operations provide good learning and training experiences for junior and middle managers.

Disadvantages of a decentralised organisation structure include:

- There will be some duplication of effort within the divisions and head office.

- It can be difficult to maintain adequate communication, especially if the separate divisions are widespread geographically.

- It can be difficult to ensure that goal congruence exists. Local managers will tend to give priority to the performance of their own responsibility centre, sometimes to the detriment of the performance of the organisation as a whole.

- Central management are not able to exercise the same level of control because decisions are delegated to the managers of the responsibility centres.

228 RESIDUAL INCOME v ECONOMIC VALUE ADDED

There are significant similarities between Residual Income (RI) and Economic Value Added (EVA). In both, the basic measure is the profit for the division less an interest charge based on the net assets that have been invested in the division. This results in an absolute value, whereas Return on Investment yields a percentage or relative measure. There are considerable theoretical advantages for the absolute measure.

The major differences between the two are that EVA has a number of complications or developments from the simple RI. RI was developed early in the twentieth century, whereas EVA became popular in the early 1990s.

EVA adjusts the operating profit to bring 'accounting profit' in line with a measure of 'economic profit'. Thus, major long-term expenditure, such as R&D or marketing costs for a new product, can be capitalised over the expected useful life of the expenditure. More complex forms of depreciation are used, and taxation is treated in a more complex manner.

EVA also calculates the interest charge in a more complex manner than was traditionally the case for RI.

229 TRANSFER PRICING (1)

An effective transfer pricing system should:

(i) be clear and well understood by all those involved in its operation;

(ii) provide motivation for divisional managers to act in the best interests of the organisation as a whole, while at the same time acting in the best interests of their own division, i.e. it should promote goal congruence;

(iii) provide a basis for fair and objective measurement each division's performance;

(iv) allow divisional autonomy and independence to be maintained;

(v) ensure that resources are used where they are most productive;

(vi) minimise the organisation's global tax liability. Multinational companies can use their transfer pricing policies to move profits around the world, from companies in countries with high tax rates to companies in countries with lower tax rates.

230 INTERNATIONAL TRANSFER PRICING

The basic analysis of transfer pricing assumes that one of the key objectives in setting such prices is that relevant divisions can be evaluated effectively, that is, that the transfer price will not distort the divisional performance evaluation. In practice, however, the existence of divisions in different countries, and particularly different systems of taxation, can add another objective. It may be valuable to the company to set transfer prices to minimise overall group tax liabilities and maximise overall group profits.

For example, profits could be reduced in a country with high taxation and increased in a country with low taxation, thus reducing the overall tax liability and increasing overall profits. If customs duties were based on the value of the goods, there would be an incentive to transfer the goods at a low transfer price to minimise customs duties. Some countries levy 'withholding taxes' on dividends paid outside the country. Here it would be possible to set transfer prices for goods in or out of the country in such a manner that minimise the profits, and thus the dividends.

Most countries have tax legislation that limits the extent to which these practices can be used, but there is still considerable scope for using transfer prices to influence the incidence of profit and, through differing tax regimes, the overall amount of group profit. Where this occurs, the effectiveness of measuring divisional performance may have been substantially reduced.

231 MARGINAL COSTS AND TRANSFER PRICING

In order to achieve goal congruence the transfer price should reflect the relevant cost of the internal transfer. The ideal transfer price could be determined as:

$$\text{Ideal transfer price} = \text{Marginal cost} + \text{Opportunity cost}$$

where the opportunity cost is the benefit forgone by the selling division if it transfers internally rather than sells externally.

If the selling division has spare capacity then the opportunity cost of an internal transfer is zero and the optimum transfer price will be the marginal cost.

The major advantage of transferring at marginal cost in this situation is that the buying division will now be using information that reflects the relevant cost of the items transferred. With this correct information goal congruent decisions should be made.

However a major disadvantage of transferring at marginal cost is that the selling division would receive no contribution for their internal sales. If the division is forced to make the transfer at marginal cost then the staff in the selling division will be demotivated.

ANSWERS TO SECTION B-TYPE QUESTIONS : SECTION 5

232 EVA®

Examiner's comments

Common errors

- Providing brief answers to part (ii) that were restricted to generalities, thus giving an impression of limited understanding.

(a) Economic Value Added (EVA®) is a similar measure to residual income. It compares the profit earned by a company, division, etc to an implied capital charge on the assets used to generate that profit. Any excess has added to the value of the company. If the profit does not cover the implied capital charge then value has been destroyed.

Residual income uses accounting values from the income statement and the balance sheet, whereas EVA adjusts those figures to get a truer indication of the economic profit and economic capital employed (for the capital charge calculation). Adjustments include:

Assets will be valued at current cost not historic cost.

Depreciation will represent the decline in the economic value of the assets.

Goodwill will be amortised over its useful life.

R & D expenditure will be written off over its life.

(b) EVA is thought by many to be the most useful measure for financial performance. If managers are being judged on their EVA, they are being judged on whether they are truly making the company financially stronger. They are not being judged on their financial performance according to book vales, but on the true underlying performance. This should encourage them to make decisions which are in the economic interests of the company and its shareholders, rather than make decisions which merely make the performance look good. EVA encourages a longer term outlook. For instance, when considering the substantial launch costs of a new product, under normal accounting rules, the entire costs would be written off in the first year, giving a big 'hit' to the income statement in the first year. Managers focusing on the short term may be reluctant to launch the new product. With EVA the launch costs would be amortised over the life of the project, without the disastrous short-term effects.

The adjustments that are made to the accounting figures are designed to minimise any benefits that managers get from manipulating the accounting figures.

The focus on one financial figure, however, may encourage managers to neglect other non-financial aspects of the business.

233 ORGANISATION STRUCTURE

Examiner's comments

Common errors

- Repeating the principles of divisionalisation learned from a textbook rather than applying these principles, with reasoning, to the circumstances described in the question.

WD sells two-thirds of its output to PD. It does so on a cost-plus basis, so it is guaranteed a profit on each unit that it transfers. PD is obliged to buy internally, so there is no pressure on WD to run its production efficiently and to be a low cost producer as PD is forced to buy internally. Indeed if WD's costs increase then, with cost plus pricing it will simply earn a bigger profit and ROI. Also as two-thirds of WD's sales are internal, then it might also not worry too much about external sales as it is guaranteed a profit on its internal transfers, which are insulated from market forces.

It is ludicrous that PD is to be treated as profit centre and to be judged on its ROI. PD has no choice but to buy from WD, and if WD is inefficient then it simply passes on its higher costs to PD (plus a mark-up). PD also has no choice but to sell internally (although it does earn a profit on those internal sales). PD can hardly be considered to be an autonomous unit and many of the behavioural benefits expected to arise from profit centre managers being able to run their part of the business as they see fit will not arise. PD could be treated as a cost centre. It could be set a target cost for its production and be judged on its costs, without worrying about the effects of transfer pricing.

TD's costs are affected by two lots of cost-plus transfer prices (from WD to PD and from PD to TD) and has no choice but to buy internally, even if it could buy cheaper externally. Again the division is not autonomous and the managers cannot affect their costs, and thus it would be unfair to judge them on their profit and thus their ROI.

234 TRANSFER PRICING (2)

Examiner's comments

Common errors

- Not justifying with reasons the transfer pricing policy suggested.
- Failing to indicate potential problems.

It would be strange to review the transfer pricing policy between PD and TD, whilst ignoring the transfer from WD to PD. If WD charges an incorrect transfer price from a decision making point of view, then PD will use this incorrect transfer price as the basis for it decisions.

As PD can only sell internally it should transfer at marginal cost (the transfer price from WD should be marginal cost if there's spare capacity or market price if any transfer to PD is at the expense of external sales). Thus TD will be making a decision as if it had made the furniture itself and will make a decision consistent with maximising group profit.

If PD does transfer at marginal cost, then it will earn no contribution on its sales, and the moment fixed costs are taken into consideration then the division will be loss making. Therefore, in order to persuade PD to transfer at the correct transfer price from a decision-making point of view, PD cannot be judged on its profit or its ROI (profit/investment).

235 T PLC

The detection of false claims could be measured by calculating the percentage of false claims to total claims. This could be compared by regional office and by type of claim or claimant. Relevant data could be obtained from similar organisations, trade journals and/or industry groups. The measure would highlight the effectiveness of the staff handling the claims and of the internal procedures and training.

The speed of processing claims could be measured by recording the time between the date of claim and the date of settlement. This could be compared by regional office and against industry averages through trade journals and published accounts.

For both areas, every effort should be made to identify best practice and to use that to establish targets that are acceptable.

Section 6

ANSWERS TO SECTION C-TYPE QUESTIONS

COST ACCOUNTING SYSTEMS

236 HENSAU

Key answer tips

This question tests the treatment of overhead costs under traditional absorption costing and under activity based costing. It is necessary to determine the overhead absorption rates per hour using the budgeted units of each product and their respective direct labour times per unit to identify the budgeted number of hours. For the costs using an activity based approach separate cost driver rates are to be used for each of the three activities.

(a) and (b) **Budgeted costs per unit**

	X (a) $	X (b) $	Y (a) $	Y (b) $	Z (a) $	Z (b) $
Direct costs						
Materials	5.00	5.00	3.00	3.00	6.00	6.00
Labour	1.60	1.60	2.67	2.67	4.00	4.00
Overheads (W2)						
Materials receipt and inspection W3)	2.40	2.52	4.00	1.68	6.00	10.06
Power (W4)	3.00	6.46	5.00	3.23	7.50	2.15
Material handling (W5)	2.10	2.81	3.50	4.22	5.25	2.11
	14.10	18.39	18.17	14.80	28.75	24.32

Workings

(W1) Direct labour hours

X	$2{,}000 \times \dfrac{24}{60}$	800
Y	$1{,}500 \times \dfrac{40}{60}$	1,000
Z	800×1	800
		2,600

(W2) Overhead absorption rates

		Per hour
Materials receipt and inspection	$15,600 / 2,600	$6.00
Power	$19,500 / 2,600	$7.50
Material handling	$13,650 / 2,600	$5.25

(W3) Materials receipt and inspection – ABC approach

Total number of batches = 31

Cost per batch = $15,600 / 31

= $503.23

Charged to

		$	$ per unit
X	(× 10)	5,032.30	2.52
Y	(× 5)	2,516.15	1.68
Z	(× 16)	8,051.68	10.06

(W4) Power – ABC approach

Total drill operations = 12,000 + 4,500 + 1,600

= 18,100

Cost per operation = $19,500 / 18,100

= $1.077

Charged to

		$ per unit
X	(× 6)	6.46
Y	(× 3)	3.23
Z	(× 2)	2.15

(W5) Material handling – ABC approach

Total quantity handled = 8,000 + 9,000 + 2,400

= 19,400 square metres

Cost per square metre = $13,650 / 19,400

= $0.704

Charged to

		$ per unit
X	(× 4)	2.81
Y	(× 6)	4.22
Z	(× 3)	2.11

(c)

	X	Y	Z
Unit cost using absorption costing	14.10	18.17	28.75
Unit cost using activity based costing	18.39	14.80	24.32
Difference	4.29	(3.37)	(4.43)

Using activity based costing the cost per unit of X increases and the cost per unit of Y and Z decreases. The ABC figures provide a much more accurate figure for the cost of each of the three products. These costs will provide a more sensible basis for production and sales planning and for pricing decisions. If the market will not bear, say, the additional cost of producing a unit of X then the company can take a more informed decision as to whether to continue with its production. Similarly, Hensau now knows that the margin on each unit of Y is higher than it had previously thought and that it might be worth either putting greater effort into selling that, or reducing the selling price in order to get some competitive advantage. It should, however, be borne in mind that this additonal information was costly to obtain. If the company cannot rearrange its production amd marketing policies then it might be unable to make much use of the new figures.

237 BRUNTI

Key answer tips

This is a basic question on overhead costs. The traditional overhead absorption rates per hour have been provided in the question and these are to be used when preparing the conventional absorption costing profit statement. For the activity based approach cost driver rates must be calculated and applied to the products' activities.

Note that the sales value and prime cost values will be the same in both profit statements. The total profit will be the same in both cases so this should provide a check on your figures.

(a) Absorption costing

	XYI	YZT	ABW	Total
Volume (000s)	50	40	30	
	$000	$000	$000	$000
Sales	2,250	3,800	2,190	
Prime cost	(1,600)	(3,360)	(1,950)	
Overheads				
Machinery at $1.20/hr(W1)	(120)	(240)	(144)	
Assembly at $0.825/hr(W2)	(289)	(99)	(49)	
Profit	241	101	47	389

(W1) Hours worked in machine department = $2 \times 50,000 + 5 \times 40,000 + 4 \times 30,000 = 420,000$

OAR = $504,000/420,000 = $1.20 per machine hour

(W2) Hours worked in assembly department = $7 \times 50,000 + 3 \times 40,000 + 2 \times 30,000 = 530,000$

OAR = $437,000/530,000 = $0.825

(b) Activity based costing

	XY1	YZT	ABW	Total
Volume (000s)	50	40	30	
	$000	$000	$000	$000
Sales	2,250	3,800	2,190	
Prime cost	(1,600)	(3,360)	(1,950)	
Overheads (W1)				
Machining $0.85/hr	(85)	(170)	(102)	
Assembly $0.60/hr	(210)	(72)	(36)	
Setups $50/set-up	(6)	(10)	(10)	
Ordering $4.875/order	(39)	(39)	(78)	
Purchasing $7.50/order	(23)	(30)	(31)	
Profit	287	119	(17)	389

Total = $389,000

Workings

(W1)

Cost pool	Machining	Assembly	Setups	Ordering	Purchasing
$000	357	318	26	156	84
Driver quantity	420,000	530,000	520	32,000	11,200
Rate	$0.85/hr	$0.6/hr	$50/setup	$4.875/order	$7.50/order

(c) The revised profit statement produced using ABC principles reveals that product ABW is making a loss and that the other two products are more profitable than had appeared to be the case with the conventional absorption costing method.

This is because product ABW is a low volume product and the conventional absorption costing approach, based on hourly rates for overhead, tends to undercharge low volume products and overcharge high volume products with overhead cost.

The data shows that product ABW generates significantly more customer and supplier orders than the other two products. When ordering and purchasing costs are traced to products using the cost drivers identified under the ABC system product ABW absorbs a more realistic share of these costs. Thus its lower profitability is revealed when overhead costs are attributed more accurately to individual products.

(d) Set-up costs

Overhead absorbed 560 × $50	28,000
Overhead incurred	30,000
Under absorption	2,000
Ordering costs	
Overhead absorbed 32,050 × 4.875	156,244
Overhead incurred	154,000
Over absorption	2,244

Purchasing costs

Overhead absorbed 11,150 × 7.50	83,625
Overhead incurred	78,000
Over absorption	5,625

238 TRIMAKE

(a) Conventional cost per unit

Key answer tips

There is less to this than meets the eye; two hourly rates are given, for labour and for overheads, standard times are supplied and thus unit costs can be found. A sub-total of direct costs may speed up (b) a little.

	X	Y	Z
	$	$	$
Materials	20	12	25
Labour ($6/hour)	3	9	6
Direct cost	23	21	31
Production overheads ($28/hour)	42	28	84
Total production cost/unit	65	49	115

(b) ABC cost per unit

Key answer tips

Each step required has been given its own sub-heading to make the procedure clear. The basic principle is to find an overhead cost per unit of activity for each element of overhead cost. In some cases it might then be possible to find an overhead cost per unit directly; here it is probably easier to split overheads between each product type first and then find a cost per unit as shown.

(i) Total overheads

Using the production and unit overhead cost information from (a):

Total overheads for a period

= (750 × $42) + (1,250 × $28) + (7,000 × $84) = $654,500.

(ii) Total machine hours

Product	Hours/unit	Production	Total hours
X	1½	750	1,125
Y	1	1,250	1,250
Z	3	7,000	21,000
Total machine hours			23,375

Both the total and the split by product will be used subsequently.

(iii) Analysis of total overheads and cost per unit of activity

Type of overhead	%	Total overhead $	Level of activity	Cost/unit of activity $
Set-ups	35	229,075	670	341.903
Machining	20	130,900	23,375	5.60
Materials handling	15	98,175	120	818.125
Inspection	30	196,350	1,000	196.35
	100	654,500		

Note: It is worth retaining the cost per set-up figure in the memory of your calculator; the memory can be used for the other unit costs in turn.

(iv) Total overheads by product and per unit

Key answer tips

Makes use of the table of total activities for the period, where it is important not to confuse rows and columns and costs per unit of activity just found

Overhead	Product X Activity	Cost $	Product Y Activity	Cost $	Product Z Activity	Cost $	Total $
Set-ups	75	25,643	115	39,319	480	164,113	229,075
Machining	1,125	6,300	1,250	7,000	21,000	117,600	130,900
M Handling	12	9,817	21	17,181	87	71,177	98,175
Inspection	150	29,453	180	35,343	670	131,554	196,350
Total o/h cost		71,213		98,843		484,444	654,500
Units		750		1,250		7,000	
Cost per unit		$94.95		$79.07		$69.21	

Notes: A little rounding has been done here.
- The unit costs could be rounded to $95, $79 and $69.
- Total costs could be split in the ratios of activities rather than finding cost per unit of activity.

(v) Cost per unit

	X $	Y $	Z $
Direct costs (from (a))	23.00	21.00	31.00
Overheads (from (iv))	94.95	79.07	69.21
	117.95	100.07	100.21

(c) Comment

The overhead costs per unit are summarised below together with volume of production.

Product	X	Y	Z
Volume	750	1,250	7,000
Conventional overheads	$42	$28	$84
ABC overheads	$95	$79	$69

The result of the change to Activity Based Costing is clear, the overhead costs of X and Y have risen whilst that of Z has fallen.

This is in line with the comments of many of those managers who have welcomed the adoption of ABC who feel that it provides a fairer unit cost reflecting better the effort required to make different products. The reason for this reaction is illustrated here with product Z being a major product line which may take longer to make than X or Y, but once production has started the process is simple to administer. Products X and Y are relatively minor products but still require a fair amount of administrative time by the production department; i.e. involve a fair amount of 'hassle'. This is explained by the following table of 'activities per 1,000 units produced'.

Materials	Set-ups	Movements	Inspections
X	100	16	200
Y	92	17	144
Z	69	12	96

This table highlights the problem.

- Product Z has fewer set-ups, material movements and inspections per 1,000 units than X or Y.
- As a consequence product Z's overhead cost per unit for these three elements has fallen.
- The machining overhead cost per unit for Z is still two or three times greater than for products X or Y.
- The machining overhead is only 20% of the total overhead.
- The overall result is Z's fall in production overhead cost per unit and the rise in those figures for X and Y.

Key answer tips

The tables provide a useful way of highlighting the relevant issues and don't take that long to produce. The paragraph between the two tables is probably surplus to requirements (or to what can be achieved in the time) but is useful background for future answers.

(d) ABC was first developed in the US where, in the 1950s – 60s, attempts were made to establish more accurate allocation and absorption of sales and distribution overheads, based on value adding activities which consume resources and the cost drivers which generate cost.

There had been general agreement that traditional methods of dealing with overheads had weaknesses, particularly in business where there was a significant shift and change in the environment where firms operate.

Traditional methods were developed at a time when many businesses had a narrow range of products, where many of the costs were direct, and manufacturing was a significant feature in many business sectors.

Business processes are now more complicated and automated, which includes a more diverse product range requiring wide support functions. Service providers have become a more significant feature in many economies. With this shift, overheads have become an increasingly larger proportion of total cost, with wide-ranging activities and drivers generating such costs. With this change has come increased competition and the need to develop models which enable management to determine more accurate product costs.

239 A PAINT MANUFACTURER

Key answer tips

Since we are given the degree of completion of each element of opening WIP, but not the cost of each element, we will need to use the FIFO valuation method.

(a) **Statement of input/output (litres)**

	Input	Output
Op WIP	5,000	
Process 1	65,000	
Normal loss		3,250
Op WIP completed		5,000
Units started and finished in month		50,000
By-product Z		7,000
Cl WIP		6,000
Abnormal gain		(1,250)
	70,000	70,000

Statement of equivalent units

	Total units	Materials	Equivalent units	Conversion cost	
Normal loss	3,250	0%	0	0%	0
Op WIP completed	5,000	0%	0	60%	3,000
Units started and finished in month	50,000	100%	50,000	100%	50,000
By-product Z	7,000	0%	0	0%	0
Cl WIP	6,000	100%	6,000	60%	3,600
Abnormal gain	(1,250)	100%	(1,250)	100%	(1,250)
			54,750		55,350

Statement of cost per equivalent unit

	$	$
Cost this month	578,500	
101,400 + 80,000 + 40,000		221,400
Less scrap value of normal loss		
3,250 litres × $2	(6,500)	
Less net income of by-product		
7,000 litres × $4 – 0.50)	(24,500)	
	547,500	221,400
Cost per equivalent unit	$10	$4

Total cost per equivalent unit = $14

ANSWERS TO SECTION C-TYPE QUESTIONS : SECTION 6

Statement of evaluation

	Equivalent units	Cost per equivalent unit	Cost
	$	$	$
Normal loss	0	14	0
Op WIP completed			
Process 1	0	10	0
Overhead	3,000	4	12,000
			12,000
+ original costs			60,000
			72,000
Units started and finished in month	50,000	14	700,000
By-product	0	14	0
Cl WIP			
Process 1	6,000	10	60,000
Overhead	3,600	4	14,400
			74,400
Abnormal gain	1,250	14	17,500

The cost of the joint products is made up of $72,000 + $700,000 = $772,000. This has to be apportioned between the joint products on the basis of the sales values at the split-off point. The sales value at the split-off point = the end sales value less further processing costs and packaging costs.

For Product X

Sales value = $15.00 − $0.50 = $14.50 per litre

For Product Y

Sales value = $18.00 − $1.50 − $0.50 = $16.00 per litre

Apportioning the joint costs:

	Sales value at split-off point		Share of joint costs
	$		$
Product X 30,000 × $14.50 =	435,000	435/835 × 772,000 =	402,180
Product Y 25,000 × $16.00 =	400,000	400/835 × 772,000 =	369,820
	835,000		772,000

(b)

Process 2 account

	Litres	$		Litres	$
Op WIP	5,000	60,000	Normal loss	3,250	6,500
Process 1	65,000	578,500	By-product Z	7,000	24,500
Direct labour		101,400	Cl WIP	6,000	74,400
Variable overhead		80,000	Joint Product X	30,000	402,180
Fixed overhead		40,000	Joint Product Y	25,000	369,820
Abnormal gain	1,250	17,500			
	71,250	877,400		71,250	877,400

Abnormal gain account

	Litres	$		Litres	$
Scrap	1,250	2,500	Process 2	1,250	17,500
Income statement		15,000			
	1,250	17,500		1,250	17,500

(c) Process accounting and throughput accounting are both techniques which can be used in a manufacturing environment where similar products pass through a series of consecutive processes. There are many differences between the approaches:

- In process costing the aim is to measure and record the cost of products. In throughput accounting costs are not allocated to product and there is no measure of product profitability.

- Throughput accounting assumes that material is the only variable cost and that labour and overhead is fixed. In process costing labour is a variable cost.

- Process costing measures the levels of abnormal loss or gain in the process and action may be taken to correct the process if these values are unacceptably high. Throughput accounting focuses attention on the bottleneck resource and attempts to alleviate it. In this way process costing is essentially reactive whereas throughput accounting focuses attention on continual improvement.

- Process costing focuses on the control of each individual process but does not consider the overall optimum production. Throughput accounting tries to optimise production by identifying the bottleneck resource and uses ratios to identify the product mix which optimises profit. The higher the TA ratio the more throughput per hour of bottleneck resource can be produced and hence contribution can be earned faster.

- Process accounting values inventory at full production cost which corresponds to the requirement for financial accounting. Throughput accounting values inventory at the purchase cost of raw materials and bought-in components.

240 CHEMICAL PROCESSING

Key answer tips

This is a relatively straight forward question because none of the outputs require further processing. The by-product is effectively treated in the same way as a normal loss which has a scrap value.

Process 2 Account

	Litres	$		Litres	$
Opening work-in-progress	1,200	7,640	Normal waste	920	nil
XP1	5,000	15,679	By-product Z	460	920
P2A	1,200	6,000	XP2	7,850	51,450
P2B	3,000	4,500			
Conversion cost		22,800			
Abnormal gain	280	1,753	Closing work in progress	1,450	6,002
	10,680	58,372		10,680	58,372

Workings

Equivalent Units Table	Process 1 and materials added	Conversion
Output:		
Started & finished this period	6,650	6,650
Completion of opening work-in-process	nil	720
Abnormal gain	(280)	(280)
Closing work-in-process	1,450	435
	7,820	7,525
Period costs ($)	26,179	22,800
By-product value ($)	(920)	
	$25,259	$22,800
Cost per equivalent unit	$3.23	$3.03

Valuation Statement

		$
Finished output:		
Started and finished 6,650 litres × ($3.23 + $3.03)	=	41,629
Opening work-in-process:		
cost brought forward	=	7,640
cost of completion 720 litres × $3.03	=	2,181
		51,450
Abnormal gain		
280 litres × ($3.23 + $3.03)	=	$1,753
Closing work-in-process:		
1,450 litres × $3.23	=	$4,684
435 litres × $3.03	=	$1,318
		$6,002

241 BIOTINCT

Key answer tips

Part (a) is process costing, involving equivalent units and in particular the FIFO method. Work your way through the statements methodically. It is important that you are aware of a set procedure for answering these questions (not necessarily the one below) as you are unlikely to be able to 'bluff' your way through the question without the background knowledge. Watch out for the further chemicals that are added after the process is 80% complete, which is a very unusual complication.

Part (b) is a discursive question inviting you to discuss the comments made by the managing director.

(a) **Statement of Input/Output**

	Input kg	Output kg	
Op WIP	40		
Base materials	80		
Op WIP completed		40	⎫
Units started and finished in month		25 Bal	⎬ Finished output 65 kg
CI WIP		50	⎭
Abnormal loss		5	
	120	120	

Statement of Equivalent Units

	Total units	Base material		Conversion costs	Equivalent units	Further chemicals	
Op WIP complete	40	0%	0	75%	30	100%	40
Units started and Finished in month	25	100%	25	100%	25	100%	25
C1 WIP	50	100%	50	90%	45	100%	50
Abnormal loss	5	100%	5	80%	4	100%	5
			80		104		120

Statement of Cost per Equivalent Unit

	$	$	$
Cost of this month	3,400	6,864	7,200
	÷ 80	÷ 104	÷ 120
Cost per equivalent unit	$42.50	$66	$60
Total cost per equivalent unit	$168.50		

Statement of Evaluation

	Equivalent units	Cost per equivalent unit	Cost
		$	$
C1 WIP			
Base material	50	42.50	2,125
Conversion costs	45	66	2,970
Further chemicals	50	60	3,000
			8,095

Op WIP completed
Base material	0	42.50	0
Conversion costs	30	66	1,980
Further chemicals	40	60	2,400
			4,380
+ original costs (1,550 + 720)			2,270
			6,650

Units started and finished in month 25 168.50 4,212.50

Abnormal loss
Base material	5	42.50	212.50
Conversion costs	4	66	264
Further chemicals	5	60	300
			776.50

Process a/c

	Kg	$		Kg	$
Op WIP	40	2,270	Cl WIP	50	8,095
Base materials	80	3,400	Finished goods		
Conversion costs		6,864	Op WIP completed	40	6,650
Further chemicals		7,200	Units started and finished in month	25	4,212.50
			Abnormal loss	5	776.50
	120	19,734		120	19,734

(b) The process accounts are not that complicated to produce and are certainly no more complicated than the reality that they are trying to represent. If there are partially completed units, then the concept of equivalent units is a logical way of taking the degree of completion into account.

We have calculated the costs per equivalent unit as $42.50, $60 and $66 for base materials, further chemicals and conversion costs respectively, giving a total cost of $168.50, compared to the target costs of $40, $70, $60 and in total $170. We can see that the total cost was actually slightly lower than expected, although the cost of the base materials and the conversion costs were slightly higher than expected.

The managing director has grossly exaggerated the cost per kilogram because he has not taken into account the true value of the work done during the period as he has ignored the substantial increase in work-in-process.

One aspect of the production efficiency that the managing director did not mention is the abnormal loss. This does indicate inefficiency. Something has gone wrong that should not have gone wrong. Hopefully, this is a one-off event and does not represent ongoing inefficiency.

When considering efficiency the MD should be looking at physical quantities. The financial values calculated above are affected by efficiency, but are also affected by price changes.

242 PHARMACEUTICAL DRUGS

Examiner's comments

Part a

Common errors

- In part (ii) making errors in the calculation of some of the cost driver rates and extending these to the respective orders.

Part b

Common errors

- In part (i), failing to apply the strengths and weaknesses to F plc.
- In part (ii), demonstrating a lack of ideas and/or failing to generate recommended action specific to F plc.

(a) (i) $\text{OAR} = \dfrac{\text{Budgeted overheads}}{\text{Budgeted level of activity}} = \dfrac{\$880,000}{£8m} = 11\%$ of list price

Selling and distribution charge for Order A = 11% of $1,200 = $132

Selling and distribution charge for Order B = 11% of $900 = $99

(ii) Cost driver rates

Invoice processing

Cost per invoice = $\dfrac{25\% \times \$280,000}{8,000 \text{ invoices}} = \$8.75$ per invoice

Cost per invoice line = $\dfrac{75\% \times \$280,000}{28,000 \text{ invoice lines}} = \$7.50$ per invoice line

Packing

$32 for large packages and $25 for small packages.

Delivery

Loading costs = $\dfrac{\$40,000}{1,000 \text{ journeys}} = \$40$ per journey

There are 12 small packages to a lorry and so the loading costs are $40/12 = $3.33 per small package.

There are 6 large packages to a lorry and so the loading costs are $6.67 per large package.

Mileage costs = $\dfrac{\$180,00 - \$40,000}{350,000 \text{ miles}} = \$0.40$ per mile

Other overheads

Cost per order = $\dfrac{\$200,000}{8,000 \text{ orders}} = \$25$ per order

		$	$
Invoice processing		8.75	8.75
$7.20 × 2		15.00	
$7.50 × 8			60.00
Packing		25.00	32.00
Delivery		3.33	6.67
$0.40 × 8		3.20	
$0.40 × 40			16.00
Other overheads		25.00	25.00
Charge for selling and distribution		80.28	148.42

(b)

Report

To   Management

From   Management Accountant

Date   May 20X5

Subject Proposed ABC system

(i) **Strengths and weaknesses of proposed system**

The present system is very simple but makes no attempt to link the selling and distribution costs to the factors which cause those costs. The present system simply charges all orders a blanket rate of 11% on list price.

The proposed ABC system is still very simple but makes some effort to determine the cost drivers, i.e. those factors which are most closely related to the way in which the costs of an activity are incurred. For instance, it has been found for the invoice processing costs that the costs are affected by the number of invoices issued, but also by how complicated the invoices are, i.e. how many different lines there are on the invoice.

Charging out the invoice processing costs on the basis of the two cost drivers above will result in more accurate costs and will give more information about the cost structure and the cost drivers in order to improve cost control. Once the cost structure is known, efforts can be made to reduce the volume of activity of the cost driver (e.g. the 28,000 invoice lines) and/or the cost of the cost driver (e.g. the $7.50 per invoice line).

It is argued by ABC supporters that the better costs calculated under ABC can then be used as the basis for fixing selling prices and that these selling prices relate to the true cost of the order and thus will prevent loss-making orders.

F plc can also compare the true costs of the different elements of the system against the costs of outsourcing.

The more accurate costs determined under an ABC system can be used to justify selling prices or selling price increases to customers.

Whilst it is undoubtedly true that ABC gives more accurate costs, it is also true that it will be more expensive to implement and the benefit may not exceed the cost.

The proposed system, here, is still very simple and it is possible that a more detailed analysis would provide further useful information.

ABC attempts to find the cost driver for each type of cost and thus avoid the arbitrariness of absorption costing but, here, some costs are still charged on an arbitrary basis, e.g. the other overheads.

(ii) **Recommendations**

In the light of the ABC information it should be determined whether any orders/customers are loss making and, if so, whether those types of order or customer should be dropped or if the costs can be reduced or the selling prices increased.

The cost per invoice line is very expensive. It should be investigated as to whether this figure can be reduced, perhaps by the purchase of a special software package.

The costs for long distance deliveries are also very high. F plc could consider only accepting orders below a certain maximum distance, or charging a selling price which takes into account the delivery costs of long distance journeys, or outsourcing the deliveries.

The present system for setting selling prices is cost based; whilst this is a simple method of setting selling prices, it does not normally lead to optimum selling prices. The proposed ABC system could be used as the basis for charging selling prices to individual customers. Whilst the proposed system is very simple, it is probably still too complex to be used for charging prices. For instance, if a new customer wants to place a new order, we would need to know how far away they are before we can calculate the cost of the order and thus the price to quote.

243 MN LTD

(a) Throughput accounting is an approach advocated as a means of applying the 'Theory of Constraints' first developed by Goldratt and Cox in the early 1980s. Notable proponents of throughput accounting are Galloway and Waldron who published a series of articles in *Management Accounting* in the late 1980s. The basic concept of throughput accounting is the notion of throughput itself. This can be defined as:

'The rate of production of a defined process over a stated period of time'

CIMA *Official Terminology*

or, to quote Galloway and Waldron:

'... throughput is the contribution remaining after material costs ... At the product level, throughput is equivalent to the rate at which money is earned. It is calculated as sales revenue minus material cost.'

Management Accounting (Jan 1989), p33

Underpinning this basic concept are three further concepts, which can be stated as follows:

(1) In the short term all manufacturing costs, with the exception of material costs, are largely pre-determined and can, therefore, be regarded as fixed.

(2) Holding and producing inventory is not regarded as a value-added activity. Profitability is seen as being inversely proportional to the time taken for production to respond to demand, i.e. throughput time. Since holding inventory lengthens throughput time, profitability can be seen as being inversely proportional to the level of inventory in the system. This supports the advocacy of a 'Just-in-Time' system of inventory management.

ANSWERS TO SECTION C-TYPE QUESTIONS : SECTION 6

(3) Overall product profitability is determined by two factors:

(i) the rate at which it contributes money – this is a measure of the product's *relative* profitability; and

(ii) the rate at which the factory spends money.

Comparing the rate at which a product contributes money to the rate at which the factory spends it determines absolute profitability.

The objective is to maximise the 'throughput' in any given time period and this automatically focuses attention on any bottleneck resource(s). If profit is to be maximised (in the short term), then the optimal utilisation of any bottleneck resources needs to be determined and, if possible, the bottleneck resource removed.

(b) Identification of the bottleneck resource

Machine X: Maximum output per week $= \dfrac{180}{4}$ TRLs

$= 45$ TRLs/week

On average 17.5 hours per month or 4.375 hours per week can be lost, reducing the maximum capacity by 10.9375% $\left(\dfrac{4.375}{40} \times 100\%\right)$. This reduces Machine X's capacity to 40 TRLs, on average, per week $(45 \times (1 - 0.109375))$.

Machine Y: Maximum output = 52 TRLs/week

Machine Z: Maximum output = 30 TRLs/week

∴ Machine Z is the key, or bottleneck resource.

(c) **Calculation of return per factory hour**

Time on key resource $= \dfrac{40 \text{ hours}}{30 \text{ TRLs}} = 1.3333$ hours/TRL

Sale price – material cost $= \$2,000 - \$600$

$= \$1,400$

∴ Return per factory hour $= \dfrac{\$1,400}{1.3333} = \$1050/\text{hour}$

Calculation of cost per factory hour

Cost per factory hour $= \dfrac{\$5,500 + \$8,000 + \dfrac{\$450,000}{48}}{40} = \$571.875/\text{hour}$

∴ **Throughput accounting ratio** $= \dfrac{\$1,050}{\$571.875}$

$= 1.836$

(d) The throughput accounting ratio, as defined, measures the rate at which the business generates money compared with the rate at which the business spends money. This ratio needs to exceed one if the business is to maintain itself as a going concern. The definition of throughput, explained in part (a), is similar to the existing concept of 'value added'.

KAPLAN PUBLISHING

In effect, MN Ltd needs to add value to the business at a greater rate than it is expending conversion costs to add that value. The ratio implies that only products with a throughput accounting ratio greater than one should be produced and that these products can be ranked in terms of profitability by their throughput accounting ratio. To maximise this throughput in the short term, the product(s) with the highest throughput accounting ratio should be produced.

However, this short-term approach may conflict with longer term measures of profitability. For instance, MN Ltd is proposing to replace machine Z with either machine F or machine G and possibly overhaul machine X. This proposal generates a positive NPV but, in the short term, the throughput accounting ratio for the TRLs may decline.

(e) Whilst throughput accounting and marginal costing have many similarities, the main difference arises from the definition of contribution or, more specifically, what can be regarded as a variable cost. The traditional marginal costing approach assumes that direct labour is a variable cost. Whilst this may have been true 30 or 40 years ago when labour was typically paid a piece rate, this is no longer the case – in the short term, throughput accounting treats labour as a fixed cost. Marginal costing also tends to emphasise cost behaviour, especially overheads, and usually attempts to separate these into fixed and variable components. As with labour costs, throughput accounting treats all production overhead costs as fixed in the short term and aggregates these with labour into what is referred to as 'total factory cost'. Consequently, in throughput accounting the only cost that is treated as variable in the short term is the direct material cost.

Furthermore, marginal costing does not provide a direct disincentive to produce for, or carry inventory. Throughput accounting discourages this by using the *total* cost of direct materials *purchased* in the period in the calculation of throughput, rather than the cost of material actually used, as is the case with marginal costing.

STANDARD COSTING

244 RS

Key answer tips

If you know your variances well, this sort of question offers some easy marks. Make sure you lay out your computations clearly, using whatever approach to variance analysis you know best. Put any subsidiary workings (standard selling price etc) in separate, cross referenced workings, to assist the clarity of your answer.

Note that in part (b) the price variance is extracted on materials *used* rather than the more common purchases. There is no overhead volume variance because actual production was as budgeted.

The requirement in (c) is very explicit – make sure you follow the instructions to the letter to get full marks. You can check your actual gross profit against the figure given in the question.

(a) **Standard product cost**

		$
Material R	10 kgs @ $30	300
Material S	6 kgs @ $45	270
Direct labour	30 hrs @ $5.50	165
Production overhead (W1)		210
		945
Standard gross profit (W3)		255
Standard selling price (W2)		1,200

ANSWERS TO SECTION C-TYPE QUESTIONS : SECTION 6

(b) Two answers have been provided for this part of the question. The first method uses a formulaic approach which many people like. The second method is a more traditional approach.

Material R variances

				$	
SQSP	10 kg/unit × 100 units ×	$30/kg	=	30,000	Usage
AQSP	1,025 kg (W4) ×	$30/kg	=	30,750	$750 A
AQAP	1,120 kg ×	$31.82/kg(W5) =		32,616	$1,866 A Price

Material S variances

				$	
SQSP	6 kg/unit × 100 units ×	$45/kg	=	27,000	Usage
AQSP	580 kg (W4) ×	$45/kg	=	26,100	$900 F
AQAP	580 kg ×	$44/kg(W5)	=	25,520	$580 F Price

Labour variances

				$	
SHSR	30 hrs/unit × 100 units ×	$5.50/hr	=	16,500	Efficiency
AHSR	3,300 hrs ×	$5.50/hr	=	18,150	$1,650 A
AHAR	×		=	17,325	$825 F Price

Fixed overhead expenditure variance

	$
Budgeted cost $252,000/12	21,000
Actual cost	22,000
	1,000 A

The variances can also be calculated in a more traditional manner as follows:

Material R

Price variance

Standard price	=	$30.00	
Actual price (W5)	=	$31.82	(rounded)
		1.82	(A)
Price variance = 1,075 kg (W4) × $1.82	=	$1,866	(A)

Usage variance

Standard usage = 100 units × 10 kgs	=	1,000	Kg	
Actual usage		1,025	Kg	
		25	Kg	(A)
Usage variance = 25 kg × $30		$750		(A)

KAPLAN PUBLISHING

Material S

Price variance

Standard price	=	$45.00
Actual price (W5)	=	$44.00
		$1.00 (F)
Price variance = 580 kg (W4) × $1	=	$580 (F)

Usage variance

Standard usage = 100 units × 6 kgs	=	600	kg
Actual usage	=	580	kg
		20	kg (F)
Usage variance = 20 kg × $45	=	$900	(F)

Direct labour

Rate variance

Standard rate	=	$5.50
Actual rate ($17,325/3,300)	=	$5.25
		0.25 (F)
Rate variance = 3,300 hrs × $0.25	=	$825 (F)

Efficiency variance

Standard hours = 100 units × 30 hrs	=	3,000
Actual hours	=	3,300
		300 (A)
Efficiency variance = 300 hrs × $5.50	=	$1,650 (A)

Fixed production overhead

Expenditure variance

Budget cost ($252,000/12)	=	$21,000
Actual cost	=	$22,000
Expenditure variance		$1,000 (A)

(c)

			$ Adv	$ Fav	$
Budgeted gross profit (W4)					25,500
Cost variances					
Material R	Price		1,866		
	Usage		750		
Material S	Price			580	
	Usage			900	
Direct labour	Rate			825	
	Efficiency		1,650		

ANSWERS TO SECTION C-TYPE QUESTIONS : SECTION 6

	Fixed overhead	Expenditure	1,000			
			5,266	2,305	2,961	(A)
	Actual gross profit				22,539	

(d) Direct labour rate variance $825 (F)

This variance is controllable by the personnel manager who appears to have settled a wage rate of 25 pence per hour less than that which was anticipated.

The manager may have employed staff of a lower grade than expected.

Direct labour efficiency variance $1,650 (A)

The variance is controllable by the production manager, it means that a total of 300 more hours were used than should have been for the output achieved.

Insufficient training may have been given to the workers.

Workings

(W1) $252,000/1,200 = $210

(W2) $120,000/100 = $1,200

(W3) Balancing figure

(W4)

	Material R Kg	Material S Kg
Op.stock	300	460
Purchases	1,100	345
	1,400	805
Less Cl. stock	375	225
Usage Qty	1,025	580

(W5) Actual prices

Material R $35,000/1,100 kg = $31.82 per kg (rounded)
Material S $15,180/345 kg = $44 per kg

(W6) Budget gross profit = 100 units × $255 = $25,500

245 DL HOSPITAL TRUST

Key answer tips

Be prepared for questions like this which test your understanding of the application of standard costing techniques to non-manufacturing scenarios. This question is set in a service industry. However, although some of the terminology may differ slightly, the basic principles are exactly the same. The starting point is the determination of the measure of activity, which you will use to flex the budget. In this case it is the number of surgical operations.

It is a good idea to show the examiner that you are flexible about the terminology you use in different situations – for example, using 'surgical team fees' instead of 'labour' variances.

The distinction between budgetary control and standard costing, part (b), is a very common exam question requirement, so make sure you are clear as to the difference. The report in (c) can only be brief for the marks given; you should recognise it as basically the introductory argument for the use of activity based costing instead of traditional labour hour absorption rates.

(a) **Cost reconciliation statement**

	$	$	$
Budget cost (20 × $5,000) (W1)			100,000
Activity adjustment (100,000 × 2/20)			10,000
			110,000
Cost variances:	*Adv.*	*Fav.*	
Surgical team fees:			
Rate variance (W2)		2,600	
Efficiency variance (W2)	3,000		
Variable overhead:			
Expenditure variance (W3)		725	
Efficiency variance (W3)	1,875		
Fixed overhead:			
Expenditure variance (W4)	1,950		
Volume variance (W4)		3,500	
	6,825	6,825	Nil
Actual cost			110,000

(b) Budgetary control is based on controlling total costs whereas standard costing is based on controlling unit costs.

In service organisations it is common for its activities to be varied and consequently it may be difficult to find a standard measure of activity. It may also be difficult to identify costs with particular activities.

The disadvantage of using only budgetary control is that, whilst it limits expenditure, it does not provide a basis for monitoring the efficiency of expenditure.

In contrast, standard costing provides a basis for monitoring such efficiency without limiting expenditure.

If possible, therefore, both budgetary control and standard costing should be used, though the latter may not be appropriate for some of the organisation's activities.

(c) **REPORT**

To: Managing Director
From: Management Accountant
Date: XX/XX/XX
Subject: Overhead absorption

Surgical team fees are representative of the direct labour cost of the DL Hospital Trust. This basis of absorption implies that all of the overhead costs arise due to the surgical team fees cost. Clearly this is likely to be an unjustifiable assumption. However, it does provide an administratively convenient method of attributing overhead costs to surgical operations.

However, management may review the causes of the overhead costs and improve their information provision by attributing costs according to various cost drivers. This would be via an Activity Based Costing system.

Workings

(W1) Standard cost per operation

	$
Surgical team fees	
10 hrs × $200/hr	2,000
Variable overhead	
10 hrs × $125/hr	1,250
Fixed overhead	
10 hrs × $175/hr	1,750
	5,000

The surgical team fees are $2,000 per operation and each operation takes 10 hours, the fees are therefore $200 per hour.

The variable overheads and the fixed overheads are 62.5% and 87.5% of surgical team fees respectively, so are 62.5% and 87.5% of $200 per hour respectively.

Two answers have been provided for this question. The first method uses a formulaic approach which many people like. The second method is a more traditional approach.

(W2) Labour variances – surgical team fees

				$	
SHSR					
10 hrs/unit × 22 operations	× $200/hr	=	44,000		Efficiency
AHSR					$3,000 A
235 hrs	× $200/hr	=	47,000		
AHAR					$2,600 F
		=	44,400		Rate

(W3) Variable overhead variances

				$	
SHSR					
10 hrs/unit × 22 operations	× $125/hr	=	27,500		Efficiency
AHSR					$1,875 A
235 hrs	× $125/hr	=	29,375		
AHAR					$725 F
		=	28,650		Rate

(W4) Fixed overhead expenditure variance

	$
Budgeted Cost 20 operations × $1,750/operation	35,000
Actual Cost	36,950
	1,950 A

Fixed overhead volume variance

	Operations
Budgeted output	20
Actual output	22
	2 F
× Std fixed overhead cost per unit	× 1,750
	$3,500 F

The variances can also be calculated in a more traditional manner as follows:

(W2) Surgical team fees:

Rate variance	=	$44,400 – ($2,000/10 × 235)
	=	$2,600 (F)
Efficiency variance	=	(235 – (22 × 10)) × $2,000/10
	=	$3,000 (A)

(W3) Variable overhead:

Expenditure variance	=	$28,650 – (235 × ($2,000/10 × 62.5%))
	=	$725 (F)
Efficiency variance	=	(235 – (22 × 10)) × $2,000/10 × 62.5%
	=	$1,875 (A)

(W4) Fixed overhead:

Expenditure variance	=	$36,950 – ($2,000 × 20 × 87.5%)
	=	$1,950 (A)
Volume variance	=	(22 – 20) × ($2,000 × 87.5%)
	=	$3,500 (F)

246 RBF TRANSPORT

Key answer tips

This is a very good test of the depth of your knowledge of variances. The basic technique is to set out your normal computations of the variances, putting in the figures you know and working back to those you don't. Often the results from one will be needed in another, so do all the related variances together.

(a) (i) Budgeted fixed overhead cost/mile

$$= \frac{(\$15,600 + \$400)}{200,000} = \$0.08/\text{mile}$$

Volume variance	=	$1,760 (A)
Volume difference	=	$1,760 ÷ $0.08
	=	22,000 miles (A)
Actual miles	=	200,000 – 22,000
	=	178,000

(ii)

Standard rate/hr	=	$\frac{\$0.08}{0.02}$
	=	$4/hour
Rate variance	=	$1,086 (F)
	=	$\frac{\$1,086}{3,620} = \$0.30/\text{hr}$ (F)
Actual rate	=	$4.00 – $0.30 = $3.70/hr

(iii)

Standard price/litre = $\dfrac{\$0.04}{0.1}$

= $0.40/litre

Actual price/litre = $0.42/litre

Price variance/litre = $0.02 (A)

Total price variance = $420 (A)

Actual number of litres = $\dfrac{\$420}{£0.02} = 21,000$

(iv) **Variable overhead variances**

$

SHSR

0.02 hrs × 178,000 delivery miles × $3/hr = 10,680 ⎤ Efficiency
AHSR   ⎬ $180 A
                                    × $3/hr =   ?   ⎦
AHAR   ⎤ $280 F
                                    =   ?   ⎦ Expenditure

We know all the above information, but are trying to find the missing information represented by question marks. In particular we are trying to find the bottom question mark, the actual hours at the actual rate, i.e. the actual variable overhead expenditure. We can do this in one step or two. Taking it in two steps, we can find the middle question mark:

SHSR

0.02 hrs × 178,000 delivery miles × $3/hr = 10,680   ⎤ Efficiency
AHSR   ⎬ $180 A
                                  × $3/hr = 10,860 Bal 1 ⎦
AHAR   ⎤ $280 F
                                  =   ?   ⎦ Expenditure

And then, the bottom question mark:

SHSR

0.02 hrs × 178,000 delivery miles × $3/h = 10,680   ⎤ Efficiency
AHSR   ⎬ $180 A
                                  × $3/hr = 10,860 Bal 1 ⎦
AHAR   ⎤ $280 F
                                  = 10,580 Bal 2   ⎦ Expenditure

The actual variable overhead expenditure is $10,580

(b) Two possible causes of an adverse fuel usage variance are:

(i) Spillage of fuel occurred on filling vehicle fuel tanks.

(ii) Vehicles are in need of servicing and as a result fuel usage is excessive.

(c) **To:** Transport Operations Manager
From: Management Accountant
Date: XX–XX–XX
Subject: Standard costs

Introduction

This report explains the type of standard cost which may be set and importance of keeping standards meaningful and relevant.

Types of standard

A standard cost is a prediction of the cost per unit expected in a future period. It is dependent on estimates of resource requirements per output unit and the price to be paid per resource unit.

There are three types of standard which may be set and these are often referred to as:

- current standard;
- attainable standard; and
- ideal standard.

The current standard uses existing efficiency and achievement levels as the standard for the future period. This does not encourage improvement and may also allow existing inefficiencies to continue unnoticed.

The attainable standard sets a target which requires improvements in performance if it is to be achieved, but these are small and are considered to be achievable (or attainable). This form of standard is believed to be the best motivator to a manager.

The ideal standard assumes a perfect working environment (which never exists for a prolonged period). This is impossible to achieve.

Keeping standards useful

Standards are useful as a basis for performance evaluation. If such comparisons are to be valid the standard must reflect the current method of working AND resource prices which are realistic. If standards are not kept up to date they are no longer meaningful and thus their usefulness is reduced.

Conclusion

I recommend that attainable standards should be used, and that they should be reviewed regularly. Please contact me if you wish to discuss this further.

247 ABC

Key answer tips

Any causes will be acceptable as your answer to part (b), as long as they are consistent with an adverse efficiency variance.

(a) (i) Budgeted volume $= \dfrac{\text{Budgeted profit}}{\text{Budgeted profit/unit}}$

$= \dfrac{\$30,000}{\$3} = 10,000$ units

Difference between actual and budget volume equals

$$\frac{\text{Fixed overhead volume variance}}{\text{Standard fixed overhead/unit}} = \frac{\$24,500}{\$14} = 1,750 \text{ units,}$$

and since the variance is adverse actual volume is less than budgeted:

Actual volume = 10,000 − 1,750 = 8,250 units

(ii) Actual production should take:

8,250 units × 4 hours/unit = 33,000 hours

Difference between actual and standard hours

$$= \frac{\text{Labour efficiency variance}}{\text{Standard labour rate}} = \frac{\$4,000}{\$4} = 1,000 \text{ hours}$$

Actual hours = 33,000 + 1,000 = 34,000 hours

(iii) Actual production should use

8,250 units × 5 litres = 41,250 litres

Difference between actual and standard usage

$$= \frac{\text{Material usage variance}}{\text{Standard material price}}$$

$$= \frac{\$400}{\$0.20} = 2,000 \text{ litres}$$

Actual usage	39,250	litres
Less:		
Decrease in inventory =	800	litres
Actual usage	38,450	litres

(iv)
	$	
Standard cost of variable overhead		
= 8,250 units × $6/unit	49,500	
Total variance ($1,000 (F) + $1,500 (A))	500	(A)
Actual cost	50,000	

(v)
	$	
Budgeted fixed overhead cost		
= budgeted units × $14/unit		
= 10,000 units × $14/unit	140,000	
Expenditure variance	500	(F)
Actual fixed overhead cost	139,500	

(b) Two possible causes of an adverse labour efficiency variance are:

(i) an ideal standard was set for labour times, which included no allowance for waiting time, etc;

(ii) employees were of a lower skill level than standard, which is also consistent with the favourable labour rate variance.

(c) Standard costs are targets per unit, whereas budgets are total costs set for a single or a range of activity levels.

This distinction means that, if using standard costs, those costs not clearly related to cost units are unitised using some form of absorption technique; this is not necessary when using budgets. However, both are used as targets against which actual values may be compared.

In manufacturing organisations it is likely that the output units will be homogeneous and easily measured whereas in non-manufacturing (service) organisations there are likely to be various forms of output which may not be easy to measure. Also non-manufacturing organisations are likely to have a greater proportion of indirect costs than manufacturing organisations. These two distinctions and difficulties make the use of standard costing in non-manufacturing organisations less appropriate than in manufacturing organisations because of the imposed attribution of standard costs to cost units.

However, a significant distinction between budgets and standard costs is that budgets set a limit on total expenditure which cannot be exceeded without authorisation whereas standard costs measure the efficiency of unit costs without limiting total expenditure.

In conclusion then, standard costs are appropriate to control variable costs in all types of organisation but budgets are a more appropriate means of controlling fixed or discretionary costs that are not related to activity. It is for these reasons that some organisations use both standard costs and budgetary control systems.

248 ZED

(a) Budgeted fixed overhead cost for October

	Alpha $	Beta $
Standard variable cost per unit	40.00	47.25
Alpha $ (10 + 8 + 5 + 14 + 3)		
Beta $ (12.5 + 12 + 10 + 10.5 + 2.25)		
Standard selling price per unit (variable costs × 2)	80.00	94.50
Standard contribution per unit	40.00	47.25
Marginal costing sales volume variance	24,000 (F)	14,175 (A)
So volume difference:	600 units	300 units
Alpha $24,000/$40.00		
Beta $14,175/$47.25		
Absorption costing sales volume variance	18,000 (F)	11,925 (A)
	$	$
So standard profit per unit:	30.00	39.75
Alpha $18,000/600		
Beta $11,925/300		
Standard fixed overhead per unit (balancing figure)	10.00	7.50
Contribution per unit (as above)	40.00	47.25
Budgeted production and sales	2,400	1,800
So budgeted fixed overheads:	$	
Alpha 2,400 × $10.00	24,000	
Beta 1,800 × $7.50	13,500	
	37,500	

ANSWERS TO SECTION C-TYPE QUESTIONS : SECTION 6

(b) Budgeted profit for October

	$
Alpha: $40.00 × 2,400	96,000
Beta: $47.25 × 1,800	85,050
Budgeted contribution	181,050
Fixed costs (from part (a))	(37,500)
Budgeted profit	143,550

(c) Actual profit for October

	Alpha	Beta
Actual production and sales	3,000	1,500
Selling price variance	($6,000)	$4,500
	$	$
Selling price variance per unit	(2.00)	3.00
Standard selling price per unit (as above)	80.00	94.50
Actual selling price	78.00	97.50

	$
Sales:	
Alpha: $78.00 × 3,000	234,000
Beta: $97.50 × 1,500	146,250
Actual sales	380,250
Less: costs ($48,890 + $44,760 + $29,850 + $67,980 + $14,300 + $72,000)	(277,780)
Actual profit	102,470

(d) Direct materials price variances:

	Usage at standard cost	Actual cost	
		$	$
X	10,150 × $5 = $50,750	48,890	1,860 (F)
Y	5,290 × $8 = $42,320	44,760	2,440 (A)
Z	2,790 × $10 = $27,900	29,850	1,950 (A)

Direct labour rate variance

9,140 × $7 = $63,980	67,980	4,000 (A)

Variable overhead expenditure variance

8,350 × ($3 / ($14/$7)) = $12,525	14,300	1,775 (A)

Fixed overhead expenditure variance

$37,500 budget as above	$72,000	34,500 (A)

Direct materials usage variances

	Standard usage for actual production	Standard rate	
X	(($10/$5 × 3,000) + ($12.50/$5 × 1,500)) = 9,750 – 10,150 = 400	$5	2,000 (A)
Y	(($8/$8 × 3,000) + ($12.00/$8 × 1,500)) = 5,250 – 5,290 = 40	$8	320 (A)
Z	(($5/$10 × 3,000) + ($10.00/$10 × 1,500)) = 3,000 – 2,790 = 210	$10	2,100 (F)

Direct labour efficiency variance

	Standard rate	
Idle time		
9,140 – 8,350 = 790 hours	$7	5,530 (A)
Efficiency		
(($14/$7 × 3,000) + ($10.50/$7 × 1,500)) =		
8,250 – 8,350 = 100 hours	$7	700 (A)

Variable overhead efficiency variance

	Standard rate	
Efficiency		
(($14/$7 × 3,000) + ($10.50/$7 × 1,500)) =		
8,250 – 8,350 = 100 hours	$3 / ($14/$7)	150 (A)

Fixed overhead volume variance

	Standard hours	
Budget output volume in standard hours:		
(2,400 × 2 hours) + (1,800 × 1.5 hours)	7,500	
Actual output volume in standard hours:		
(3,000 × 2 hours) + (1,500 × 1.5 hours.)	8,250	
Volume variance in standard hours	750	
Standard fixed overhead per hour	$5	3,750 (F)

Absorption cost reconciliation statement for October

	Favourable $	Adverse $	$
Budgeted profit			143,550
Sales volume variance ($18,000 – $11,925)			6,075 (F)
Actual sales at standard profit			149,625
Selling price variance ($6,000 – $4,500)			1,500 (A)
Actual sales actual price less standard costs			148,125
Cost variances:			
Price/rate variances:			
Material X	1,860		
Material Y		2,440	
Material Z		1,950	
Direct labour		4,000	
Variable overheads		1,775	
Fixed overheads		34,500	
Usage/efficiency variances:			
Material X		2,000	
Material Y		320	
Material Z	2,100		
Direct labour idle time		5,530	
Direct labour efficiency		700	
Variable overhead efficiency		150	
Fixed overhead volume	3,750		
	7,710	53,365	45,655 (A)
Actual profit			102,470

(e) When materials are mixed together in a production process and the output is homogenous, then it is appropriate to calculate mix and yield variances. For instance, more of Material A may be used and less of Material B to yield a smaller quantity of the product than would be expected. Calculating the mix and yield variance breaks down the basic usage variance to show what has happened in more detail.

ANSWERS TO SECTION C-TYPE QUESTIONS : SECTION 6

In the case of ZED plc it is clear that Materials X, Y and Z are not homogenous since they are measured in metres, litres and kilograms respectively.

249 SALES/OVERHEAD VARIANCES

Key answer tips

This question concentrates on sales and overhead variances, with which students are perhaps less comfortable than with labour, materials etc. You are given comparatively little data from which to work, and you need to do quite a bit of manipulation to get to the required numbers in part (a).

The remainder of the question is largely written, although you can (and should) use the data from the question to illustrate your points. Part (b) tests your understanding of the different effects of marginal and absorption costing systems on variances and profits – here, you must bring in your earlier computations to gain full marks.

(a) (i) Under marginal costing the difference between the budgeted and actual number of units sold is valued using the standard contribution per unit to determine the sales volume variance, so:

Budgeted sales (units)	10,000
Actual sales (units)	9,500
Difference	500

$$\frac{\text{Sales volume variance (marginal)}}{\text{Difference}} = \text{Standard contribution/unit}$$

$$= \frac{\$7{,}500}{500} = \$15$$

(ii) Under absorption costing the sales volume variance is the difference between the actual and budgeted units sold valued at the standard profit per unit, so

$$\frac{\text{Sales volume variance (absorption)}}{\text{Difference}} = \text{standard profit/unit}$$

$$= \frac{\$4{,}500}{500} = \$9$$

(iii) The fixed overhead absorption rate (based on budgets) is the difference between the standard contribution per unit and the standard profit per unit:

$15 – $9 = $6

The absorption rate is $6 per unit

Budgeted production = 10,000 units

So budgeted cost	=	10,000 units × $6/unit
	=	$60,000
Expenditure variance	=	2,500 (F) (deduct because it is favourable)
Actual cost	=	$57,500

(iv)
Fixed overhead volume variance	=	Production shortfall × fixed overhead rate per unit
Production shortfall	=	$1,800
		$6
	=	300 units
Actual production volume	=	10,000 budget – 300 shortfall
	=	9,700 units

KAPLAN PUBLISHING

(b) Variances are calculated in order to reconcile the budgeted profit with the actual profit. This reconciliation is achieved by comparing the actual and budgeted levels of activity, and the actual costs incurred and resources used with the costs and resources expected for the actual level of activity achieved.

Absorption and marginal costing take differing views on the treatment of fixed production overhead costs. Under absorption costing such costs are considered to be necessarily incurred by production, and consequently they are attributed to individual cost units using an absorption rate based on budgeted expenditure and activity levels. The effect of this treatment is that under absorption costing inventories are valued at their total production cost (including a share of fixed production overhead costs).

Under marginal costing the fixed production overhead costs are not recognised as being necessarily incurred by production because the cost is fixed, and therefore its total value is not affected by the level of production activity. Consequently the fixed production overhead cost is not attributed to individual cost units. Instead it is treated as an expense of the period in which it is incurred, and wholly written off in the period's income statement. The effect of this treatment is that inventories are valued at variable production cost only.

The effect of these **different inventory valuations** is that in periods when the level of inventory increases or decreases (as occurs in this question) the profit reported by the two systems will be different. Since the purpose of variances is to reconcile profits then if the profits reported are different then at least some of the variances are different.

In fact most of the variances calculated in respect of these two systems are the same. All of the variable cost variances are the same, and as is shown by the data in the question the selling price variance and fixed production overhead expenditure variance are the same. But **under marginal costing there is no fixed production overhead volume variance.** It is not applicable to marginal costing because it arises due to the attribution of such costs to cost units, and marginal costing does not do this. Instead marginal costing emphasises contribution and thus the sales volume variance is valued differently.

(c) The **fixed overhead volume variance** under absorption costing arises due to the use of an absorption rate based on budgeted costs and activity levels. This is used to attribute fixed production overhead costs to cost units as they are produced.

The rate is designed so that, if the actual costs and activity levels are exactly as predicted, then there will be no variances. In practice of course this is rarely the case, and it is a difference between the actual and budgeted production volume which gives rise to the fixed overhead volume variance.

The variance is calculated by multiplying the difference in units by the absorption rate per unit, hence in the question:

(10,000 units − 9,700 units) × $6/unit = $1,800

The variance in the question is adverse because the actual units produced were less than budgeted. The important thing is to establish why there is this difference in volume. Only then will the full consequences of the variance be understood and the usefulness to management be derived.

For example was the lower level of activity deliberate? The level of actual sales was lower than budgeted and lower than the actual production achieved – was a decision made to lower production in order to avoid increasing inventory levels, or was there a machine breakdown which prevented production from taking place?

In the question the variance was adverse; this is usually thought of as being inefficient because profits will be lower than expected with the opposite view being taken of favourable variances. However, a favourable fixed overhead volume variance means that more units have been produced than expected – is this a benefit if they cannot be sold?

In conclusion it is not the variance itself which is useful to management but the reason why the production volume achieved differs from that budgeted and the consequential effects of that volume difference.

(d) **Activity Based Costing** (ABC) is a system of full costing which recognises that the more traditional method of absorption costing using cost centre absorption rates may not provide accurate product costs.

ABC identifies the activities of a production process and the extent to which individual products make use of those activities. Costs are then estimated for each of these activities which are referred to as cost pools. The number of times which the activity is expected to be carried out is also estimated and a cost driver rate calculated:

$$\frac{\text{Estimated cost of cost pool}}{\text{Estimated number of times activity is to be performed}}$$

An individual product will probably make use of a number of different activities, and a proportion of the cost of each activity will be attributed to the product using these pre-determined cost driver rates.

The **actual costs** of each cost pool together with the number of times the activity is performed will be collected and a comparison made with the corresponding estimated values. This is similar to the comparison of actual and budgeted costs and volumes using the **traditional absorption costing approach** except that there are likely to be a greater number of cost driver rates using ABC than the one per cost centre absorption rate found in traditional absorption costing.

250 FB

Key answer tips

The planning variances may be based upon budget or actual level of activity, depending upon at what point the sales volume variance was calculated. If the first calculation is sales volume variance, then ALL variances AFTER this should be based upon the actual output of 9,000 units. However, if the first calculations are the planning variances, these would be based upon the budget volume of 10,000 units. Full marks should be obtained using either approach.

The mix variance may be calculated using either the individual units method or the weighted average price method. The total result, which is the important figure in this question, will be the same.

(a)		$000		$000	
Original budgeted contribution (10,000 × $158)				1,580	
Planning variances					
Material A price ($25 – $21) × 5 kg × 10,000		200	F		
Material B price ($22 – $19) × 3 kg × 10,000		90	F		
				290	F

Revised budgeted contribution (10,000 × $187) (W1)			1,870
Operational variances			
Sales volume (contribution) (10,000 – 9,000) × $187	187	A	
Selling price ($400 – $495) × 9,000	855	F	
Material A price (35,000 × $21) – $910,000	175	A	
Material B price (50,000 × $19) – $1,050,000	100	A	
Mix variance (W2)	36.25	F	
Yield variance (W3)	263.25	A	
Direct labour rate (30,000 hr × $10) – $385,000	85	A	
Direct labour efficiency (9,000 × 3 – 30,000) × $10	30	A	
Variable overhead expenditure (30,000 hr × $7) – $230,000	20	A	
Variable overhead efficiency (9,000 × 3 – 30,000) × $7	21	A	
Total operational variances			10 A
			1,880

The above variances can also be calculated as follows:

Material A variance

```
                              $
AQSP
    35,000 kg  ×  $21/kg  =  735,000  ⎫
AQAP                                  ⎬  $175,000 A
                          =  910,000  ⎭   Price
```

Material B variance

```
                              $
AQSP
    50,000 kg  ×  $19/kg  =  950,000   ⎫
AQAP                                   ⎬  $100,000 A
                          = 1,050,000  ⎭    Price
```

Labour variances

```
                                    $
SHSR
  3 hrs/unit × 9,000 units × $10/hr  =  270,000  ⎤  Efficiency
AHSR                                             ⎬  $30,000 A
    30,000 hrs        ×  $10/hr      =  300,000  ⎦
AHAR                                             ⎤  $85,000 A
                                     =  385,000  ⎦   Rate
```

ANSWERS TO SECTION C-TYPE QUESTIONS : SECTION 6

Variable overhead variances

		$	
SHSR 3 hrs/unit × 9,000 units × $7/hr	=	189,000	⎫ Efficiency
AHSR 30,000 hrs × $7/hr	=	210,000	⎬ $21,000 A
AHAR	=	230,000	⎭ $20,000 A Rate

Sales price variance

	$
Std selling price	400
Actual selling price $4,455,000/9,000 units	495
	95 F
× Actual no of units sold	× 9,000
	$855,000 F

Sales volume contribution variance

	Units
Budgeted sales	10,000
Actual sales	9,000
	1,000 A
× Std contribution per unit	× 187
	$187,000 A

Workings

(W1) *Revised contribution per unit*

		$
Selling price		400
Material A	5 kg × $21	(105)
Material B	3 kg × $19	(57)
Direct labour	3 hr × $10	(30)
Variable overhead	3 hr × $7	(21)
Contribution		187

(W2) *Mix variance*

Note: A method is not specified. Use individual units method if given a choice as it is quicker and easier than the weighted average price method.

Material	Standard mix	Actual mix	Difference	@ Standard price	Variance
	000s	000s	000s		$000
A	53.125	35	18.125 F	$21	380.625 F
B	31.875	50	18.125 A	$19	344.375 A
	85	85	Nil		36.25 F

KAPLAN PUBLISHING

Standard mix of A : B is 5 kg : 3 kg
Hence, standard mix of actual input is:

$A = 85 \times \dfrac{5}{8} = 53.125$

$B = 85 \times \dfrac{3}{8} = 31.875$

(W3) *Yield variance*

Standard yield from actual input 85,000 kg ÷ 8 kg pu	10,625	units
Actual yield (output)	9,000	units
	1,625	units
@ Average price per unit of **output** (5 kg × $21) + (3 kg × $19)	$162	
Variance	$263,250	A

(W4)

	$000
Sales revenue	4,455
Less: Material A	(910)
Material B	(1,050)
Labour cost	(385)
Variable overhead	(230)
	1,880

(b) **Planning and operational variances**

The actual contribution is $300,000 higher than budget, despite sales volume falling from 10,000 units to 9,000 units. At first this appears to be an extraordinarily strong result. However, by calculating planning variances a new perspective emerges.

Both materials A and B were originally budgeted at prices that were quite substantially higher than the general market prices that emerged during the period. Material A could be bought at $4 less per kg than originally planned. This reduction in general market price immediately leads to a saving of $200,000 on the original budgeted cost. This is a significant saving. Similarly, material B's reduction in market price lead to a saving in the budget of $90,000. Planning variances indicate this large uncontrollable saving experienced by FB.

Once the budget is amended to reflect the new standard costs of the materials, actual results can be compared to the new budget. This exercise involves calculating operational variances. The operational variances for FB are quite revealing. There was a selling price variance of $855,000 favourable. However, virtually all the other variances were adverse. This would seem to indicate that FB did not perform particularly well in the latest period.

Planning and operational variances are useful for several reasons:

(1) They permit actual results to be compared to realistic up-to-date standards.

(2) The system is likely to provide more useful information for management.

(3) Operational staff may be more motivated by the feedback information, as their performance is judged against realistic standards.

(4) The importance of the planning function is emphasised – poor forecasting may be highlighted.

Mix and yield variances

The mix variance was $36,250 favourable. This was due to a far smaller proportion of the more expensive material A being used than was standard. The standard stated that 62.5% of material input should be material A. During the period, however, only 41% of input was material A. This is a significant difference. In each case the balance of material was material B (cheaper than A).

It *is* possible for FB to vary the input mix of raw materials. As this is the case, it would seem to be a useful exercise to examine how a deviation of the actual material mix from the expected mix has had an impact on costs.

Perhaps because of this mix variance there has been a massive drop in expected output. 85,000 kg of input should have produced 10,625 units of output. During the period only 9,000 units of output were produced. This is 15% below expectations. This has given rise to an adverse variance of $263,250 adverse. FB should investigate this significant variance and discover whether this variance was partly caused by the unusual mix in the period. It is probably important that FB correct the problems behind the yield variance and avoid it recurring in the future.

251 SATELLITE NAVIGATION SYSTEMS

Examiner's comments

Part a

Common errors

- Demonstrating an inability to link the variances reported to the possible causes, many of which were alluded to in the scenario.
- Not offering in the candidates' discussion many of their own ideas.
- Not developing the report comprehensively.

Part b

Common errors

- Demonstrating very limited ideas in any direction or at any level about how to increase motivation and improve performance through enhancing the budgeting system.

(a) **Report**

To Operations Manager

From Management Accountant

Date May 2005

Subject Performance of S Limited for four months to 31 December

Production and sales

Production and sales were 1,100 units in September and October, 950 units in November and 900 units in December. There has thus been a marked decline over the four-month period. This good performance in the first two months and poor performance in the latter two months may be due to a seasonal variation. If this is the case, it would be good for the budget to reflect the expected seasonal variation, rather than just being a flat 1,000 units per month.

Tutorial note: The output was calculated by taking the standard cost of actual output and dividing by the standard cost per system, i.e. $1,276,000/$1,160 = 1,100 units, $1,102,000/$1,160 = 950 units and $1,044,000/$1,160 = 900 units.

Materials

The material price variance was favourable for the first two months, and then very adverse for November and December. This was possibly due to the exchange rate movement if the systems are imported. The effect of the exchange rate variations should be quantified. Any remaining adverse variances may be due to inefficient purchasing by the purchasing manager. It should be investigated as to whether there are alternative suppliers for the systems.

The material usage variance was adverse in every month, but was particularly bad in October and even worse in December. In October the variance was $7,200 A and as the material cost was $400 per unit, this meant that an extra $7,200/$400 = 18 units were used on a production of 1,100 units. In December, the variance was $16,000/$400 = 40 extra units on production of 900 units. This variance could possibly be due to the large batch of systems which did not have the correct adaptors. The variance needs careful investigation in order to find out where the excess units were used, which systems and which teams of fitters were involved.

Labour

The labour rate variance was adverse in September and October and substantially adverse in November and December. Expressing the variances as percentages, for September the standard labour cost was $320 × 1,100 units = $352,000 and thus the variance was $4,200 A/$352,000 = 1.1% A. In November the variance was $5,500 A/$352,000 = 1.6% A. These minor variances could be explained by more overtime than expected being worked, especially as production was high in the first two months. Then things were much worse in the latter two months, for November the variance was $23,100 A/($320 per unit × 950 units) = 7.6% A and in December the variance was $24,000 A/($320 per unit × 900 units) = 8.3%. These substantial variances are almost certainly due to higher wage rates being offered in order to retain the staff and lower the labour turnover. It would be very useful to have information on the number of staff leaving the business. Overtime is unlikely to be the cause for the variances in November and December as production was lower than budget.

The labour efficiency variance was $16,000 favourable in September ($16,000/$352,000 = 4.5% F), zero in October and $32,000 adverse in November and December ($32,000 A/$320 per unit × 950 units) = 10.5% A, and $32,000 A/$320 per unit × 900 units) = 11.1% A). It would be expected that some of this variance was due to the large batch of systems which did not have the correct adaptors. This problem was not apparent until fitting was attempted, thus involving the fitters in extra work. If this were the case then we would expect the labour efficiency variance to tie up with the material usage variance, but it does not. We are also told that there is a fluctuation of ± 25% in the fitting times, so even the substantial variances for November and December fall within this range and thus might not represent inefficiency, but simply the fitting of a higher proportion of more labour intensive systems. It would be useful to have information on the standard times for different systems and the numbers of the different systems, instead of treating all systems alike. The high labour turnover also means that experienced workers are leaving and that new workers are constantly having to be trained. The efficiency of the new workers would be poor to start off with.

Variable overheads

The variable overhead efficiency variance is based on labour hours and thus simply moves in line with the labour efficiency variance.

The expenditure variance was $7,000 A in September, improved to $2,000 A in October and then $2,000 F in November. It was zero in December. For this variance to have any meaning it must be sub-analysed into its different components in order to determine which ones are being overspent and which ones underspent.

Taking the variable overheads as a whole, the variance gets worse as production levels fall, perhaps indicating that the variable overheads are not entirely variable but may include a fixed element.

Fixed overheads

The fixed overhead volume variance simply reflects the better than expected production in the first two months and the worse than expected production in the latter two months. The fixed overhead volume variance has no significance as it does not represent a cash flow (if we make more or less units than expected then the fixed overheads do not change), but is simply a mathematical device to reconcile budgeted profit with actual profit in an absorption costing system.

The fixed overhead expenditure variance is $5,000 A, $10,000 A, $20,000 A and $20,000 A over the four months and thus shows a worsening pattern, but again in order to understand where things are going wrong we need to sub-analyse the fixed overhead into their different components. We have been told that rent, rates insurance and computing costs have risen in price noticeably; these costs may be regarded as uncontrollable. Managers' attention should be devoted to investigating the controllable costs and reducing any overspend.

Conclusion

Overall the actual cost was 4.4% worse than expected (($4,906,201 − $4,698,000)/ $4,698,000). Whilst this variance might not be regarded as significant, the individual variances in many cases are much bigger and should be investigated. There is a marked decline in performance in November and December. It is important that the individual variances are investigated and their causes understood so that future performance improves.

(b)

Report

To Operations Manager

From Management Accountant

Date May 2005

Subject Using the budgeting system to increase motivation and improve performance

One way to increase motivation is to allow managers to participate in the setting of their budgets. If the managers and the fitters are allowed some say in the setting of their budget, they will be more likely to accept the standards and strive to achieve those standards. If the standards were set by a senior manager, there would be resistance to the standard imposed. Managers/fitters would feel that the standard was set by someone removed from the work, who did not have the detailed knowledge of the job and who is simply unqualified to produce a reasonable standard. The problem of an imposed budget can be overcome if the senior managers take the time to explain the budget, consult with the managers/fitters and gain their acceptance.

Also participation in the budget makes the managers feel that their opinion is listened to, that they have some say in the running of the business and that they are a valued part of the business.

A reward system could be linked to the budgeting system. This can then improve performance, but care must be taken in a participative system that the managers then do not build in budgetary slack in order to make the budget easy to achieve. Also the reward system should be based on clear relevant objectives – that managers are only judged on controllable factors and that gaming behaviour is not encouraged. Gaming behaviour occurs when managers are rewarded on the basis of one measure and they then focus on that one measure at the expense of other important factors which are not being measured.

When judging performance it is important that the feedback is clear and rapid. There is strong evidence that people like to know how well they are performing and that feedback increases the motivation to do well.

(c)

	September $	October $	November $	December $
Standard cost of actual output	1,276,000	1,276,000	1,102,000	1,044,000
Standard cost per unit	1,160	1,160	1,160	1,160
Actual units of output	1,100	1,100	950	900
Standard material usage (×$400)	440,000	440,000	380,000	360,000
Price % variance	1.25 F	0.76 F	2.51 A	2.87 A
Usage % variance	0.09 A	1.6 A	0.21 A	4.4 A

Percentage variance chart for September to December

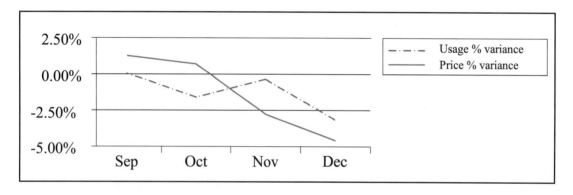

The percentage variance chart can be used to monitor the trend of variances. Significant variances may be identified by setting a control limit. If variances exceed the control limit then action is taken. Alternatively variances which show a worrying trend, such as the material usage variance for S limited, may be investigated before the variance exceeds the control limit.

252 X LTD

EXAMINER'S COMMENTS

Part a) was done well with the most common errors being that students duplicated variances by including the material usage and mix and yield variances, included a fixed overhead volume variance (which is not applicable in a marginal costing environment), used sales price rather than contribution to value the sales volume variance and made errors in showing a variance as favourable or adverse. The main error in part b) was that students gave a general answer rather than describing their answers to part a).

(a) **Workings**

(W1) Standard price = $234 × 1.8 = $421.20

Standard profit = $421.20 − $234 = $187.20 per unit

5,000 × 187.20 − 350,000 = $586,000

(W2)

Budgeted sales		5,000
Actual sales		5,450
Difference		450 F
× standard profit		$187.20
Sales volume variance		$84,240 F

(W3) Sales price variance = ($445 − $421.20) × 5,450 = $129,710 F

(W4)

Material price variance $ $

Material A	43,000 kg should cost (× 15)		645,000	
	did cost		688,000	
				43,000 A
Material B	37,000 kg should cost (× 8)		296,000	
	did cost		277,500	
				18,500 F
Material C	23,500 kg should cost (× 4)		94,000	
	did cost		99,875	
				5,875 A
				30,375 A

(W5)

	Standard mix	Actual material usage (Kg)	Actual usage at standard mix (Kg)	Mix variance (Kg)	Standard price per kg	Mix variance
A	10/23	43,000	45,000	2,000 F	15	30,000 F
B	8/23	37,000	36,000	1,000 A	8	8,000 A
C	5/23	23,500	22,500	1,000 A	4	4,000 A
Total		103,500	103,500			18,000 F

103,500 kg of input should produce   (/23)   4,500 units of product P
                  did produce   5,450 units of product P

Difference   950 F
Value at standard cost   × $234
Yield variance $222,300

(W6)

	$
Sales revenue	2,425,250
Less material cost	(1,065,375)
Overhead	(385,000)
Actual profit	974,875

Operating statement

		$
Budgeted profit (W1)		586,000
Sales volume variance (W2)		84,240 F
Sales price variance (W3)		129,710 F
Actual sales less standard cost of sales		799,950

Cost variances

	F	A	
Material price (W4)		30,375	
Material mix (W5)	18,000		
Material yield (W5)	222,300		
Fixed production expenditure		35,000	
	240,300	65,375	174,925 F
Actual profit (W6)			974,875

(b) **REPORT**

To: Production Manager

From: Management Accountant

Date: November 2006

Subject: Material mix and Yield variances

Introduction

This report explains the meaning of the material price, mix and yield variances included in the operating statement attached. It also explains the merits of calculating mix and yield variances for X Ltd.

Meaning of material price, mix and yield variances for the period

The material price variance measures the impact on profit when the actual price paid for materials is different to standard. This period the total price variance is $30,375 A which has been caused by materials A and C costing more than standard and material B costing less than standard.

The mix variance measures the impact of a change in material mix on profit. This period the mix variance is $18,000 F which has been caused by more of the cheaper materials B and C being used than standard.

The yield variance measures the impact on profit of different output being produced from a given input than standard. This period the yield variance is $222,300 F which has been caused by a much greater level of output being produced than expected from the given input.

It is possible that the higher price paid for material A may have reduced the quantity required in the mix and increased the yield. This may have led to the favourable mix and yield variance.

Merits of mix and yield variances for X Ltd

Mix and yield variances are useful to sub-analyse the material usage variance when material inputs to a product can be varied. X Ltd uses an automated manufacturing process to produce a chemical and it appears that the mix of materials can be varied, so the analysis is appropriate. It is common for mix and yield to be interrelated and, by analysing the variances, an optimal mix can be selected.

BUDGETING

253 PUBLIC SECTOR ORGANISATION

Key answer tips

In this sort of question, where there is quite a lot of initial information to read through, it is often a good idea to read the requirements first. The requirements are very explicit, telling you both what is and, importantly, what *isn't* required. This sets the context of your read-through – make notes under each of the headings prescribed by the requirement as you pick up relevant information.

(a) **Budget preparation**

It would be in line with the principles of modern management if the department manager was encouraged to participate more in setting the budget. In this way his commitment to the organisational goals in general and the budget in particular would be more likely to occur. He is closer to the activity and hence the relevance and accuracy of the budget should be improved. This involvement should extend also to discussion of the form and frequency of the reporting which is to take place for his/her department.

Activity volume

The volume of visits undertaken is 20% greater than that budgeted. It is inappropriate to compare the actual costs of visiting 12,000 clients with a budget for 10,000 clients. Costs such as wages, travel expenses and consumables would be expected to be higher than the fixed budget in these circumstances.

One way to deal with this is to adjust or flex the budget to acknowledge the cost implications of the higher number of visits, or to be aware of it when making any comparison. If a factor of 1.2 is applied to the overall wages budget (i.e. on the assumption that it is a variable cost) the flexed budget $5,040 ($4,200 × 1.2) is greater than the actual cost of $4,900. On a similar basis actual travel expenses are exactly in line with the flexed budget, but the consumables seem to be highly overspent, though the nature of this cost item may make expenditure on it difficult to predict.

To circulate a report as originally constructed seems to highlight and publicise some invalid comparisons on which inappropriate conclusions may be drawn. It is recommended that for cost control purposes a report is prepared which compares actual spending with a flexible budget based on the actual activity. This would require an estimate of the variable, fixed and semi-variable nature of the cost items.

Controllability

It is possible to question whether all the costs shown need to feature on the report. For example, the allocated administrative costs and equipment depreciation are book entries which do not directly affect the department and are not likely to be controllable by members of the department. There are, therefore, adverse variances on the report contributing to the overall overspend which are not the responsibility of the departmental manager. The difference between actual and budgeted cost of administration serves no useful purpose on this report, as the manager can take no action to directly influence this. The only justification to include this is if the manager can bring about some pressure to reduce this spending by someone else.

It may be unwise to adopt the guide of a 5% deviation to judge variances. The key is whether a cost is out of control and can be corrected by managerial action. Also, 5% of some values can be significant whilst on others are of little consequence.

Funding allocation

The Director is correct in pointing out that 'the department must live within its funding allocation'. It is not like a commercial organisation where more output can result in more revenue and hence more money to spend. Increased funding will only be achieved if this organisation and the department is allocated more funds as a result of National or Local Government decisions to support an increase in services.

It would be appropriate for the funding allocation to be compared with the flexible budget (based on actual activity) to encourage the managers to be aware of and live within the budget allocation. Ways can always be found to spend more money and so authority structures must be in place to ensure that requests to spend have been budgeted and appropriately funded. Hence the organisational arrangements which authorised the increased visits would be examined.

The nature of the activity for which the budget is being developed should not be lost sight of. It is more complex to deal with budget decisions related to the welfare needs of society than those for a typical manufacturing firm. There are no clear input-output relationships in the former and hence it is difficult to judge what is justifiable spending for the department compared with other departments and Public Sector organisations.

Other aspects

One possible outcome from discussion over the appropriate form of report would be the use of non-financial measures. The total staff hours worked, client satisfaction and size of the potential client population are all examples of extensions to the reporting procedure which would help to place the results in context.

The style of the approach adopted by the Director may show some lack of behavioural insight. The despatch of a memo to deal with a prototype report may result in lower staff morale and increased tension in the Homecare department. This may lead to inappropriate future decisions on spending and budget 'game playing' within the department. It may, of course, be a conscious decision of the Director to place the manager in the position of having to reduce spending to the allocated level.

Although this is the first month's report, in the future it may be helpful to use an additional column of the report to show the year to date figures. This would help to identify trends and assist discussion of whether costs are being controlled over the longer term. To show results for only one month may be insufficient; for example, the repairs to equipment may not follow a regular pattern and this would be revealed if cumulative data existed.

(b) Traditional budgeting, sometimes called incremental budgeting, takes a current level of spending as a starting point. Discussion then takes place on any extra expenditure or what, of the current expenditure, to cut. Zero Based Budgeting (ZBB) is an approach which takes nothing for granted; it requires justification of all expenditure. This technique would not suit expenditure planning in line departments of a manufacturing company because clear relationships of input and output will exist and be defined by standard values. In less clearly defined areas such as service departments or non-profit orientated businesses ZBB might have some value if selectively applied.

ZBB would involve describing all of the organisation's activities in a series of decision packages, for example, visit frequency, level of eligibility for visit, type of support (medical care, food preparation, wash and clean, shopping needs, etc). The packages can then be evaluated and ranked: what is essential, highly desirable, desirable and so on. The resources would be allocated according to the packages selected, discussion could also take place between other departments so that a wider allocation of funding is brought into the discussion. Once the budget is set, the packages are adopted up to the spending level indicated – this is the cut-off point.

It is possible that economies and increased efficiency could result if departments were to justify all, not just incremental, expenditure. It is argued that, if expenditure were examined on a cost/benefit basis, a more rational allocation of resources would take place. Such an approach would force managers to make plans and prioritise their activities before committing themselves to the budget. It should achieve a more structured involvement of departmental management and should improve the quality of decisions and management information, enabling such questions as: Should this be done?, At what quality/quantity?, Should it be done this way?, What should it cost?

ZBB may not be simple and easy to install. It could be expensive in time and effort to analyse all expenditure and difficult to establish priorities for the activities or decision packages. Managers are often reluctant to commit themselves to ZBB because they believe they already do it. Critics of ZBB have asserted that no real change in funding allocation takes place as a result of the exercise. However, any system which encourages managers to examine, and communicate about, their spending and performance levels must be useful providing it does not prevent individuals fulfilling their other duties and responsibilities.

254 AHW

Key answer tips

Part (a) involves a lot of number crunching, and a clear layout should help you here in saving time and avoiding silly mistakes. Parts (b) to (d) are fairly straightforward knowledge-type questions, though you should try to apply your knowledge to AHW to gain extra marks.

(a) First we need to calculate the budgeted cost driver rates:

Budgeted total activities

Activity	Budgeted cost $	Product A	Product B	Product C	Product D	Product E	Total	Rate $
W	160,000	80	150	30	120	25	405	395
X	130,000	60	60	75	40	100	335	388
Y	80,000	60	90	30	160	50	390	205
Z	200,000	80	180	120	80	75	535	374

Now we calculate the actual number activities and the flexible budget figures:

Actual total activities

Activity	Product A	Product B	Product C	Product D	Product E	Total	Flexible budget (rate × actual activities) $000
W	72	165	32	105	28	402	159
X	54	66	80	35	112	347	135
Y	54	99	32	140	56	381	78
Z	72	198	128	70	84	552	206

PAPER P1 : MANAGEMENT ACCOUNTING – PERFORMANCE EVALUATION

Budgetary control statement for October 20X2

Activity	Original budget	Flexible budget	Actual	Variance (actual from flexible)
	$000	$000	$000	$000
W	160	159	158	1 F
X	130	135	139	4 A
Y	80	78	73	5 F
Z	200	206	206	0
Total	570	578	576	2 F

(b) The main reasons why it may be preferable for managers NOT to be involved in the setting of budgets are as follows:

- Budget setting is often a very time-consuming task and it may be that operational managers do not have the time available to make a significant contribution to the budget-setting process.

- Budget setting in complex environments such as that of AHW is a skilled task and it may be that operational managers do not have the necessary skills to take part, and that time is not available to provide them with those skills.

- Budget setting is often a very political process with operational managers trying to lay off responsibility for 'difficult' areas onto their colleagues or superiors. Centralised budgeting prevents this, and the resultant bad feeling, from happening.

- There is always a very strong temptation for operational managers to set as 'soft' a budget as possible, so they cannot fail to meet it and so will be assessed positively by senior managers. Soft budgets means that there is a degree of slack in there, so managers are not motivated to achieve their best possible performance, but rather one that is simply adequate.

(c) (i) A fixed budget is one that is typically set at the beginning of the budget period, based on a particular level of activity. A flexible budget, on the other hand, takes account of the fact that the actual level of activity achieved affects the level of costs, and adjusts the fixed budget costs accordingly. Thus the rates and efficiency targets may be maintained, but the total figures are adjusted for the actual level of activity achieved.

Flexible budgets are particularly useful for monitoring the costs which are directly affected by changes in activity levels. Fixed budgets, however, are better placed to help monitor costs which are unaffected by the level of activity, i.e. non-production costs. Hence in AHW plc, a flexible budget is useful for activities W to Z, while a fixed budget will help to control discretionary non-production costs such as marketing costs.

(ii) As AHW is a manufacturer serving the retail trade, it will probably be able at the beginning of a period to set a fixed amount of money to be spent on advertising. Even if actual activity levels fluctuate over the period, this fixed budget should represent the maximum expected expenditure. In some organisations it would be possible to talk about 'having funds left in the budget' to allocate to a particular campaign. Once these funds are spent, there will be no more available.

Another example of a cost that falls into this category is training. Usually the training budget is set at the beginning of the period and it is then up to the training managers to allocate the funds as they see fit.

ANSWERS TO SECTION C-TYPE QUESTIONS : SECTION 6

(d) y denotes the total cost of the period in question

a denotes the variable cost per unit of activity

x refers to the level of activity in the period in question

b denotes the fixed cost incurred in the period

255 ST

Key answer tips

The key to answering questions such as this which requires the processing of a large volume of data is to produce clear and well laid out workings. This makes it easier to find the figures you need when you are in a rush. It also makes it easier for the marker to see what you have done in deriving your answer. This is particularly important if your final answer is wrong. At least you will earn marks for your workings.

(a) (i) *Budgeted processing hours* $= (10 \times 100) + (30 \times 375) + (200 \times 80)$

$= 28,250$

Budgeted overhead cost $= \$500,000$

Budgeted absorption rate per processing hour $= \dfrac{\$500,000}{28,250} = \$17.70$

Budgeted overhead cost per batch of A $= \$17.70 \times 10 = \$177$

(ii) *Number of activities*:

Preparation $= (100 \times 5) + (30 \times 9) + (200 \times 12) = 3,170$
Cooking $\quad\, = (100 \times 2) + (30 \times 1) + (200 \times 4) = 1,030$
Packaging $= (100 \times 15) + (30 \times 2) + (200 \times 6) = 2,760$

Activity	Budgeted cost	Number of activities	Cost driver rate
$000	$000	$000	$000
Preparation	100	3,170	31.546
Cooking	350	1,030	339.806
Packaging	50	2,760	18.116

Budgeted overhead cost per batch of A = [(31.546 × 5) + (339.806 × 2) + (18.116 × 15)] = $1,109.08

(b) An activity based costing (ABC) approach attributes overhead costs to individual products on a fairer basis.

In part (a) it can be seen that the overhead cost of a batch of food A is considerably higher using ABC than with traditional absorption costing.

This is because Food A utilises relatively little processing time per batch, particularly the packaging activity. ABC recognises this different level of activity generation and accordingly attributes more overhead cost to food A.

(c) *Initial workings*

Food		Preparation $
A	(120 × 5 × 31.546)	18,928
B	(45 × 9 × 31.546)	12,776
C	(167 × 12 × 31.546)	63,218
		94,922

Food		Preparation
		$
A	(120 × 2 × 339.806)	81,553
B	(45 × 1 × 339.806)	15,291
C	(167 × 4 × 339.860)	226,990
		323,834

Food		Packaging
		$
A	(120 × 15 × 18.116)	32,609
B	(45 × 2 × 18.116)	1,630
C	(167 × 6 × 18.116)	18,152
		52,391

Flexed budget

Activity	A	B	C	Total
	$	$	$	$
Preparation	18,928	12,776	63,218	94,922
Cooking	81,553	15,291	226,990	323,834
Packaging	32,609	1,630	18,152	52,391
	133,090	29,697	308,360	471,147

256 PRODUCTS R, S AND T

(a) A cost driver is any factor that causes a change in the cost of an activity, so the most important factor when selecting a cost driver is to identify a *causal* relationship between the cost driver and the costs. Such a relationship may arise because of some physical relationship or because of the logic of the situation.

For example, quality inspection costs are caused by the action of carrying out an inspection to ensure quality standards are being achieved, so the appropriate cost driver would be the number of inspections carried out. Some activities may have multiple cost drivers associated with them; in such a situation it is best if the costs can be analysed into separate cost pools for each of which a single driver can be identified.

(b) (i) The budgeted costs are:

Activity	Total	Appropriate cost driver
	$000	
Power	1,250	Power (kj) per batch
Stores	1,850	Purchase orders per batch
Maintenance	2,100	Machine hours per batch
Machinery cleaning	800	Machine set-ups per batch
Indirect labour	1,460	Standard labour hours per batch

For each activity we must calculate a cost driver rate.

ANSWERS TO SECTION C-TYPE QUESTIONS : SECTION 6

Power

Total budgeted power = $(1.4 \times 36) + (1.7 \times 10) + (0.8 \times 40)$
= 99.4 kj

∴ Cost driver rate = $\dfrac{\$1.25m}{99.4}$ = \$12,575 per kj

Stores

Total budgeted purchase orders = $(5 \times 36) + (3 \times 10) + (7 \times 40)$
490 orders

∴ Cost driver rate = $\dfrac{\$1.85m}{490}$ = \$3,776 per order

Maintenance

Total budgeted machine hours = $(10 \times 36) + (7.5 \times 10) + (12.5 \times 40)$
935 hours

∴ Cost driver rate = $\dfrac{\$2.1m}{935}$ = \$2,246 per machine hour

Machinery cleaning

Total budgeted machine set-ups = $(3 \times 36) + (2 \times 10) + (5 \times 40)$
328 set-ups

∴ Cost driver rate = $\dfrac{\$0.8m}{328}$ = \$2,439 per set-up

(ii) The actual output is 30 batches of R, 12 batches of S and 40 batches of T.

∴ Actual output uses $(1.4 \times 30) + (1.7 \times 12) + (0.8 \times 40)$

= 94.4 kj of power

and $(5 \times 30) + (3 \times 12) + (7 \times 40)$

= 466 purchase orders

and $(10 \times 30) + (7.5 \times 12) + (12.5 \times 40)$

= 890 machine hours

and $(3 \times 30) + (2 \times 12) + (5 \times 40)$

= 314 machine set-ups

The production overhead budgetary control report can therefore be redrafted using an activity based approach as follows:

Production overhead budgetary control report
April

	Original budget $000		Flexed budget $000	Actual $000	Variances $000
Power	1,250	($12,575 × 94.4)	1,187	1,295	108 (A)
Stores	1,850	($3,776 × 466)	1,760	1,915	155 (A)
Maintenance	2,100	($2,246 × 890)	1,999	2,100	101 (A)
Machinery cleaning	800	($2,439 × 314)	766	870	104 (A)
Indirect labour	1,460	($1,460 × $\dfrac{1,710}{1,800}$)	1,387	1,510	123 (A)
	7,460		7,099	7,690	591 (A)

KAPLAN PUBLISHING

(c) An organisation such as X plc should benefit from an activity based approach to budgetary control since it offers a conceptually valid method of flexing a budget. The method recognises that different costs have different causes, rather than assuming that all costs can be absorbed on the basis of labour hours (the more traditional approach). The ABB approach should therefore produce more accurate budgeted figures against which actual costs can be compared, to yield meaningful variances.

Looking at the figures above, we can see that the ABB variances for power, stores and maintenance are significantly different to what was reported originally, although all the reported variances remain adverse. These more accurate ABB variances should enable management to concentrate their attention on the areas of the business where costs should be reduced – a message that might be lost using the less accurate variances produced using the traditional approach

257 PMF

Key answer tips

The trend calculations are very straightforward as you do not have to do any smoothing. The question tests your understanding of why trend analysis is used in forecasting and performance measurement.

(a) Quarter 3 year 1 = period 3 = Q3
Quarter 3 year 2 = period 7 = Q7
Quarter 3 year 3 = period 11 = Q11

Trend values for quarter 3 of each year:

$10,000 + 4,200 Q$

The trend value for passenger numbers per quarter (x) can be calculated as fractions.

Year 1 Q3 $10,000 + (4,200 \times 3) = 22,600$

Year 2 Q3 $10,000 + (4,200 \times 7) = 39,400$

To identify the seasonal variation these figures need to be compared with the historical data provided.

	Historical data	Trend value	Q3 Seasonal variation %
Year 1 Q3	16,950	22,600	75
Year 2 Q3	29,550	39,400	75

Adjust the trend value for Year 3 Q3 (11):

$((10,000 + (4,200 \times 11)) \times 75\% = 42,150$ passengers to be carried in the third quarter of year 3.

(b) The transit staff cost item is a semi-variable cost, comprising a fixed element of $32,000 and a variable element of $3 for each passenger. Hence the cost equation is in the form $32,000 + 3x$. The reason for this is most likely that transit staff receive a fixed basic salary but are awarded bonuses according to how many passengers are carried as a motivational tool.

(c) $x = 42,150$

Cost item	Relationship	Cost $
Premises cost	y = 260,000	260,000
Premises staff	y = 65,000 + 0.5x	86,075
Power	y = 13,000 + 4x	181,600
Transit staff	y = 32,000 + 3x	158,450
Other	y = 9,100 + x	51,250
Total costs expected in year 3 Q3		737,375

(d) It is highly unlikely that the actual data for Year 3 Quarter 3 will be the same as that predicted by the calculations for the following reasons:

- The key variable is the number of passengers predicted. The relationships show that any change in the value of x will have an effect on all the cost items except for the premises costs. While trend value calculations are very useful they are necessarily based on historical data and it is always true that past events are not guaranteed to be replicated. It is therefore possible that the predicted growth in passenger numbers will not happen.

- All the cost relationships apart from premises costs are related to the number of passengers. It may well be that, currently or in the future, other cost drivers might affect the costs. For instance, the number of transit units run on time might be the cost driver for penalties charged by the industry regulator.

- It is also possible that the historical seasonal variation from the trend value of 75% in quarter 3 will also not be replicated. This seasonal variation could have been due to factors that happened in Years 1 and 2 and which might fail to recur in Year 3.

- The derivation of the cost relationships may be flawed, either by particular events that will not be repeated or by failure to include some relationships or the inclusion of others that actually are not true.

- All the cost relationships are linear which, while being a useful approximation for reality, rarely reflect real life. For instance, it may be that once a certain level of passengers is reached there may need to be a step change in the number of staff employed, or the amount of power used as more transit units are run.

- The effect of cost increases unrelated to the number of passengers has not been taken into account. Penalties and staff costs have already been mentioned. Another possibility is that the unit cost of power might change.

(e) The difference between the multiplicative and additive models is the way in which the seasonal variations are expected to impact on the data. The multiplicative model assumes that the variations will be in the form of fixed proportionate increases/decreases from the basic trend figures.

The additive model assumes that the variations will be absolute.

If, as in this case, the underlying trend is upward, the absolute variations under the additive model will get less and less significant over time. The multiplicative model is thus considered generally more appropriate.

258 MARSHALL

Key answer tips

The actual costs to date can be derived by calculating the standard cost of 29,600 services, then adjusting for the variances. The budget figure for 29,600 services should be shown, for a valid comparison.

(a) **Summary statement for six months to 30 September**

	Cumulative actual to date	Cumulative budget to date	Total variance	Price/spending variance	Efficiency variance
				$	$
Production	29,600	30,000	400		
Costs	$	$	$	$	$
Materials	1,207,100	1,184,000	(23,100)	(1,100)	(22,000)
Labour	846,129	976,800	130,671	130,671	0
Variable overheads	455,000	444,000	(11,000)	(11,000)	0
Fixed overheads	738,000	710,400	(27,600)	(18,000)	(9,600)
Total costs	3,246,229	3,315,200	68,971	100,571	(31,600)

( ) = Adverse variance

Note: Alternative statements that summarise the performance of the Service Department would be acceptable.

(b) **Report to the operations director of marshall**

Re: Performance of the Service Department for six months to 30 September 20X3

A summary performance statement is attached to this report. The main features are set out below, along with issues that require further explanation or information.

- There has been a rise, then fall in volumes. Is this seasonal variation, such as less services required during the summer, or the result of other factors, such as action from competitors in months 4 to 6? If the trend in the last three months continues, this could be a serious problem that needs to be addressed promptly.

- A favourable material usage variance, as occurred in month 2 must mean that some parts were not replaced during the service. Is this acceptable? There seems to be a general inefficiency in material usage. Is this caused by a lack of care by service engineers, or by poor quality sets? The price variance – see below – does not indicate cheap parts are being purchased.

- Material prices are on a general upward path. Is there a general drift in material prices or is there a material shortage? Are there other suppliers offering a better price?

- Labour price is massively out of line with budget yielding large favourable variances. Is this caused by a mistake in the budget or an unexpected change in the price, for example, using different grades/mix of labour. This variance is more than 13% of budgeted cost and thus must be investigated quickly and thoroughly.

- Labour efficiency gets seriously worse after month 4. Has something unusual happened to labour during this month, perhaps a dispute? Is this significantly worse labour efficiency linked to the fall in output over the same months?

- Month 4 is significantly out of line with other months. What happened? Was production disrupted; was there a labour dispute or supplier problems or did another factor affect the result? It is important to find satisfactory explanations for the results in this month and attempt to ensure this performance is not repeated.

- Only total variable overhead variance has meaning and reveals a worsening position after the disaster in month 4, giving further evidence for some unusual circumstances.

- Fixed overhead spending seems to come under control from month 5, but what caused the problems in the early months? Has management acted to remedy matters?

- The fixed overhead volume variance is purely technical and represents differences between planned and actual production.

- Overall costs are 2% below budget, but this apparently satisfactory position masks considerable variation. Nevertheless, the general performance of the Service Department has been close to budget.

259 KEY METRICS

Key answer tips

There are sometimes different opinions as to how some of these metrics are calculated. The safest thing would be to show your formulae as well as clear workings, so that the marker can see how you have derived your results.

(a) (i) Return on capital employed $= \dfrac{\text{Profit}}{\text{Net assets}} \times 100\%$

$= \dfrac{295}{(1{,}280 + 800 - 280 - 50)} \times 100\%$

$= 16.9\%$

This is lower than the target and would not be acceptable.

(ii) Profit/sales ratio $= \dfrac{\text{Profit}}{\text{Revenue}} \times 100\%$

$= \dfrac{295}{4{,}885} \times 100\%$

$= 6.0\%$

This is exactly as required, therefore the profitability of sales is acceptable.

(iii) Net asset turnover $= \dfrac{\text{Revenue}}{\text{Net assets}}$

$= \dfrac{4{,}885}{(1{,}280 + 800 - 280 - 50)}$

$= 2.8 \text{ times}$

This is lower than the target and would not be acceptable.

(iv) Non-current asset turnover $= \dfrac{\text{Revenue}}{\text{Non - current assets}}$

$= \dfrac{4{,}885}{1{,}280}$

$= 3.8 \text{ times}$

This is lower than the target and would not be acceptable.

(v) Current ratio $= \dfrac{\text{Current assets}}{\text{Current liabilities}}$

$= \dfrac{800}{(280 + 50)}$

$= 2.4 \text{ times}$

This is higher than the target. Although this is acceptable from a point of view of liquidity, it may indicate a wasteful level of current assets which requires further investigation.

(vi) Quick ratio $\quad=\quad\dfrac{\text{Current assets excluding inventory}}{\text{Current liabilities}}$

$\qquad\qquad\qquad\qquad\qquad =\ \dfrac{465}{330}$

$\qquad\qquad\qquad\qquad\qquad =\ 1.4\text{ times}$

This is exactly equal to the target and so would be acceptable.

(b) The key metrics which are not acceptable can be summarised as follows.

Key metric	Target	Master budget result
Return on capital employed	19.0%	16.9%
Net asset turnover	3.2 times	2.8 times
Non-current asset turnover	4.5 times	3.8 times
Current ratio	2.1 times	2.4 times

The return on capital employed should be higher. The profitability of sales is acceptable therefore an improvement is needed in the net asset turnover, as indicated above. These two ratios could both be increased by generating higher sales for a given level of net assets, or by reducing the level of net assets without affecting sales.

Opportunities for increasing sales without the need for further investment in net assets should be investigated.

The non-current asset turnover ratio indicates again that insufficient sales are being generated compared to the investment in the assets. An increase in sales would help again here and in addition the utilisation of every group of non-current assets should be investigated to see whether the non-current asset base can be reduced or alternatively used more effectively.

Although the current ratio is higher than target it may indicate a wasteful level of investment in current assets compared with the commitment to current liabilities. When the inventory is removed from the calculation the quick ratio reveals an acceptable level of current assets relative to current liabilities. This suggests that inventory levels are unnecessarily high.

If inventory levels can be reduced this would also lead to an improvement in the net asset turnover and the return on capital employed.

(c) Critical success factors are those areas of a business and its environment which are critical to the achievement of its goals and objectives. A company may, for example, express its main goal as being a world-class business in its chosen areas of operation. Management should identify critical success factors since failure in any one such factor may prevent or inhibit the advancement of the company and the achievement of its goals.

The balanced scorecard is one approach where managers identify critical success factors in four different aspects of performance – customer perspective, internal business perspective, innovation and learning perspective and the financial perspective.

The key metrics calculated in (a) are examples of financial measures. Critical success factors can be identified in the other areas and performance measures developed to monitor their progress.

260 M PLC

EXAMINER'S COMMENT

Students found part a) difficult. Many did not appreciate that the first task was to identify cost behaviour and separate fixed and variable, controllable and uncontrollable costs. When using the high low method on variable overheads many students were unable to correctly deal with the stepped fixed cost. In part b) many students did not provide evidence from the scenario to support their answer. In part c) many students gave descriptive answers rather than discussing the pros and cons of a change and making a recommendation.

(a) The current statement is against an original fixed budget which needs to be flexed to reflect the increased assembly hours.

	Original budget	Flexed budget	Actual	Variance	
Assembly labour hours	6,400	7,140	7,140		
Variable costs	$	$	$	$	
Assembly labour	49,920	55,692	56,177	485	Adv
Furniture packs	224,000	249,900	205,000	44,900	Fav
Other materials	23,040	25,704	24,100	1,604	Fav
Variable overheads (W1)	34,560	38,556	76,340(W2)	37,784	Adv
Total variable costs	331,520	369,852	361,617	8,235	Fav
Departmental fixed costs					
Manager	2,050	2,050	2,050	-	
Overheads (W1)	18,500	27,000	27,000	-	
Total departmental fixed costs	20,550	29,050	29,050	-	
Central costs	9,000	9,000	9,000	-	
	361,070	407,902	399,667	8,235	Fav

Note: The variable costs have been flexed in relation to the number of assembly hours worked.

Workings

(W1)

Using the high low method at 10,000 and 7,500 units so that the impact of the stepped fixed cost does not distort the analysis.

	Units	$
	10,000	90,000
	7,500	76,500
Difference	2,500	13,500

Variable cost = $13,500/2,500 = $5.40 per unit

Fixed cost = 90,000 − (10,000 × 5.40) = 36,000. This is made up of a fixed cost of $9,000 for services from head office which are uncontrollable and should therefore be shown separately in the statement.

Overhead at 5,000 units = 5,000 × $5.40 + Fixed cost = $54,500

Fixed cost = $27,500 − $9,000 = $18,500

(W2)

Actual overhead cost $112,340

Less fixed cost 36,000 ($27,000 controllable cost + $9,000 HQ cost)/76,340

(b) (i) The revised format of the statement is more helpful to the management and managers of M plc for performance measurement because:

- it is flexed to the actual level of activity and therefore actual costs are measured against expected costs for the level of output achieved;
- it separates controllable and uncontrollable items to facilitate responsibility accounting;
- it separates variable and fixed costs so that managers are more aware of how a change in activity levels will impact on profit.

(ii) The company has used labour hours to flex all variable costs but it is possible that furniture packs do not vary directly with labour hours as the furniture made varies considerably in size and complexity. There is a significant favourable variance for furniture packs and this may reflect more labour-intensive work (hence more labour hours) in producing more complex but less furniture. The company may consider identifying the activities that drive costs to allow for flexing to be more accurate.

(c) Benefits of participative budgeting for M plc potentially include:

- improved communication of aims and objectives which can lead to improved goal congruence;
- managers can widen their experience and develop the skills necessary for more senior posts;
- improved accuracy as managers will have better knowledge of operations;
- improved motivation if targets are discussed and agreed.

The main disadvantages of a participative approach are:

- budgetary slack. Managers may include allowances for unforeseen events to make achievement of the budget easier;
- managers may not be sufficiently skilled to participate in the budgetary process.

CONTROL AND PERFORMANCE MEASUREMENT OF RESPONSIBILITY CENTRES

261 KDS

(a) **Divisional administrator's proposal**

Effect on 20X5 ROCE

It will have been assumed in arriving at the 31/12/X5 net assets that the debt will have been paid. Reversing this assumption has the effect of increasing liabilities and has no effect on assets, as cash is excluded. Thus net assets will be reduced by $90,000 (to $4,310,000).

Whether the $2,000 late payment penalty is accounted for in 20X5 or 20X6 will depend to some extent on the company's accounting policy. The accruals concept would, however, lean towards it being accounted for in 20X5. Thus operating profits would be reduced by $2,000 (to $647,000).

The new ROCE would thus be $\dfrac{\$647,000}{\$4,310,000} \times 100 = 15.01\%$

Thus the target will have been achieved and bonuses paid. This is, of course, no indication of improved performance, but simply an arithmetical anomaly arising as a result of one side of the transaction being ignored in the calculation. In fact, the finance cost of the late payment is extremely high.

Longer term effects

There would be no quantifiable long-term effects, although relationships with the supplier may be adversely affected by the late payment.

The works manager's proposal

Effect on 20X5 ROCE

Assuming no depreciation charge in 20X5, net assets would be increased by the cost of the new assets, $320,000 (to $4,720,000), and operating profits would be unaffected.

The new ROCE would thus be $\dfrac{\$649,000}{\$4,720,000} \times 100 = 13.75\%$

This represents a reduction of ROCE in the short term.

Longer term effects

In 20X6 and beyond, the full impact of the cost savings and depreciation charge would be felt – operating profits would be increased by a net $(76,000 – 40,000) = $36,000. Net assets value will be increased, but the increase will be smaller each year as the asset is depreciated.

In 20X6, the equipment's own ROCE would be $\dfrac{\$36,000}{\$(320,000 - 40,000)} \times 100 = 12.86\%$

This will still not help the division to achieve its target of 15%, although it does exceed the company's cost of capital and thus may be desirable overall.

However, by the end of 20X7, the equipment WDV will be $(320,000 – 80,000) = $240,000, giving a ROCE of 15%, exactly on target. As it increases above this level it will help the division to achieve its overall target.

This illustrates one of the major problems with using book values for assets in performance measures – as the assets get older, they appear to give better performance. This can have the effect of deterring managers from replacing assets even though this may be of benefit in the long term through cost savings (as above), increased productivity etc.

(b) Residual income (RI) is an absolute measure of performance, and is arrived at by deducting a notional interest charge at the company's cost of capital on the net assets. Appraising the two divisions' performance forecasts under this method would have the following results:

	20X5 operating profit	Interest charge (12% net assets)	Residual income
	$	$	$
Division K	649,000	528,000	121,000
Division D	120,000	57,600	62,400

The performance rankings of the two divisions are now apparently reversed. However, the RIs of the two divisions are not directly comparable – whilst Division K has produced nearly twice the level of RI than that of Division D, the net asset base required to do this is over nine times as large. RI cannot be meaningfully used to compare investments of differing sizes, as ROCE can.

One could also question the use of the company's average cost of money in computing the notional interest charge. The two divisions have been set a target well above this - this may be because they are considered riskier than average. If 15% had been used in the computation, Division K would have negative RI, whilst Division D has positive RI - reflecting the same information as the ROCE, that K is not achieving its target return.

The RI uses the same principles for establishing profit and asset values as the ROCE, and thus shares the same problems. As assets get older and their WDV falls, the imputed interest falls and RI rises.

However, RI can be of greater benefit than ROCE in management decision making. Management may only feel inclined to undertake new investment if doing so improves their performance measure. For example, Division D currently enjoys a ROCE of 25% and its manager may only consider new projects that give a return at least as good as this (although this may depend upon the particular structure of the bonus scheme - a fixed bonus provided the target of 15% is reached may not provoke such an attitude).

However, the RI measure will improve with new investment, i.e. increase, provided the investment's returns are at least covering the rate used in computing the notional interest (12% or 15%). This will ensure that projects that are worthwhile from the company's point of view will also be seen as such by the divisional manager (goal congruence).

In summary, RI has advantages and disadvantages over ROCE as a performance measure, and both suffer from common valuation problems. One of these can be used as part of a package of performance indicators – market share, productivity, employee satisfaction, technological advancement, etc – but neither is perfect in isolation.

(c) Financial measures taken in isolation are unlikely to tell the whole story of a division's or company's performance. They must be put into context, taking account of the circumstances in which they were achieved – new products being introduced, market changes, technological changes, competitors' moves, availability of resources, etc.

For example, one might question why the two divisions in KDS are apparently performing at such different levels. Whilst quality of management may well be a contributory factor, it is unlikely to explain a difference of over 10 percentage points in ROCE.

The age profile of assets used should be considered, as discussed above. Division K may have recently invested in new machinery, possibly in response to technological advances. Not to do so would put them at a disadvantage over their competitors, and thus is for long-term benefit. The industry of the much smaller Division D may be more static, requiring less asset changes.

Performance relative to the market and competitors should be considered (market share, product leadership, etc) and the degree of innovation achieved. Level of complaints received may also be monitored.

Finally, employee measures are relevant when assessing the effectiveness of a manager – labour turnover, staff morale, managers' relationships with both subordinates and superiors. The level of job satisfaction felt by employees at all levels is an important consideration in the plan for achievement of company objectives.

ANSWERS TO SECTION C-TYPE QUESTIONS : SECTION 6

262 Y AND Z

Key answer tips

This was not a popular question; many students dislike this part of the syllabus. There are 4 marks available for the computations in part (a), which are straightforward, but don't forget to convert the monthly profit into an annual profit and don't ignore the discussion, which is worth more marks than the computations. Part (b) gave 3 marks for the calculations, which were again straightforward, and 3 marks for the discussion. Part (c), for 5 marks, wanted a discussion of the strengths and weaknesses of the two methods and an explanation of two other performance measures that could be used. This should have been fairly easy for the well-prepared student.

(a) Return on Investment (ROI) = $\dfrac{\text{Profit}}{\text{Investment}}$

Unfortunately, both the top and the bottom of the equation can be calculated in different ways. There is no ambiguity, here, for the value of the investment, we shall use the $9.76m and the $1.26m. The profit figure, however, involves a choice – should we use the controllable income of $460,000 and $201,000 or should we use the $122,000 and $21,000 which are the net income before tax figures? If you think a question is ambiguous, you must state your assumption and choose whichever figures you think are appropriate.

One trick here is that, whichever profit figure you choose, it is expressed per month and has to be annualised as made clear in the requirement.

	Division Y $000	Division Z $000
Net income before tax		
122 × 12	1,464	
21 × 12		252
Investment	÷ 9,760	÷ 1,260
ROI	15%	20%

On the basis of ROI, division Z is performing better than division Y.

Division Y's net income before tax is almost six times as much as division Z's, and its ROI does exceed the target, so division Y does increase the wealth of the shareholders to a greater extent than division Z. This is not reflected in the ROI, and indeed is a well-known flaw of the method, in that it is only a measure of relative profitability, not absolute profitability.

If the target return on capital of 12% is raised, then division Z has the greater margin of safety, whereas division Y's performance with its ROI of 15% would quickly become less and less attractive.

The net income before tax figures are very much affected by the apportioned central costs. It would be nice to know on what basis the apportionment has been made. Indeed a very convincing argument could be made that, if we are trying to judge performance in the two divisions, then we should only be looking at controllable profit as it would be unfair to judge managers on factors over which they have no control.

If there are unlimited funds available for investment, then both divisions earn above the target return and, provided they can find projects with similar returns to their existing projects, then they should seek additional funds. If there are limited funds available and division Z can find new projects with returns similar to its existing projects, then division Z will be the more attractive destination for funds.

KAPLAN PUBLISHING

PAPER P1 : MANAGEMENT ACCOUNTING – PERFORMANCE EVALUATION

	Division Y $000	Division Z $000
Controllable income		
460 × 12	5,520	
201 × 12		2,412
Investment	÷ 9,760	÷ 1,260
	56.6%	191.4%

The controllable income return on net assets is very much higher for Z than for Y and, compared to the ROIs calculated on the basis of net income before tax, show Z to be performing better than Y to a much greater extent. This is an indication than Z is earning its income with much less use of divisional net assets.

(b)

	Division Y $000	Division Z $000
Net income before tax	1,464	252
Imputed interest		
12% × $9.76m	1,171.2	
12% × $1.26m		151.2
Residual income	292.8	100.8

Division Y has a better performance on the basis of residual income, but residual income is not a useful comparator when comparing divisions of different sizes. Division Y has a bigger residual income, but so it should as it is a much bigger division.

All in all division Y does increase the wealth of the shareholders to a greater extent than division Z, but division Z does earn its income at a better rate than division Y.

(c) ROI is expressed as a percentage and is more easily understood by non-financial managers.

ROI can be used to compare performance between different sized divisions or companies.

It is not necessary to know the cost of capital in order to calculate ROI.

ROI may lead to dysfunctional decisions. For instance, if a division has a very high ROI of say 40% and is considering a project with an ROI of 30% which is still well above the cost of capital of say 10%, then the project should be accepted as it provides a return well in excess of the cost of capital. The division may quite possibly reject the project, however, as when added to its existing operations it will reduce the ROI from 40%.

Using residual income as a performance measure should ensure that divisions make decisions which are in the best interests of the group as a whole and should eliminate the problem outlined in the previous paragraph.

Different divisions can use different rates to reflect different risk when calculating residual income.

Residual income is not useful for comparing divisions of different sizes.

Both residual income and ROI improve as the age of the assets increase and both provide an incentive to hang onto aged possibly inefficient machines.

Other methods of assessment that could be used in addition to ROI or residual income include:

- EVA which is similar to residual income except that, instead of using book values for profit and capital employed, the figures are adjusted to reflect the true economic value of the profit and of the capital employed;
- the Balanced Scorecard, which still looks at financial performance, perhaps using residual income or ROI, but also encompasses three other perspectives: the customer perspective, the internal business process perspective, and the learning and growth perspective.

263 CTD

Key answer tips

The calculations involved in this question are very straightforward, but don't be deceived – the real thrust of this question is to make sure that you both understand the principles of different transfer pricing methods, and can apply them to a situation.

(a) The current transfer price is ($40 + $20)) × 1.1 = $66.

		FD		TM	
		$000	$000	$000	$000
Internal sales	15,000 × $66		990		
External sales	5,000 × $80		400		
	15,000 × $500				7,500
			1,390		7,500
Production variable costs	20,000 × $40	(800)			
	15,000 × $366			(5,490)	
Selling/distribution variable costs	5,000 × $4	(20)			
	15,000 × $25			(375)	
			820		5,865
			570		1,635
Production overheads	20,000 × $20	(400)			
	15,000 × $60			(900)	
Administration overheads	20,000 × $4	(80)			
	15,000 × $25			(375)	
Net profit			90		360
Interest charge	$750,000\$1,500,000 × 12%		(90)		(180)
Residual income (RI)			0		180
Target RI			85		105
Bonus	$180,000 × 5%		0		9

Implications of the current reward system

While the TM manager has received a bonus and presumably will be pleased about it, the FD manager has received nothing. This will not be very motivating and may lead to problems within the division as a whole, such as inefficiency, staff turnover and unreliability. Since the TM division relies so completely on the FD division, this situation is clearly unacceptable.

(b) (i) In order to achieve a 5% bonus, the manager of TM division will be willing to accept a decrease in residual income of $(180,000 – 105,000) = $75,000. This is an increase in transfer price of the 15,000 units transferred of $75,000/15,000 = $5. Thus the transfer price would rise to $66 + $5 = $71.

(ii) In order to achieve a 5% bonus, the manager of FD division will want an increase in residual income of $85,000. This is an increase in transfer price of the 15,000 units transferred of $85,000/15,000 = $5.67. Thus the transfer price would have to rise to $66 + $5.67 = $71.67.

(c) **REPORT**

To: CTD management
From: Management accountant
Date: XXXX
Subject: Transfer pricing for profit maximisation

At present the transfer price for the moulding from FD to TM is set at variable costs plus 10%. In many companies it has been found that this approach leads to sub-optimal decisions, and less profit being made than possible. This report sets out how the right transfer price can lead to profit maximisation.

One method is for the transfer price to be set at the marginal cost of production in FD division (namely variable cost without any mark-up) plus the opportunity cost of the fact that the company as a whole is supplying the moulding internally. As FD has the capacity for making 25,000 mouldings, 15,000 of which are supplied to TM, the opportunity cost of the 20,000 units actually made is zero. Thus the transfer price should be $40. If TM division could source the moulding externally at less than $40, then doing so is not a sub-optimal decision for the company.

If FD found external markets for the extra 5,000 units then it should increase production, selling 10,000 externally at $80 and transferring 15,000 internally at $40. If, however, external demand at $80 per moulding exceeded 10,000 units, and assuming that TM still need 15,000 units, for each unit over 10,000 that FD is not selling externally, the transfer price to TM should be $80. This reflects the opportunity cost to the company of the fact that the units are not being sold at a contribution of $40.

At a transfer price of $40, FD will not be covering its fixed costs, and the manager will not be receiving a bonus. The division would then aim to sell all its production externally at $80, which will leave TM short of its supplies and therefore would deprive the company of all the TM profit. This is clearly sub-optimal, but the scenario depends on the idea that TM cannot source externally. If it can, then the whole scenario changes.

The FD manager will only get a bonus if the transfer price is set at $71.67, which is 67c more than the maximum transfer price that the TM manager is prepared to accept. But if the TM manager finds a source of mouldings externally at a price that is between $40 and $71.67, and takes the supply (i.e. is not forced to buy internally), then this is a sub-optimal decision for the company as a whole as mouldings are being acquired at a cost which exceeds the cost of internal manufacture. In addition, if FD cannot sell externally all its 15,000 production that TM is no longer taking, then the company as a whole is diminishing.

There is thus a conflict of interests on a number of fronts between the two divisions. Below are some possible alternative methods of transfer pricing that could help resolve these conflicts:

- Dual pricing – there are two possible approaches:
  - TM accounts for transfers at $4, but FD accounts for transfers at $80. Head office keeps an account of the discrepancy that therefore arises. Divisional autonomy is preserved and both divisions will make optimal decisions. The method is awkward to administer, however, and would require some adjustment of the residual income performance measure.

ANSWERS TO SECTION C-TYPE QUESTIONS : SECTION 6

- Mouldings are transferred at marginal cost ($40), but at the end of each period a share of the profit that TM makes on its external sales of the TX is transferred back to FD. Again this is administratively tricky, and does not clearly address the issue of divisional autonomy, since the decision as to what share should be given back to FD would have to be made *post hoc* by head office.

- Two-part tariff system – this is similar to the second kind of dual pricing, in that mouldings are transferred at $40, and at the end of the period an amount is credited back to FD. However, under this system, the amount is a fixed fee that reflects the fixed costs incurred by FD in making the transfers. Again this undermines divisional autonomy, since the decision as to what share should be given back to FD would have to be made by head office.

- Negotiated transfer price – if the managers get on and fully understand the complexity of the issues facing both divisions and, more importantly, their impact on the performance of the company as a whole, they may be able to negotiate a transfer price that satisfies both of them. Provided the compromise is reflected in the bonus system, then this is probably the most desirable approach. However, if they cannot agree, then head office will simply have to impose a transfer price which will possibly fail to satisfy either side, and will be demotivating.

264 DIVISION A

(a) (i) Profit required by division A to meet RI target:

Cost of capital $3.2m @ 12%	384,000
Target RI	180,000
Target profit	564,000
Add fixed costs	1,080,000
Target contribution	1,644,000
Contribution earned from external sales 90,000 @ ($35-$22)	1,170,000
Contribution required from internal sales	474,000
Contribution per bit on internal sales ($474,000/ 60,000)	$7.90
Transfer price to division C $22.00 + $7.90	$29.90

(ii) The two transfer prices based on opportunity costs:

40,000 units (150,000 – 110,000) at the marginal cost of $22.00

20,000 units (110,000 – 90,000) at the external selling price of $35.00

(b) Where divisional managers are given total autonomy to purchase units at the cheapest price and where divisional performance is assessed on a measure based on profit, sub-optimal behaviour could occur i.e. divisional managers could make decisions that may not be in the overall interests of the group.

Impact of group's current transfer pricing policy

Division C's objective is to maximise its RI in order to achieve its target RI. It will therefore endeavour to find the cheapest source of supply for Bits. As C requires 60,000 Bits and X is willing to supply them at $28 each, C would prefer to buy them from X rather than division A. However this will not benefit the group, as division A will be unable to utilise its spare capacity of 40,000 Bits. The effect on the group's profit will be as follows:

	$
Additional payment by division C 60,000 Bits @ ($28 – $22)	(360,000)
Gain in contribution by Division A 20,000 Bits @ $13	260,000
Net loss to group	(100,000)

Impact of group's proposed transfer pricing policy

If division A was to set transfer prices based on opportunity costs the effect on its divisional profit would be as follows:

	$
Reduction in profit 40,000 Bits @ ($29.90 – $22.00)	(316,000)
Increase in profit 20,000 Bits @ ($35 – $29.90)	102,000
Net loss to division	(214,000)

Division C has the following two purchase options:

	$
Purchase from division A 40,000 Bits @ $22	880,000
Purchase from Z 20,000 Bits @ $33	660,000
Total cost of Bits	1,540,000
Or Purchase 60,000 from X 60,000 Bits @ $28	1,680,000

As division C will opt to source the Bits from the cheapest supplier/s it will choose to purchase 40,000 Bits from division A at $22 per Bit and the remaining 20,000 Bits from Z at $33 per Bit. This also benefits the group, as there is no opportunity cost to division A on the 40,000 units transferred to division C.

When marginal cost is used as the transfer price division C will make the correct decision and the group will maximise profits. However division A would suffer. This can be overcome by changing the way it measures the performance of its divisions – rather than using a single profit based measure it needs to introduce a variety of quantitative and qualitative measures.

(c) **Purchase of 60,000 Bits from division A**

	Contribution $	Taxation $	Net effect $
A – external sales 90,000 Bits @ ($35 – $22)	1,170,000		
– internal sales 60,000 Bits @ ($30 – $22)	480,000		
Total contribution from A	1,650,000		
Taxation @ 55%		(907,500)	
C – purchases 60,000 Bits @ $30	(1,800,000)		
Taxation @ 25%		450,000	
Net effect	(150,000)	(457,500)	(607,500)

Purchase of 60,000 Bits from X

	Contribution $	Taxation $	Net effect $
A – external sales 110,000 Bits @ ($35 – $22)	1,430,000		
Taxation @ 55%		(786,500)	
C – purchases 60,000 Bits @ $28	(1,680,000)		
Taxation @ 25%		420,000	
Net effect	(250,000)	(366,500)	(616,500)

The group will maximise its profits if division C purchased the Bits from division A.

ANSWERS TO SECTION C-TYPE QUESTIONS : **SECTION 6**

265 MOBILE PHONES

Key answer tips

Remember to relate both parts of your answer to the question scenario wherever possible. Very few marks are awarded for purely theoretical answers.

(a) Traditional absorption costing is the system currently used by Division Y. All overheads are absorbed on the basis of labour hours. This system is clearly a very straightforward procedure that will be simple to operate.

However, it is unlikely that this system will provide useful information for decision making purposes. The current system treats all overheads as if they vary with labour hours. This is unlikely to be the case. Indeed, Professors Cooper and Kaplan argue that it is **support activities** that cause overhead costs to arise, not direct labour hours.

When overhead costs are investigated, it is often found that activities such as material handling, setting up of machinery, quality control work, etc actually cause costs. Furthermore, it is known that cost drivers exist for each activity. These cost drivers influence the level of cost.

ABC establishes a cost driver rate, for example a rate per customer order. The overheads are then charged to the products by applying the cost driver rates to the products as they consume the support activities.

The cost driver rates reflect the behaviour of the overhead cost.

ABC tends to provide more accurate product cost information than traditional absorption costing.

More accurate information will provide managers with the tools to make better, more informed decisions for the firm.

Division Y has produced a budgeted income statement showing mobile phone Q as a loss making product line. However, the overheads charged to Q are unlikely to reflect the actual work involved in making Q. At present managers may be tempted to delete product Q. This decision may alter if ABC is implemented.

(b) (i) The current transfer pricing system in operation involves Division X setting the price at the total cost of the chips plus a 20% mark-up.

This price will allow Division X to generate some profit on internal sales to Division Y. It may also be a price that is acceptable to both selling and buying divisions. It may be seen as a 'fair' price.

However, the price is unlikely to encourage goal congruent behaviour from the divisional managers. The manager of Division Y has already asked permission to purchase the chips from an external supplier. This may or may not be in the best interest of M.

To bring about goal congruent behaviour, the transfer price should reflect the opportunity cost of the transfer. This relevant cost will depend upon the circumstances within the division. Cost plus 20% will not reflect the **relevant** cost.

The transfer price set by Division X should either be:

(1) the marginal cost of the chip – if spare capacity is used to manufacture the chips; or

PAPER P1 : MANAGEMENT ACCOUNTING – PERFORMANCE EVALUATION

(2) marginal cost plus contribution forgone from other products – if chips for Division Y are manufactured by producing and selling less of one of its existing products. Division X must be compensated for the loss in contribution from the other product. This opportunity cost is built into the transfer price.

If marginal cost, in particular, is used as the transfer price, the manager of Division X will be demotivated as no benefit (contribution) is received from internal sales.

If this proves to be the case, a dual pricing system may be implemented. This is where the selling division and buying division record different transfer prices.

Division X may record sales at cost plus 20%, but Division Y records purchases at marginal cost. This system will motivate the manager of X and encourage goal congruent decisions from the manager of Y.

An alternative to dual pricing would be a two-part tariff system. Under this method Division Y would pay a transfer price equal to the marginal cost per unit, but then a fixed fee would be paid to Division X each period to provide them with some benefit.

(ii) Once ABC has been introduced within the organisation, the total cost of individual product lines is likely to alter. This will then require a re-evaluation of current transfer prices. The direct costs of products will remain the same. However, overheads charged to products are likely to change.

Whichever transfer pricing system is used, be it total cost plus 20%, marginal cost, marginal cost plus contribution forgone, two-part tariff or dual pricing, a change in product costs will necessitate a change in transfer price.

If transfer prices are altered then revenues of Division X and costs of Division Y will be affected. Hence, divisional profits will be affected as well.

266 FP

EXAMINER'S COMMENT

Part a) was the least well done part of this question and many students did not attempt an answer. The remainder of the question was answered better with the main problem being that students did not link their answer closely enough to the scenario given

(a)

	$ per repair	Total cost for 500 repairs
		$
Parts	54	
Labour 3 hours @ $15 each	45	
Variable overhead 3 hours at $10 per hour	30	
Marginal cost	129	64,500
Fixed overhead 3 hours at $22 per hour	66	33,000
Total cost	195	97,500
Mark-up	78	39,000
Selling price	273	136,500

Transfers at 40% mark-up

	Sales $	Service $	FP $
Sales	120,000	136,500	120,000
Costs	136,500	97,500	97,500
Profit	(16,500)	39,000	22,500

Transfers at marginal cost

	Sales $	Service $	FP $
Sales	120,000	64,500	120,000
Costs	64,500	97,500	97,500
Profit	55,500	(33,000)	22,500

Repairs carried out by RS

	Sales $	Service $	FP $
Sales	120,000	0	120,000
Costs	90,000	33,000	123,000
Profit	30,000	(33,000)	(3,000)

(b) (i) Transfers at full cost plus may not be appropriate for FP because, at this price, the Sales Department can buy more cheaply from external suppliers and will not wish to purchase from the Service Department. This decision would be dysfunctional for the company as a whole as an overall loss is made.

It would also lead to any inefficiencies of the Service Department being passed on to the Sales Department which would give no incentive to control costs.

(ii) Issues to consider include:

- Can RS guarantee the quality and reliability of the repairs?
- Is the offer by RS a short-term offer? Would the price rise in the longer term?
- Can the Service Department find other work to take up the capacity released if RS does the guarantee repairs?
- Can the Service Department find cost savings to reduce costs?

(c) Operating the two departments as profit centres may have the following advantages:

- If managers are given autonomy to take decisions, this may lead to improved profitability owing to specialist knowledge and the ability to make decisions quickly.
- If realistic targets are set which are within managers' control, then managers may be motivated to improve performance.
- Head office time may be freed up to focus on strategic issues.
- Profit centres may provide a training ground for senior management positions.

There could also be disadvantages as follows:

- loss of control by head office;
- dysfunctional decision making;
- duplication of functions such as personnel and administration.

267 ZZ GROUP

EXAMINER'S COMMENT

This was a very unpopular choice in the exam but those students who chose this question did it very well. The main error was in the calculation of asset turnover.

(a) Increasing the transfer price of internal sales from $10 per unit to $20 per unit, results in sales of Division X increasing by $30,000 and variable costs of Division Y increasing by a corresponding amount. Revised profit is calculated as follows:

	Division X	Division Y
Sales	100,000	270,000
Variable cost	50,000	144,000
Contribution	50,000	126,000
Fixed cost	15,000	100,000
Profit	35,000	26,000
RI	29,000	15,000
ROCE	58.33%	23.64%
Operating profit margin	35.00%	9.63%
Asset turnover	1.67	2.45

(b) Changing the transfer price to $20 per component results in an improvement in many of the performance measures of Division X and a deterioration in the performance measures of Division Y.

The sales revenue of Division X increases by $30,000 with no corresponding change in costs, so profit increases by the same amount. This leads to an improvement in all of the profit measures so RI, ROCE and the operating profit margin all improve. Asset turnover also improves as this measures the level of sales generated by the capital employed.

The variable cost of Division Y increases by $30,000. This leads to a fall in all of the profit measures, but asset turnover remains the same as sales do not change.

If profit measures are used to evaluate managerial performance and rewards, changing the transfer price would be unfair as appears to impact on performance whereas in reality overall profit is unchanged.

(c) (i) If full autonomy was given to Divisional Managers, then the manager of Division X would prefer to satisfy external demand at a price of $20 than supply Division Y at a marginal cost of $10. This would result in only 2,000 units being available for internal transfer and Division Y would have to buy externally or lose sales. Division X will be reluctant to transfer internally at marginal cost as no contribution towards fixed cost or profit will be earned. Division Y will be reluctant to pay a price above marginal cost as this will have a detrimental effect on existing performance measures as shown in (a).

From a group perspective, if Division X charges the external price for all components, then this will lead to a reduction in profit for the group as a whole.

(ii) The problems could be resolved by allowing divisions to set the transfer price at full external cost for the first 3,000 units. As Division X faces excess demand, any price below market price would be unacceptable for the first 3,000 units. The remaining 2,000 units could be transferred at a price at marginal cost plus a contribution towards fixed cost and profit. This could be negotiated or a two-part tariff could be used.

Performance targets should be adjusted to reflect the change in the share of profits.

Section 7

MAY 2007 EXAM QUESTIONS

SECTION A – 40 MARKS

[The indicative time for answering this section is 72 minutes]

Answer ALL fifteen sub-questions.

QUESTION ONE

1.1 **Which of the following best describes an investment centre?**

   A   A centre for which managers are accountable only for costs.

   B   A centre for which managers are accountable only for financial outputs in the form of generating sales revenue.

   C   A centre for which managers are accountable for profit.

   D   A centre for which managers are accountable for profit and current and non-current assets. **(2 marks)**

1.2 **A flexible budget is**

   A   a budget which, by recognising different cost behaviour patterns, is designed to change as volume of activity changes.

   B   a budget for a twelve month period which includes planned revenues, expenses, assets and liabilities.

   C   a budget which is prepared for a rolling period which is reviewed monthly, and updated accordingly.

   D   a budget for semi-variable overhead costs only. **(2 marks)**

1.3 **The term 'budget slack' refers to the**

   A   lead time between the preparation of the master budget and the commencement of the budget period.

   B   difference between the budgeted output and the actual output achieved.

   C   additional capacity available which is budgeted for even though it may not be used.

   D   deliberate overestimation of costs and/or underestimation of revenues in a budget.

   (2 marks)

PAPER P1 : MANAGEMENT ACCOUNTING – PERFORMANCE EVALUATION

1.4 PP Ltd is preparing the production and material purchases budgets for one of their products, the SUPERX, for the forthcoming year.

The following information is available:

SUPERX
Sales demand (units)   30,000
Material usage per unit   7 kgs
Estimated opening inventory   3,500 units
Required closing inventory   35% higher than opening inventory

How many units of the SUPERX will need to be produced?

A   28,775

B   30,000

C   31,225

D   38,225

(2 marks)

The following data are given for sub-questions 1.5 and 1.6 below

X Ltd operates a standard costing system and absorbs fixed overheads on the basis of machine hours. Details of budgeted and actual figures are as follows:

	Budget	Actual
Fixed overheads	$2,500,000	$2,010,000
Output	500,000 units	440,000 units
Machine hours	1,000,000 hours	900,000 hours

1.5 The fixed overhead expenditure variance is

A $190,000 favourable

B $250,000 adverse

C $300,000 adverse

D $490,000 favourable

(2 marks)

1.6 The fixed overhead volume variance is

A $190,000 favourable

B $250,000 adverse

C $300,000 adverse

D $490,000 favourable

(2 marks)

1.7 A company operates a standard absorption costing system. The budgeted fixed production overheads for the company for the latest year were $330,000 and budgeted output was 220,000 units. At the end of the company's financial year the total of the fixed production overheads debited to the Fixed Production Overhead Control Account was $260,000 and the actual output achieved was 200,000 units.

The under / over absorption of overheads was

A $40,000 over absorbed

B $40,000 under absorbed

C $70,000 over absorbed

D $70,000 under absorbed

(2 marks)

1.8 A company operates a standard absorption costing system. The following fixed production overhead data are available for the latest period:

Budgeted Output 300,000 units
Budgeted Fixed Production Overhead $1,500,000
Actual Fixed Production Overhead $1,950,000
Fixed Production Overhead Total Variance $150,000 adverse

The actual level of production for the period was nearest to

A   277,000 units

B   324,000 units

C   360,000 units

D   420,000 units   (2 marks)

1.9 Which of the following best describes a basic standard?

A   A standard set at an ideal level, which makes no allowance for normal losses, waste and machine downtime.

B   A standard which assumes an efficient level of operation, but which includes allowances for factors such as normal loss, waste and machine downtime.

C   A standard which is kept unchanged over a period of time.

D   A standard which is based on current price levels.   (2 marks)

1.10 XYZ Ltd is preparing the production budget for the next period. The total costs of production are a semi-variable cost. The following cost information has been collected in connection with production:

Volume (units)	Cost
4,500	$29,000
6,500	$33,000

The estimated total production costs for a production volume of 5,750 units is nearest to

A $29,200

B $30,000

C $31,500

D $32,500   (2 marks)

1.11 S Ltd manufactures three products, A, B and C. The products use a series of different machines but there is a common machine, P, that is a bottleneck.

The selling price and standard cost for each product for the forthcoming year is as follows:

	A	B	C
	$	$	$
Selling price	200	150	150
Direct materials	41	20	30
Conversion costs	55	40	66
Machine P – minutes	12	10	7

Calculate the return per hour for each of the products.   (4 marks)

KAPLAN PUBLISHING

1.12 The following data have been extracted from a company's year-end accounts:

	$
Turnover	7,055,016
Gross profit	4,938,511
Operating profit	3,629,156
Non-current assets	4,582,000
Cash at bank	4,619,582
Short term borrowings	949,339
Trade receivables	442,443
Trade payables	464,692

Calculate the following four performance measures:

(i) Operating profit margin;

(ii) Return on capital employed;

(iii) Trade receivable days (debtors days);

(iv) Current (Liquidity) ratio. **(4 marks)**

1.13 PQR Ltd operates a standard absorption costing system. Details of budgeted and actual figures are as follows:

	Budget	Actual
Sales volume (units)	100,000	110,000
Selling price per unit	$10	$9.50
Variable cost per unit	$5	$5.25
Total cost per unit	$8	$8.30

(i) Calculate the sales price variance. **(2 marks)**

(ii) Calculate the sales volume profit variance. **(2 marks)**

1.14 WX has two divisions, Y and Z. The following budgeted information is available.

Division Y manufactures motors and budgets to transfer 60,000 motors to Division Z and to sell 40,000 motors to external customers.

Division Z assembles food mixers and uses one motor for each food mixer produced.

The standard cost information per motor for Division Y is as follows:

	$
Direct materials	70
Direct labour	20
Variable production overhead	10
Fixed production overhead	40
Fixed selling and administration overhead	10
Total standard cost	150

In order to set the external selling price the company uses a 33.33% mark up on total standard cost.

(i) Calculate the budgeted profit/(loss) for Division Y if the transfer price is set at marginal cost.

(ii) Calculate the budgeted profit/(loss) for Division Y if the transfer price is set at the total production cost. **(4 marks)**

1.15 RF Ltd is about to launch a new product in June 2007. The company has commissioned some market research to assist in sales forecasting. The resulting research and analysis established the following equation:

$Y = A x^{0.6}$

Where Y is the cumulative sales units, A is the sales units in month 1, x is the month number.
June 2007 is Month 1.
Sales in June 2007 will be 1,500 units.

Calculate the forecast sales volume for each of the months June, July and August 2007 and for that three month period in total. **(4 marks)**

(Total for Section A : 40 marks)

SECTION B – 30 MARKS

[The indicative time for answering this section is 54 minutes]

Answer ALL six sub-questions. Each sub-question is worth 5 marks.

QUESTION TWO

(a) A company uses variance analysis to monitor the performance of the team of workers which assembles Product M. Details of the budgeted and actual performance of the team for last period were as follows:

	Budget	Actual
Output of product M	600 units	680 units
Wage rate	$30 per hour	$32 per hour
Labour hours	900 hours	1,070 hours

It has now been established that the standard wage rate should have been $31.20 per hour.

(i) Calculate the labour rate planning variance and calculate the operational labour efficiency variance.

(ii) Explain the major benefit of analysing variances into planning and operational components. **(5 marks)**

(b) Briefly explain three limitations of standard costing in the modern business environment.
(5 marks)

(c) Briefly explain three factors that should be considered before deciding to investigate a variance. **(5 marks)**

(d) G Group consists of several autonomous divisions. Two of the divisions supply components and services to other divisions within the group as well as to external clients. The management of G Group is considering the introduction of a bonus scheme for managers that will be based on the profit generated by each division.

Briefly explain the factors that should be considered by the management of G Group when designing the bonus scheme for divisional managers. **(5 marks)**

(e) Briefly explain the role of a Manufacturing Resource Planning System in supporting a standard costing system. **(5 marks)**

(f) Briefly explain the main differences between the traditional manufacturing environment and a just-in-time manufacturing environment. **(5 marks)**

(Total : 30 marks)

(Total for Section B : 30 marks)

PAPER P1 : MANAGEMENT ACCOUNTING – PERFORMANCE EVALUATION

SECTION C – 30 MARKS

[The indicative time for answering this section is 54 minutes]

Answer ONE of the two questions.

QUESTION THREE

RJ produces and sells two high performance motor cars: Car X and Car Y. The company operates a standard absorption costing system. The company's budgeted operating statement for the year ending 30 June 2008 and supporting information is given below:

Operating statement year ending 30 June 2008

	Car X $000	Car Y $000	Total $000
Sales	52,500	105,000	157,500
Production cost of sales	40,000	82,250	122,250
Gross profit	12,500	22,750	35,250
Administration costs			
Variable	6,300	12,600	18,900
Fixed	7,000	9,000	16,000
Profit/(loss)	(800)	1,150	350

The production cost of sales for each car was calculated using the following values:

	Car X Units	$000	Car Y Units	$000
Opening inventory	200	8,000	250	11,750
Production	1,100	44,000	1,600	75,200
Closing inventory	300	12,000	100	4,700
Cost of sales	1,000	40,000	1,750	82,250

Production costs

The production costs are made up of direct materials, direct labour, and fixed production overhead. The fixed production overhead is general production overhead (it is not product specific). The total budgeted fixed production overhead is $35,000,000 and is absorbed using a machine hour rate. It takes 200 machine hours to produce one Car X and 300 machine hours to produce one Car Y.

Administration costs

The fixed administration costs include the costs of specific marketing campaigns: $2,000,000 for Car X and $4,000,000 for Car Y.

Required:

(a) Produce the budgeted operating statement in a marginal costing format. **(7 marks)**

(b) Reconcile the total budgeted absorption costing profit with the total budgeted marginal costing profit as shown in the statement you produced in part (a). **(5 marks)**

The company is considering changing to an activity based costing system. The company has analysed the budgeted fixed production overheads and found that the costs for various activities are as follows:

	$000
Machining costs	7,000
Set up costs	12,000
Quality inspections	7,020
Stores receiving	3,480
Stores issues	5,500
	35,000

The analysis also revealed the following information:

	Car X	Car Y
Budgeted production (number of cars)	1,100	1,600
Cars per production run	10	40
Inspections per production run	20	80
Number of component deliveries during the year	492	900
Number of issues from stores	4,000	7,000

Required:

(c) Calculate the budgeted production cost of one Car X and one Car Y using the activity based costing information provided above. **(10 marks)**

(d) Prepare a report to the Production Director of RJ which explains the potential benefits of using activity based budgeting for performance evaluation. **(8 marks)**

(Total : 30 marks)

QUESTION FOUR

RF Ltd is a new company which plans to manufacture a specialist electrical component. The company founders will invest $16,250 on the first day of operations, that is, Month 1. They will also transfer fixed capital assets to the company.

The following information is available:

Sales

The forecast sales for the first four months are as follows:

Month	Number of components
1	1,500
2	1,750
3	2,000
4	2,100

The selling price has been set at $10 per component in the first four months.

Sales receipts

Time of payment	% of customers
Month of sale	20*
One month later	45
Two months later	25
Three months later	5

The balance represents anticipated bad debts.

*A 2% discount is given to customers for payment received in the month of sale.

Production

There will be no opening inventory of finished goods in Month 1 but after that it will be policy for the closing inventory to be equal to 20% of the following month's forecast sales.

Variable production cost

The variable production cost is expected to be $6.40 per component.

	$
Direct materials	1.90
Direct wages	3.30
Variable production overheads	1.20
Total variable cost	6.40

Notes:

Direct materials: 100% of the materials required for production will be purchased in the month of production. No inventory of materials will be held. Direct materials will be paid for in the month following purchase.

Direct wages will be paid in the month in which production occurs.

Variable production overheads: 60% will be paid in the month in which production occurs and the remainder will be paid one month later.

Fixed overhead costs

Fixed overhead costs are estimated at $75,000 per annum and are expected to be incurred in equal amounts each month. 60% of the fixed overhead costs will be paid in the month in which they are incurred and 30% in the following month. The balance represents depreciation of fixed assets.

Calculations are to be made to the nearest $1.

Ignore VAT and Tax.

Required:

(a) Prepare a cash budget for each of the first three months and in total. **(15 marks)**

(b) There is some uncertainty about the direct material cost. It is thought that the direct material cost per component could range between $1.50 and $2.20.

Calculate the budgeted total net cash flow for the three month period if the cost of the direct material is:

(i) $1.50 per component; or

(ii) $2.20 per component.

(6 marks)

(c) Using your answers to part *(a)* and *(b)* above, prepare a report to the management of RF Ltd that discusses the benefits or otherwise of performing 'what if' analysis when preparing cash budgets. **(9 marks)**

(Total : 30 marks)

(Total for Section C : 30 marks)

Section 8

ANSWERS TO MAY 2007 EXAM QUESTIONS

SECTION A

QUESTION ONE

1.1 D

An investment centre has responsibility for sales, costs and net assets.

1.2 A

Option B is a fixed budget and option C is a rolling budget. Option D is incorrect as a flexible budget includes all costs.

1.3 D

This is the definition of budgetary slack.

1.4 C

Note that the material usage figure is not required.

	Units
Sales	30,000
Add closing inventory (3,500 × 1.35)	4,725
Less opening inventory	(3,500)
Production	31,225

1.5 D

	$
Budget overhead	2,500,000
Actual overhead	2,010,000
Expenditure variance	490,000 F

1.6 C

OAR = $2,500,000/500,000 = $5 per unit

Budgeted volume	500,000 units
Actual volume	440,000 units
	60,000 units
× OAR per unit	× $5
Volume variance	$300,000 A

1.7 A

OAR = $330,000/220,000 = $1.50 per unit

	$
Overhead absorbed (200,000 units × $1.50)	300,000
Actual overhead	260,000
Over absorbed	40,000

1.8 C

OAR = $1,500,000/300,000 = $5 per unit

Fixed production overhead variance is the level of over/under absorption. An adverse variance means that overhead is under absorbed.

	$
Overhead absorbed	?
Actual output x $5	
Actual overhead	1,950,000
Under absorbed	150,000

Working backwards, Overhead absorbed = 1,950,000 – 150,000 = 1,800,000 and actual output = 1,800,000/5 = 360,000 units

1.9 C

Option A is an ideal standard, option B is an attainable standard and option D is a current standard.

1.10 C

High Low Method	Activity	$	
	6,500	33,000	
	4,500	29,000	
Difference	2,000	4,000	
So the variable cost	= $4,000/2,000	= $2 per unit	
Substitute into either activity	6,500	33,000	Total cost
	6,500 × $2	13,000	Variable cost
	Difference	$20,000	Fixed cost

The estimated production cost for 5,750 units = 5,750 x $2 + $20,000 = $31,500

1.11

	A	B	C
	$	$	$
Selling price	200	150	150
Direct materials	41	20	30
Throughput	159	130	120
Machine P – minutes per unit	12	10	7
Return per factory minute	159/12	130/10	120/7
	13.25	13	17.14
Return per factory hour × 60 minutes	**$795**	**$780**	**$1,028**

Note Product C return per factory hour = $1,029 with no rounding

1.12

(i) Operating profit margin
= operating profit/sales × 100% $(3,629,156/7,055,016) \times 100 = 51.44\%$

(ii) Capital employed =
total assets – current liabilities $4,582,000 + 4,619,582 + 442,443 - 949,339 - 464,692$
   $= 8,229,994$

Return on capital employed =
Operating profit/capital
employed × 100% $(3,629,156/8,229,994) \times 100 = 44.10\%$

(iii) Trade receivable days = $(442,443/7,055,016) \times 365$ days = 22.89 days
trade receivables/turnover × 365

(iv) Current/liquidity ratio
= current assets/current $(4,619,582 + 442,443)/(949,339 + 464,692) = 3.58:1$
liabilities

1.13

Sales price variance
Budgeted selling price	$10.00	
Actual selling price	$9.50	
	$0.50	adverse
Actual sales volume (units)	110,000	
	$55,000	adverse

Sales volume profit variance
Budgeted sales volume (units)	100,000	
Actual sales volume (units)	110,000	
	10,000	favourable
Standard profit per unit ($10 – $8)	$2	
	$20,000	favourable

1.14

(i) Marginal (variable) cost = 70 + 20 + 10 = $100

External selling price = 150 × 1.3333 = $200

			$000
Sales			
Internal	60,000 × $100		6,000
External	40,000 × $200		8,000
			14,000
Variable cost	100,000 × $100		10,000
Contribution			4,000
Fixed costs			
Production	100,000 × $40		4,000
Administration	100,000 $10		1,000
Loss			(1,000)

(ii) The total production cost = $140 (not $150 as this includes selling and administration overhead). This means that sales revenue increases by $40 × 60,000 = $2,400,000 and costs stay the same. Profit is now (1,000,000) + 2,400,000 = $1,400,000.

1.15 Forecast sales volume for June, July and August is:

Month		Cumulative sales (units)		Monthly sales (units)
June		1,500		1,500
July	$1,500 \times 2^{0.6}$	2,274	2,274 – 1,500	774
August	$1,500 \times 3^{0.6}$	2,900	2,900 – 2,274	626

SECTION B

QUESTION TWO

(a) (i) Budgeted wage rate = $30 per hour

Revised wage rate = $31.20 per hour

Standard hours for actual output = 680 × 900/600 = 1,020

Planning labour rate variance = standard hours for actual output × difference in wage rate = 1,020 × $1.20 = $1,224 Adverse

Operational labour efficiency variance

680 units should take	1,020 hours
did take	1,070 hours
	50 A
Value at revised rate per hour	$31.20
Operational labour efficiency variance	**$1,560 Adverse**

Tutorial note: **Planning variance**

The original labour rate variance is;

1,070 hours should cost $30 per hour $32,100
             did cost $32 per hour $34,240
                                     $ 2,140 A

It may be tempting to split this variance into a planning variance (1,070 × $1.20 = $1,284 A) and an operational variance (1,070 × $0.80 = $856 A). This approach ignores part of the effect of the revision to the wage rate; the part that impacts on the calculation of the efficiency variance. The original labour efficiency variance is 50 hours Adverse × $30 = $1,500 A. By revising the wage rate the operational efficiency variance increases to $1,560 A. There is a 'planning effect' of $60 F to reconcile back to the original variance. The net planning effect is $1,284 A − $60 F = $1,224 A. This is all caused by the revision to the wage rate and is therefore a planning labour rate variance.

(ii) The major benefit of analysing the variances into planning and operational components is that the revised standard should provide a realistic standard against which to measure performance. Any variances should then be a result of operational management efficiencies and inefficiencies and not faulty planning.

(b) Limitations of standard costing in the modern business environment include:

- Standard costs are long run average costs which are most suited to the production of many similar items. In the modern environment products have short life cycles and may be adapted to be suitable in different markets. Standards will therefore be difficult to set and will become out of date quickly.

- The focus of the modern environment is on quality and customer care. Companies may prefer to have long run contracts with few suppliers which may make material standards redundant. It may be preferable to pay higher wages for more skilled labour to avoid inefficiency and loss of quality.

- It may be difficult to decide on a basis for standard costs. Ideal standards would be more suitable in a TQM environment but may be demotivating if used for performance measurement.

(c) Three factors that should be considered before deciding to investigate a variance are:

- The benefit should exceed the cost. This may depend on the importance (materiality) of the variance in the business and whether the cost can be controlled

- Trend. Actual costs will be expected to fluctuate around the standard from period due to it being a long run average. If there appears to be a trend of a variance steadily worsening this maybe an indication that the cost is out of control.

- Interrelationships. Some variances may be caused by the same factor. For example, purchasing cheaper material may lead to a favourable material price variance, an adverse material usage variance and an adverse labour efficiency variance. The net impact may be considered before deciding whether action is necessary.

(d) A bonus scheme based on profit generated by each division must;

- be clearly understood by all personnel involved

- motivate the personnel. In order to be motivating a bonus scheme must be linked clearly to controllable costs and revenues

- not cause sub-optimal behaviour.

Ensuring goal congruence can be difficult when a transfer pricing system is in place.

If there is unlimited demand for the output of the two divisions in the market then the transfer price should equal the market price less any savings as a result of internal transfer. This then allows the divisions to report a profit on the transfers and will not cause any issue for the calculation of the bonus.

However, if there is a limit on the amount that can be sold on the external market and the supplying divisions have spare capacity then the transfer price should be based on marginal cost for the resulting decisions to be goal congruent. In this case they will have no contribution towards fixed costs or profit. This will mean that if the bonus is awarded on profit the divisional manager will not receive a bonus despite the fact that they have made internal supplies.

Therefore the company must ensure that in order for decisions to remain goal congruent the bonus scheme must allow for internal transfers that impact on the divisions' ability to earn bonuses.

(e) A manufacturing resource planning system contains details of all of the inputs into production, including raw materials, components, labour and machine capacity, and coordinates these to provide an optimal production and purchasing plan.

In order to ensure that a manufacturing resource planning system operates effectively it is essential to have:

- A master production schedule, which specifies both the timing and quantity demanded of each product.

- A bill of materials file for each sub-assembly, component and part, containing details of the number of items on hand, scheduled receipts and items allocated to released orders but not yet drawn from inventories.

- A master parts file containing planned lead times of all items to be purchased and sub-assemblies and components to be produced internally.

- A master labour and machine capacity file which specifies both the timing and quantity demanded to achieve planned production levels.

- Details of inputs can then be used in a standard costing system to set parameters for materials, labour and overhead capacity. These will then be used to measure performance through variance analysis.

(f) Just-in-time (JIT) is a system whose objective is to produce or procure products or components as they are required by a customer or for use, rather than for inventory. It is a philosophy which aims to eliminate all waste and non value adding activities in an organisation. The main differences between JIT and a traditional manufacturing environment are:

- JIT is a 'pull system' which responds to demand, in contrast to a 'push system' in a traditional manufacturing environment, in which inventories act as buffers between the different elements of the system, such as purchasing, production and sales.

- The main focus in a traditional manufacturing environment is on maximising output and minimising costs. In a JIT environment it may be more cost effective to allow resources to stand idle than to produce goods for inventory.

- In a traditional manufacturing environment labour are organised into specialist roles and performance is measured against pre determined standards. In a JIT environment labour are multi skilled and carry out routine maintenance tasks as well as working on products. They are empowered to find methods of cost reduction.

- In a traditional manufacturing environment quotes will be taken from several suppliers for raw materials and the cheapest option chosen. In a JIT environment companies are likely to have long term contracts with few suppliers who are located near to the manufacturing operation and can guarantee delivery times and quality of components.

SECTION C

QUESTION THREE

(a) Fixed production overhead = $35,000,000

Budgeted machine hours = (1,100 × 200) + (1,600 × 300) = 700,000 machine hours
Fixed production overhead absorption rate = $35,000,000/700,000 = $50 per machine hour.

	Car X $ per car	Car Y $ per car
Total production cost per unit		
($44,000,000/1,100)	40,000	
($75,200,000/1,600)		47,000
Fixed overhead absorbed		
(200 × $50)	10,000	
(300 × $50)		15,000
Variable production cost per car	30,000	32,000

Marginal costing operating statement – year ending 30 June 2008

	Car X $000	Car Y $000	Total $000
Sales	52,500	105,000	157,500
Variable production costs			
(1,000 × $30,000)	30,000		
(1,750 × $32,000)		56,000	86,000
Variable administration costs	6,300	12,600	18,900
Contribution	16,200	36,400	52,600
Specific fixed costs			
Marketing	2,000	4,000	6,000
Contribution to general fixed costs	14,200	32,400	46,600
General fixed costs			
Production			35,000
Administration ($16,000 – $6,000)			10,000
Profit			**1,600**

(b) The difference in the profit figures will be caused by the fixed production overheads that are absorbed into closing inventories. If inventory levels increase, the absorption costing profit will be higher than the profit calculated using marginal costing since a proportion of fixed overhead will be carried forward to be charged against future revenue.

	Car X	Car Y
Change in inventory (units)	+100	−150
Fixed production overhead per car	$10,000	$15,000
Total difference in profits	$1,000,000	$2,250,000

Reconciliation

	$000
Absorption costing profit	350
Car X: inventory impact	(1,000)
Car Y: inventory impact	2,250
Marginal costing profit	1,600

(c)

Activity	Cost Driver		Drivers
Machining costs	Machine hours	From part a)	700,000
Set up costs	No. of production runs	(1,100/10) + (1,600/40)	150
Quality inspections	No. of inspections	(110 × 20) + (40 × 80)	5,400
Stores receiving	No. of deliveries	492 + 900	1,392
Stores issues	No. of issues	4,000 + 7,000	11,000

Activity	$000	Driver	Cost per driver
Machining costs	7,000	700,000	$10 per machine hour
Set up costs	12,000	150	$80,000 per set up
Quality inspections	7,020	5,400	$1,300 per inspection
Stores receiving	3,480	1,392	$2,500 per delivery
Stores issues	5,500	11,000	$500 per issue

	Car X		Car Y	
	Driver	$000	Driver	$000
Machining costs	220,000	2,200	480,000	4,800
Set up costs	110	8,800	40	3,200
Quality inspections	2,200	2,860	3,200	4,160
Stores receiving	492	1,230	900	2,250
Stores issues	4,000	2,000	7,000	3,500
Total overhead		17,090		17,910
Direct costs		33,000		51,200
Total production costs		50,090		69,110
Cars produced		1,100		1,600
Cost per car		**$45,536**		**$43,194**

(d)

Report

To: Production Director

From: Management Accountant

Date: 22 May 2007

Subject: Activity Based Budgeting – Performance Evaluation

Introduction

This report presents the potential benefits of adopting an activity based budgeting approach for performance evaluation.

Benefits of activity based budgeting

(1) *Better understanding of activities which cause costs*

Activity based budgeting provides a clear framework for understanding the link between costs and the level of activity. This would allow us to evaluate performance based on the activity that drives the cost.

The modern business environment has a high proportion of costs that are indirect and the only meaningful way of attributing these costs to individual products is to find the root cause of such costs, that is, what activity is driving these costs. The traditional absorption costing approach collects overhead costs using functional headings which may make many overhead costs appear to be fixed as they are not linked to the volume of output but they may be related to other activities which are variable for a batch or product line.

(2) *Clearer responsibility for costs*

With an activity based costing approach responsibility for activities and therefore costs can be broken down and assigned accordingly. Individual managers can provide input into the budgeting process and subsequently be held responsible for the variances arising.

(3) *More detailed analysis of overhead costs*

There is greater transparency with an ABB system due to the level of detail behind the costs. The traditional absorption costing approach combines all of the overheads together using a machine hour basis to calculate an overhead absorption rate and uses this rate to attribute overheads to products. ABB will drill down in much more detail examining the cost and the driver of such costs and calculate a cost driver rate which will be used to assign overheads to products. Therefore ABB has greater transparency than absorption costing and allows for much more detailed information on overhead consumption and so on. This then lends itself to better performance evaluation.

Conclusion

The traditional absorption costing approach to product costing does not enable us to provide a satisfactory explanation for the behaviour of costs. In contrast ABB will provide such details which will allow us to have better cost control, improved performance evaluation and greater manager accountability.

If you require any further information please do not hesitate to contact me.

QUESTION FOUR

(a)

Cash Budget

	Month 1 $	Month 2 $	Month 3 $	Total $
Sales receipts (W1)	2,940	10,180	15,545	28,665
Capital	16,250			16,250
Total receipts	**19,190**	**10,180**	**15,545**	**44,915**
Outflow				
Material purchases (W2)	0	3,515	3,420	6,935
Labour (W3)	6,105	5,940	6,666	18,711
Variable overhead (W4)	1,332	2,184	2,318	5,834
Fixed overhead (W5)	3,750	5,625	5,625	15,000
Total payments	**11,187**	**17,264**	**18,029**	**46,480**
Net cash flow	8,003	(7,084)	(2,484)	(1,565)
Bal b/fwd	0	8,003	919	0
Bal c/fwd	8,003	919	(1,565)	(1,565)

Workings

W1 Sales receipts	1	2	3
Sales units	1,500	1,750	2,000
Sales (Units x $10)	15,000	17,500	20,000
Paid in month – 20% x 0.98	2,940	3,430	3,920
45% in the following month		6,750	7,875
25% in 3rd month			3,750

Receipts	2,940	10,180	15,545	
W2 Production	1	2	3	4
	units	*units*	*units*	*units*
Required by sales	1,500	1,750	2,000	2,100
Opening inventory		(350)	(400)	
	1,500	1,400	1,600	
Closing inventory (20% × following month's sales)	350	400	420	
Production	1,850	1,800	2,020	
Material price	$1.90	$1.90	$1.90	
Material cost	$3,515	$3,420	$3,838	
Payment		£3,515	$3,420	
W3 Labour				
Production units	1,850	1,800	2,020	
Rate per unit	$3.30	$3.30	$3.30	
Payment	$6,105	$5,940	$6,666	
W4 Variable Overhead				
Production units	1,850	1,800	2,020	
Rate per unit	$1.20	$1.20	$1.20	
Variable overhead cost	$2,220	$2,160	$2,424	
60% in month	1,332	1,296	1,454	
40% in following month		888	864	
Payment	1,332	2,184	2,318	
W5 Fixed overhead	6,250	6,250	6,250	
60% in month	3,750	3,750	3,750	
30% in following month		1,875	1,875	
Payment	3,750	5,625	5,625	

(b) (i)

	Month 1	Month 2	Month 3
Production	1,850	1,800	2,020
Material price saving ($1.90 – $1.50)	$0.40	$0.40	$0.40
Total saving ($)	740	720	808
Received		740	720
Total cash benefit	$1,460		
Current cash flow at $1.90	$(1,565)		
Revised cash flow at $1.50	**$(105)**		

(ii)

	Month 1	Month 2	Month 3
Production units	1,850	1,800	2,020
Additional cost ($2.20 – $1.90)	$0.30	$0.30	$0.30
Total additional cost ($)	555	540	606
Payment ($)		555	540
Total additional payment	$1,095		
Current cash flow at $1.90	$(1,565)		
Revised cash flow at $2.20	**$(2,660)**		

(c) **Report**

To: Management

From: Management Accountant

Date: 22 May 2007

Subject: 'What if' analysis and cash budgets

Introduction

This report evaluates 'what if' analysis in relation to cash budgets.

Benefits of 'what-if' analysis

(1) It provides an assessment of how responsive the cash flows are to changes in variables.

For example, in preparing the cash budgets it has been identified that there is a degree of uncertainty concerning the direct material cost. The following results have been calculated:

Direct material cost per component	Increase/(decrease) in cash flow	Budgeted cash flow
$2.20	($1,095)	($2,660)
$1.50	$1,460	($105)
$1.90		($1,565)

A 16% increase in material cost to $2.20, results in a negative cash flow of -$2,660. This is a 70% increase in the closing cash negative balance. A 21% decrease in direct material cost to $1.50, results in a revised cashflow of -$105. This is a 93% reduction in the closing cash negative balance. It can be seen that the closing cash balance is sensitive to changes in the price of materials because a small change in price results in a large change in the total cash balance.

(2) *Directs attention to critical variables*

The sensitivity of each variable can be calculated and the most sensitive variables identified. These can be closely monitored and action taken quickly if they vary from forecast.

(3) *Assess the risk to the closing cash balance*

'What-if' analysis can be used to assess how likely the expected cash balance is to occur. Managers may decide to take an alternative course of action if the outcome is very risky. For example they may negotiate an overdraft limit if there is a possibility of a cash deficit.

Limitations of 'what-if' analysis

(1) *Only one variable changes at a time*

'What-if' analysis assesses the impact on the outcome of one variable changing at a time and assumes that each variable is independent. In reality variables are likely to be interdependent.

(2) *Probabilities of changes unknown*

There is no indication of the likelihood of a key variable changing and therefore the use of 'what if' analysis is limited.

Conclusion

Despite the limitations of 'what-if' analysis it can provide an insight into key variables which can impact on an outcome and give managers a better understanding of the risks involved in a cash budget.

Section 9

NOVEMBER 2007 EXAM QUESTIONS

SECTION A – 40 MARKS

[The indicative time for answering this section is 72 minutes.]

Answer ALL 16 sub-questions.

Instructions for answering Section A:

For sub-questions **1.11 to 1.16** you should show your workings as marks are available for the method you use to answer these sub-questions.

QUESTION ONE

1.1 T uses a standard labour hour rate to charge its overheads to its clients' work. During the last annual reporting period production overheads were under-absorbed by $19,250. The anticipated standard labour hours for the period were 38,000 hours while the standard hours actually charged to clients were 38,500. The actual production overheads incurred in the period were $481,250.

The budgeted production overheads for the period were

   A $456,000

   B $462,000

   C $475,000

   D   None of the above   (2 marks)

1.2 Operation B, in a factory, has a standard time of 15 minutes. The standard rate of pay for operatives is $10 per hour. The budget for a period was based on carrying out the operation 350 times. It was subsequently realised that the standard time for Operation B included in the budget did not incorporate expected time savings from the use of new machinery from the start of the period. The standard time should have been reduced to 12 minutes.

Operation B was actually carried out 370 times in the period in a total of 80 hours. The operatives were paid $850.

The operational labour efficiency variance was:

   A $60 adverse

   B $75 favourable

   C $100 adverse

   D $125 adverse   (2 marks)

PAPER P1 : MANAGEMENT ACCOUNTING – PERFORMANCE EVALUATION

1.3 JP manufactures two joint products (X and Y) and a by-product (Z), in a single continuous process. The following information is available for period 3:

Raw materials input	20,000 litres
Raw material costs	$52,000
Conversion costs	$56,000
Outputs	10,000 litres of X, selling price $8 per litre
	8,000 litres of Y, selling price $6 per litre
	2,000 litres of Z, selling price $1 per litre

Process costs are apportioned on a sales value basis. There was no opening and closing inventory of raw materials. The revenue from the by-product is used to reduce the process costs.

What was the cost per litre of joint product X?

A $5.889

B $6.523

C $6.625

D $6.646

(2 marks)

1.4 A company has budgeted breakeven sales revenue of $800,000 and fixed costs of $320,000 for the next period.

The sales revenue needed to achieve a profit of $50,000 in the period would be:

A $850,000

B $925,000

C $1,120,000

D $1,200,000

(2 marks)

1.5 The production volume ratio in a period was 95%.

Which statement will always be true?

A Actual hours worked exceeded the budgeted hours

B Actual hours worked exceeded the standard hours of output

C Budgeted hours exceeded the standard hours of output

D Budgeted output was less than the actual output

(2 marks)

1.6 Two CIMA definitions follow:

(1) A system that converts a production schedule into a listing of the materials and components required to meet that schedule so that adequate inventory levels are maintained and items are available when needed.

(2) An accounting-oriented information system, generally software-driven, which aids in identifying and planning the enterprise-wide resources needed to resource, make, account for and deliver customer orders.

Which of the following pairs of terms matches the definitions?

	Definition 1	*Definition 2*
A	Material requirements planning	Enterprise resource planning
B	Manufacturing resource planning	Material requirements planning
C	Material requirements planning	Manufacturing resource planning
D	Manufacturing resource planning	Enterprise resource planning

(2 marks)

1.7 The fixed overhead volume variance is defined as:

A the difference between the budgeted value of the fixed overheads and the standard fixed overheads absorbed by actual production

B the difference between the standard fixed overhead cost specified for the production achieved, and the actual fixed overhead cost incurred

C the difference between budgeted and actual fixed overhead expenditure

D the difference between the standard fixed overhead cost specified in the original budget and the same volume of fixed overheads, but at the actual prices incurred

(2 marks)

1.8 Overheads will always be over-absorbed when:

A actual output is higher than budgeted output

B actual overheads incurred are higher than the amount absorbed

C actual overheads incurred are lower than the amount absorbed

D budgeted overheads are lower than the overheads absorbed

(2 marks)

The following data are given for sub-questions 1.9 and 1.10 below.

A manufacturing company recorded the following costs in October for Product X:

	$
Direct materials	20,000
Direct labour	6,300
Variable production overhead	4,700
Fixed production overhead	19,750
Variable selling costs	4,500
Fixed distribution costs	16,800
Total costs incurred for Product X	72,050

During October 4,000 units of Product X were produced but only 3,600 units were sold. At the beginning of October there was no inventory.

1.9 The value of the inventory of Product X at the end of October using marginal costing was:

A $3,080

B $3,100

C $3,550

D $5,075

(2 marks)

1.10 The value of the inventory of Product X at the end of October using throughput accounting was:

A $630

B $1,080

C $1,100

D $2,000

(2 marks)

1.11 A company has the following budgeted sales figures:

Month 1 $90,000

Month 2 $105,000

Month 3 $120,000

Month 4 $108,000

80% of sales are on credit and the remainder are paid in cash. Credit customers paying within one month are given a discount of 1.5%. Credit customers normally pay within the following time frame:

Within 1 month   40% of credit sales

Within 2 months   70% of credit sales

Within 3 months   98% of credit sales

There is an expectation that 2% of credit sales will become irrecoverable (bad) debts.

Outstanding receivables at the beginning of month 1 includes $6,000 expected to be received in month 4.

Calculate the total receipts expected in month 4.

(4 marks)

1.12 The budgeted total costs for two levels of output are as shown below:

Output	25,000 units	40,000 units
Total cost	$143,500	$194,000

Within this range of output it is known that the variable cost per unit is constant but fixed costs rise by $10,000 when output exceeds 35,000 units.

Calculate for a budgeted output of 36,000 units:

(i) the variable cost per unit

(ii) the total fixed costs. **(3 marks)**

1.13 A company can produce many types of product but is currently restricted by the number of labour hours available on a particular machine. At present this limitation is set at 12,000 hours per annum. One type of product requires materials costing $5 which are then converted to a final product that sells for $12. Each unit of this product takes 45 minutes to produce on the machine. The conversion costs for the factory are estimated to be $144,000 per annum.

Calculate the throughput accounting ratio for this product and state the significance of the result. **(3 marks)**

1.14 A company manufactures three joint products in a continuous single process. Normal losses are 10% of inputs and do not have any value. Budget data is available for the month of January as follows:

Opening and closing work in progress	Nil
Direct materials input	20,000 kg at a cost of $36,000
Direct labour costs	3,000 hours @ $6 per hour
Variable production overheads	3,000 hours @ $1 per hour

Fixed production overheads are absorbed at a rate of $8 per direct labour hour.

	Expected outputs	Selling price per kg
Joint product A	9,000 kg	$8
Joint product B	6,000 kg	$6
Joint product C	3,000 kg	$4

Joint costs are apportioned on a physical unit basis.

Calculate the gross profit margin for each of the joint products. **(3 marks)**

1.15 A company has the following balance sheet totals at the end of its most recent financial year:

	$million
Non-current assets	3.64
Current assets	0.42
Share capital and reserves*	2.69
Long-term debt	1.00
Current liabilities	0.37

* Includes retained profit for the year of $320,000 after deducting:

Ordinary share dividends	$200,000
Interest on long-term debt	$100,000
Taxation	$70,000

Calculate the Return on Investment (ROI) of the company for the year (using end-year balance sheet values for investment). **(3 marks)**

1.16 A division is considering the purchase of a new machine which costs $1,500,000 and is expected to generate cost savings of $450,000 a year. The asset is expected to have a useful life of five years with no residual value. Depreciation is charged on a straight line basis. Divisional performance is evaluated on Residual Income (RI). The division's cost of capital is 10%.

Calculate for this machine for each of the five years:

(i) the Residual Income (RI)

(ii) the Return on Investment (ROI).

Note: When calculating performance measures the division always uses capital values as at the start of the year.

(4 marks)

(Total for Section A: 40 marks)

SECTION B – 30 MARKS

[The indicative time for answering this section is 54 minutes.]

Answer ALL six sub-questions. Each sub-question is worth 5 marks.

QUESTION TWO

The following data are given for sub-questions 2(a) and 2(b) below.

QBQ produces one type of product. Details of the budgeted sales and production are given below.

Selling price and costs per unit

	$
Selling price	40
Material FX: 1.5kg @ $6 per kg	9
Conversion costs (variable)	8
Fixed production overheads	15

The fixed production overhead absorption rate is based on annual production overheads of $720,000 and budgeted annual output of 48,000 units. The fixed overheads will be incurred evenly throughout the year.

The company also incurs fixed costs for administration of $200,000 per year.

Budgeted sales

Quarter	Units
1	10,000
2	12,000
3	14,000
4	12,000

Inventory

It has been decided that inventory levels are to be reduced. Details are as follows:

Finished goods: 5,500 units are currently held but it has been decided that the closing inventories for Quarters 1, 2 and 3 will be 45%, 40% and 35% of the following quarter's sales respectively.

Raw materials: 4,500 kg are currently held but it has been decided that the closing inventories for Quarters 1 and 2 will be 25% and 20% of the following quarter's production requirements respectively.

Required:

(a) Prepare a materials purchase budget for Quarter 1. **(5 marks)**

(b) In Quarter 3 the opening and closing inventories of finished goods will be 5,600 units and 4,200 units respectively. QBQ adjusts for any under- or over-absorption of overheads at the end of each quarter.

Assume that production and sales volumes were as budgeted and that inventory levels were as planned. Also assume that all costs and revenues were as budgeted.

(i) Calculate using marginal costing the profit for Quarter 3.

(ii) Calculate using absorption costing the profit for Quarter 3.

(iii) Explain the difference, if any, in the profits you have calculated. **(5 marks)**

Budget for Period 3

Nursing costs split (Period 1):
- Let V = variable, F = fixed, V + F = 280,000
- Period 2 nursing: (V × 1.25 + F) × 1.08 = 324,000
- ⇒ V × 1.25 + F = 300,000
- ⇒ 0.25V = 20,000 ⇒ V = $80,000, F = $200,000

Period 2 split (after cost index 108):
- Variable: 80,000 × 1.25 × 1.08 = $108,000
- Fixed: 200,000 × 1.08 = $216,000

Period 3 Budget:

Cost	Workings	$
House-keeping (variable)	125,000 × 0.90 × 1.06	119,250
Nursing – variable	108,000 × 0.90 × 1.05	102,060
Nursing – fixed	216,000 × 1.05	226,800
Administration (fixed)	100,000 × 1.04	104,000
Total		**552,110**

SECTION C – 30 MARKS

[The indicative time for answering this section is 54 minutes.]

ANSWER ONE OF THE TWO QUESTIONS

QUESTION THREE

WC is a company that installs kitchens and bathrooms for customers who are renovating their houses. The installations are either pre-designed 'off-the-shelf' packages or highly customised designs for specific jobs.

The company operates with three divisions: Kitchens, Bathrooms and Central Services. The Kitchens and Bathrooms divisions are profit centres but the Central Services division is a cost centre. The costs of the Central Services division, which are thought to be predominantly fixed, include those incurred by the design, administration and finance departments. The Central Services costs are charged to the other divisions based on the budgeted Central Services costs and the budgeted number of jobs to be undertaken by the other two divisions.

The budgeting and reporting system of WC is not very sophisticated and does not provide much detail for the Directors of the company.

Budget details

The budgeted details for last year were:

	Kitchens	Bathrooms
Number of jobs	4,000	2,000
	$	$
Average price per job	10,000	7,000
Average direct costs per job	5,500	3,000
Central Services recharge per job	2,500	2,500
Average profit per job	2,000	1,500

Actual details

The actual results were as follows:

	Kitchens	Bathrooms
Number of jobs	2,600	2,500
	$	$
Average price per job	13,000	6,100
Average direct costs per job	8,000	2,700
Central Services recharge per job	2,500	2,500
Average profit per job	2,500	900

The actual costs for the Central Services division were $17.5 million.

Required:

(a) Calculate the budgeted and actual profits for each of the profit centres and for the whole company for the year. **(4 marks)**

(b) Calculate the sales price variances and the sales mix profit and sales quantity profit variances. **(6 marks)**

(c) Prepare a statement that reconciles the budgeted and actual profits and shows appropriate variances in as much detail as possible. **(10 marks)**

(d) Using the statement that you prepared in part (c) above, discuss:

  (i) the performance of the company for the year; and

  (ii) potential changes to the budgeting and reporting system that would improve performance evaluation within the company. **(10 marks)**

(Total: 30 marks)

QUESTION FOUR

A multinational computer manufacturer has a number of autonomous subsidiaries throughout the world. Two of the group's subsidiaries are in America and Europe. The American subsidiary assembles computers using chips that it purchases from local companies. The European subsidiary manufactures exactly the same chips that are used by the American subsidiary but currently only sells them to numerous external companies throughout Europe. Details of the two subsidiaries are given below.

America

The American subsidiary buys the chips that it needs from a local supplier. It has negotiated a price of $90 per chip. The production budget shows that 300,000 chips will be needed next year.

Europe

The chip production subsidiary in Europe has a capacity of 800,000 chips per year. Details of the budget for the forthcoming year are as follows:

Sales	600,000 chips

	$ per chip
Selling price	105
Variable costs	60

The fixed costs of the subsidiary at the budgeted output of 600,000 chips are $20 million per year, but they would rise to $26 million if output exceeds 625,000 chips.

Note: The maximum external demand is 600,000 chips per year and the subsidiary has no other uses for the current spare capacity.

Group directive

The Managing Director of the group has reviewed the budgets of the subsidiaries and has decided that, in order to improve the profitability of the group, the European subsidiary should supply chips to the American subsidiary. She is also thinking of linking the salaries of the subsidiary managers to the performance of their subsidiaries but is unsure which performance measure to use. Two measures that she is considering are 'profit' and the 'return on assets consumed' (where the annual fixed costs would be used as the 'assets consumed').

The Manager of the European subsidiary has offered to supply the chips at a price of $95 each. He has offered this price because it would earn the same contribution per chip that would be earned on external sales (this is after adjusting for increased distribution costs and reduced customer servicing costs).

Required:

(a) Assume that the 300,000 chips are supplied by the European subsidiary at a transfer price of $95 per chip. Calculate the impact of the profits on each of the subsidiaries and the group.

(5 marks)

(b) Calculate the minimum unit price at which the European subsidiary would be willing to transfer the 300,000 chips to the American subsidiary if the performance and salary of the Manager of the subsidiary is to be based on:

   (i) the profit of the subsidiary (currently $7 million)

   (ii) the return on assets consumed by the subsidiary (currently 35%). **(9 marks)**

(c) Write a report to the Managing Director of the group that discusses issues raised by the directive and the introduction of performance measures. (You should use your answers to parts (a) and (b), where appropriate, to illustrate points in your report.) **(10 marks)**

(d) Briefly explain how multinational companies can use transfer pricing to reduce their overall tax charge and the steps that national tax authorities have taken to discourage the manipulation of transfer prices. **(6 marks)**

(Total: 30 marks)

(Total for Section C: 30 marks)

Section 10

ANSWERS TO NOVEMBER 2007 EXAM QUESTIONS

SECTION A

1.1 A

	$
Actual overhead incurred	481,250
Less under-absorbed overhead	19,250
Overhead absorbed	462,000

Overhead absorbed = Actual standard hours charged × OAR
So OAR = overhead absorbed/actual standard hours charged = $462,000/38,500 = $12

OAR = Budgeted overheads/budgeted labour hours
So budgeted overheads = OAR × budgeted labour hours = $12 × 38,000 = $456,000

1.2 A

The operational labour efficiency variance uses the revised standard time of 12 minutes.

SHSR
$12/60 \times 370 \times \$10/\text{hr} = \$740$

AHSR
$80 \text{ hrs} \times \$10/\text{hr} = \$800$

Efficiency $60 A

1.3 C

Total process costs	$
Raw material costs	52,000
Conversion costs	56,000
Less by-product revenue	(2,000)
	106,000

Sales values	$
Product X	80,000
Product Y	48,000
Total	128,000

Process costs apportioned to product X = 80,000/128,000 × $106,000 = 66,250

Cost per litre of product X = $66,250/10,000 = $6.625

KAPLAN PUBLISHING

1.4 B

$$\text{Breakeven sales revenue} = \frac{\text{fixed costs}}{\text{C/S ratio}}$$

$$800{,}000 = \frac{\$320{,}000}{\text{C/S ratio}}$$

$$\text{C/S ratio} = \frac{\$320{,}000}{\$800{,}000} = 40\%$$

Sales revenue required to achieve a target profit of $5,000

$$= \frac{\$320{,}000 + 50{,}000}{40\%} = \underline{\$925{,}000}$$

1.5 C

Production volume ratio = standard hours produced/budgeted capacity = 95 %

So budgeted hours > standard hours

1.6 A

These are the official CIMA definitions for material requirements planning and enterprise resource planning respectively.

1.7 A

The fixed overhead volume variance is the difference between budgeted and actual production volume multiplied by the standard absorption rate per unit. This is the same as the difference between budgeted value of fixed overheads (budgeted volume × standard absorption rate per unit) and standard fixed overheads absorbed by actual production (actual volume × standard absorption rate per unit).

1.8 C

Over-absorption occurs when the amount absorbed is greater than the actual overheads incurred.

1.9 B

Using marginal costing inventory is valued at the variable production cost per unit

	$
Direct materials	20,000
Direct labour	6,300
Variable production overhead	4,700
Total variable cost	31,000

Inventory value = 400 units × 31,000/4,000 = $3,100

1.10 D

Using throughput accounting inventory is valued at material cost

Inventory value = 20,000/4,000 × 400 units = $2,000

1.11

	Sales	Receipts $
Month 4	$108,000 × 20%	21,600
Month 3	$120,000 × 80% × 40% × 0.985	37,824
Month 2	$105,000 × 80% × 30%	25,200
Month 1	$90,000 × 80% × 28%	20,160
Pre month 1		6,000
Total sales receipts in month 4		110,784

1.12

It is known that there is a stepped fixed cost of $10,000 above 35,000 units. Removing the stepped fixed cost at 40,000 units leaves $184,000.

(i) Variable cost per unit = $\dfrac{\$184{,}000 - \$143{,}500}{40{,}000 - 25{,}000} = \$2.70$

(ii) At 25,000 units

Total cost	143,500
Total variable cost $2.70 × 25,000	67,500
Fixed cost	76,000

Therefore fixed cost at 36,000 units = $76,000 + $10,000 = $86,000

1.13

Return per factory hour = $\dfrac{\$12 - \$5}{0.75\,\text{hrs}} = \$9.333$

Cost per factory hour = $144,000/12,000 = $12

TA ratio = 9.3333/12 = 0.778

A profitable product should have a ratio greater than 1. This product is making a loss as cost per hour is exceeding throughput per hour.

1.14

	$
Direct materials	36,000
Direct labour	18,000
Variable production overheads	3,000
Fixed production overheads	24,000
Total process costs	81,000

Cost per kg = $81,000/ 18,000 = $4.50

Joint Products	A	B	C
Sales price ($)	8.00	6.00	4.00
Cost per kg ($)	4.50	4.50	4.50

Gross profit/(loss)	3.50	1.50	(0.50)
Gross profit margin	43.75%	25%	(12.5)%

1.15

Return on investment = profit before interest and tax (PBIT)/ capital employed

PBIT = $320,000 + $200,000 + $100,000 + $70,000 = $690,000
Capital employed = $2.69m + $1.00m = $3.69m

ROI = 690,000/3,690,000 × 100% = 18.7%

1.16 (i)

Profit per year = cost savings − depreciation = $450,000 − $300,000 = $150,000

Residual income = profit − imputed interest (10% × opening capital)

ROI = profit/opening capital × 100%

Year	1	2	3	4	5
	$000	$000	$000	$000	$000
Capital Employed (at start of year)	1,500	1,200	900	600	300
Profit	150	150	150	150	150
Imputed interest	150	120	90	60	30
Residual income	–	30	60	90	120

(ii)

	1	2	3	4	5
Profit	150	150	150	150	150
Capital Employed	1,500	1,200	900	600	300
ROI	10%	12.5%	16.7%	25%	50%

ANSWERS TO NOVEMBER 2007 EXAM QUESTIONS : SECTION 10

SECTION B

QUESTION 2

(a) *Tutorial note:* First produce a production budget and a materials usage budget. Then adjust for changes in raw material inventories to arrive at a material purchase budget. The budget for Quarter 1 is required but this often requires production figures for the next period to arrive at a closing inventory value. Leave space to add additional workings if required.

Quarter	1	2
Sales (units)	10,000	12,000
Add closing inventory (finished goods)		
45% × 12,000	5,400	
40% × 14,000		5,600
Less opening inventory (finished goods)	(5,500)	(5,400)
Production budget (units)	9,900	12,200
Material usage budget (× 1.5kg)	14,850	18,300
Add closing inventory (raw materials)		
25% × 18,300	4,575	
Less opening inventory (raw materials)	(4,500)	
Materials purchase budget (kg)	14,925	
Materials purchase budget ($) (× $6)	$89,550	

(b) Quarter 3

Sales units 14,000 units
Opening inventory 5,600 units
Closing inventory 4,200 units
So production is 14,000 – 5,600 + 4,200 = 12,600 units

(i) Using marginal costing, production and inventory are valued at the variable production cost per unit = 9 + 8 = $17 per unit

	$
Sales (14,000 × 40)	560,000
Variable cost of sales (14,000 × $17)	238,000
Contribution	322,000
Less fixed costs	
Production ($720,000/4)	(180,000)
Administration ($200,000/4)	(50,000)
Profit	92,000

(ii) Using absorption costing production and inventory are valued at the full production cost = 17 + 15 = $32.

In addition profit must be adjusted for any over/under absorption of overhead. Overhead is absorbed by $15 for each unit of production.

Overhead absorbed (12,600 × $15)	189,000
Overhead incurred	180,000
Over-absorption	9,000

KAPLAN PUBLISHING 287

	$
Sales (14,000 × 40)	560,000
Cost of sales (14,000 × $32)	448,000
	112,000
Administration cost	(50,000)
Add overabsorption	9,000
Profit	71,000

(iii) The profit calculated using marginal costing is greater than the profit calculated using absorption costing by $21,000. This is due to inventory decreasing by 1,400 units. Using absorption costing, each unit of inventory includes $15 of fixed overhead which is carried forward to a future period to be matched against sales. This is a total of 1,400 × $15 = $21,000. Using marginal costing fixed overhead is treated as a period cost and charged against sales for the current period.

(c) Feedback control is the comparison of actual results with a budget or target. Corrective action is then taken if necessary. Flexible budgeting is used for feedback control. The original budget is adjusted to reflect the actual volume of output to make comparisons more meaningful. Any variances which arise can be investigated and action taken to prevent these occurring again.

Feed-forward control is the comparison of forecasts with targets. If there is a gap between the forecast and target, action can be taken to reduce the difference before it occurs. An example may be a cash budget. This is often used to forecast cash requirements and the outcome compared to a predetermined finance limit. If the closing cash balance is forecast to exceed the overdraft limit action can be taken to slow payments and improve cash collection. Alternatively additional sources of finance can be negotiated.

(d) Budgetary planning and control might be inappropriate in a rapidly changing business environment because;

– Budgets may provide static targets which stifle innovation. Managers' attention may be focused on achieving the budget targets rather than responding to opportunities which may arise.

– Budgets may become quickly out of date and therefore be misleading for control purposes. Rolling budgets may allow targets to be updated more regularly but are time consuming. Constantly changing targets may be confusing and demotivating for managers if they feel that the 'goal posts' are constantly moving.

– It may be difficult to incorporate cost reduction in a budget. As long as budget targets are achieved there is no incentive for managers to continually seek methods of improving efficiency and removing any non-value added activities. In a rapidly changing business environment these may be the key to success.

(e) The objective of JIT is to remove all non value added activities from the production system. This includes reducing inventory to as close to zero as possible. Raw materials are ordered only when they are required for production and products are only produced when demanded by a customer. Production systems are arranged in an optimal layout to reduce material movements. Labour are multi skilled to allow production or routine maintenance to be carried out and high quality material is important to prevent wastage and rejects.

To be successful there must be:

– High quality suppliers willing to deliver material as required. Suppliers must be located nearby to achieve short lead times.

– Predictable demand patterns. Uneven demand would make it very difficult to operate with low inventories.

- Sophisticated real time ordering systems to link customers with the production facility and to be able to order materials when required.

(f) Administration costs = $100,000 \times \dfrac{104}{100}$ = $104,000

House-keeping costs = $125,000 \times \dfrac{90}{100} \times \dfrac{106}{100}$ = $119,250

The nursing costs are more of a problem, because they are semi-variable. We will need to use the high/low method to break the cost into its fixed and variable elements. Before we do that we will need to strip out the effects of inflation, i.e. we will need to deflate the period 2 figures to period 1 prices (we could, alternatively, inflate the period 1 figures to period 2 prices).

$324,000 \times \dfrac{100}{108}$ = $300,000 in period 1 prices

Variable costs = $\dfrac{\$300,000 - \$280,000}{125 - 100}$

= $800 per index point (in period 1 prices)

	High level $	OR	Low level $
Semi-variable cost	300,000		280,000
Variable part			
$800 × 125	100,000		
$800 × 100			80,000
Fixed cost	200,000		200,000

	Period 1 $	Period 2 $	Period 3 $
Variable cost	$80,000 \times \dfrac{125}{100} \times \dfrac{108}{100}$	$108,000 \times \dfrac{90}{100} \times \dfrac{105}{100}$	102,060
Fixed cost	$200,000 \times \dfrac{108}{100}$	$216,000 \times \dfrac{105}{100}$	226,800
	280,000	324,000	328,860

Period 3 Budget

	$
House-keeping	119,250
Nursing	328,860
Administration	104,000
	552,110

PAPER P1 : MANAGEMENT ACCOUNTING – PERFORMANCE EVALUATION

SECTION C

QUESTION 3

(a)

Budget	Kitchens $	Bathrooms $	Total $
Sales	40	14	54
Direct costs	(22)	(6)	(28)
Central services	(10)	(5)	(15)
Budget profit	8	3	11

Actual	Kitchens $	Bathrooms $	Total $
Sales	33.8	15.25	49.05
Direct costs	(20.8)	(6.75)	(27.55)
Central services	(6.5)	(6.25)	(17.5)
Actual profit	6.5	2.25	4

Note: The information given in the question suggests that an OAR of $2,500 per job is used to absorb central services costs. This means that there is under absorbed central services cost of 17.5 – 6.5 – 6.25 = $4.75m. There is no indication that this is charged to profit centres but total costs must be shown to arrive at total profit.

(b)

	Kitchens $	Bathrooms $	Total $
Standard selling price	10,000	7,000	
Actual selling price	13,000	6,100	
	3,000 F	900 A	
× Actual no. of units sold	× 2,600	× 2,500	
	7,800,000 F	2,250,000 A	5,550,000 F

Sales mix profit variances

	Actual Sales	Standard Mix of Actual sales	Difference	Value at standard profit	Mix Variance $m
Kitchens	2,600	3,400	800 A	$2,000	1.6 A
Bathrooms	2,500	1,700	800 F	$1,500	1.2 F
	5,100	5,100			0.4 A

Sales quantity profit variances

	Budget Sales	Standard Mix of Actual sales	Quantity Variance	Value at standard profit	Mix Variance $
Kitchens	4,000	3,400	600 A	$2,000	1.2 A
Bathrooms	2,000	1,700	300 A	$1,500	0.45 A
	6,000	5,100			1.65 A

ANSWERS TO NOVEMBER 2007 EXAM QUESTIONS : SECTION 10

Check

Sales volume variances

Kitchens $(4,000 - 2,600) \times \$2,000 = \$2.8m$ A
Bathrooms $(2,000 - 2,500) \times \$1,500 = \$0.75m$ F   Total $2.05m

Sales volume variance   = mix variance + quantity variance
                        = $0.4m A + $1.65m A = $2.05 m

Tutorial Note: Interestingly, Sales Mix and Qty variances are clearly not in the syllabus

(c)

	F ($m)	A ($m)	$m
Budgeted profit (from part a)			11
Sales mix variance (from part b)			
– kitchens		1.6	
– bathrooms	1.2		
Sales quantity variance (part b)			
– kitchens		1.2	
– bathrooms		0.45	
Sales price variances (part b)			
– kitchens	7.8		
– bathrooms		2.25	
Direct costs (W1)			
– kitchens		6.5	
– bathrooms	0.75		
Central services (W2)			
– volume (kitchens)		3.5	
– volume (bathrooms)	1.25		
– expenditure		2.5	
	11	18	7 A
Actual profit (from part a)			4

Workings

(W1)

Direct cost variances
   Kitchens $2,600 \times (5,500 - 8,000) = \$6.5m$ A
   Bathrooms $2,500 \times (3,000 - 2,700) = \$0.75m$ F

(W2)

Central services volume variances
   Kitchens $(4,000 - 2,600) \times \$2,500 = \$3.5m$ A
   Bathrooms $(2,500 - 2,000) \times \$2,500 = \$1.25m$ F
Central services expenditure variance = $15m – $17.5m = $2.5m A

KAPLAN PUBLISHING

(d) (i) Actual profit at $4m is $7m below budgeted profit, a shortfall of 64%. The main causes are as follows:

- an overall fall in the total volume of sales resulting in a sales quantity variance of $1.65m A. The lower than expected volume has also resulted in central services costs being under absorbed as shown by the volume variances (net impact $2.25A).

- the sales mix has also switched from more profitable kitchens to less profitable bathrooms and this is reflected in the sales mix variance of $0.4m A.

- the impact of the lower volume of kitchen sales has been partially offset by the favourable price variance for kitchens. It is possible that a higher proportion of jobs are of the highly customised category rather than the 'off the shelf' packages. This has led to higher average prices being charged but also higher direct costs being incurred. The opposite seems to have occurred with bathrooms.

- Central services costs have exceeded budget by $2.5m. This may be due to higher costs incurred designing customised jobs.

It would be worth investigating whether the extra price charged for customised designs is covering all of the additional costs incurred. Higher prices may be necessary or better control of costs.

(ii) Potential changes include;

- to separate the revenues and costs relating to 'off the shelf' packages and highly customised jobs for both the kitchens and bathrooms divisions so that their profitability can be more closely analysed.

- to analyse the activities that cause central services costs and trace as many as possible to product lines rather than using a budgeted overhead absorption rate based on the number of jobs. The current approach is likely to be very inaccurate as customised jobs are likely to use a far greater level of central services than 'off the shelf' jobs.

- restructure the central services division as a profit centre and allow it to charge competitive rates for services. This may motivate the manager to control costs and improve service. Alternatively prepare an activity based budget for the central services division and monitor actual costs on this basis.

QUESTION 4

(a) Without the transfer the European subsidiary would make a profit of

($105-$60) × 600,000 − $20m = $7m

With the transfer the profit would increase to

$45 × 800,000 − $26m = $10m

The internal transfer would lead to an increase in cost for the American subsidiary of

300,000 × $5 = $1.5m

The net impact on profit for the group would be

European subsidiary	American subsidiary	Group
Increase of $3m	Reduction of $1.5m	Increase of $1.5m

(b) (i) Let TP = transfer price required

Maximum capacity is 800,000 units so to supply the American subsidiary with 300,000 units only 500,000 units can be sold externally.

Contribution per unit on external sales = $105 − $60 = $45

If contribution remains the same when the transfer price is $95 then the variable cost per unit relating to internal transfers must be $95 − $45 = $50

$300{,}000 \times (TP - 50) + 500{,}000 \times \$45 - \$26m = \$7m$
$TP - 50 = \$7m + \$26m - \$22.5m/300{,}000 = \$35$
So TP = $85

(ii) $\dfrac{300{,}000 \times (TP - 50) + 500{,}000 \times \$45 - \$26m}{\$26m} \times 100 = 35\%$

$300{,}000 \times (TP - 50) = 35\% \times \$26m - 500{,}000 \times \$45 + \$26m = \$12.6m$
$TP - 50 = \$12.6m/300{,}000 = \$42$
So TP = $92

(c)

REPORT

To: Managing Director
From: Management Accountant
Date:
Subject: Group Directive

This report discusses issues raised by the directive and the introduction of performance measures.

Internal transfer of chips

The European subsidiary has 200,000 units of spare capacity and should, in principle, be prepared to supply these at any price which exceeds incremental costs. For 200,000 units this would be $50 + $6m/200,000 = $80 per unit. (Note that the variable cost of internal transfers is lower than that of external sales – see part b). The American subsidiary would be prepared to accept any price under $90, the price at which the chips can be purchased from a local supplier. For the first 200,000 units there is a range of possible transfer prices which would be acceptable to both subsidiaries of $80 to $90.

The American subsidiary requires 300,000 units however and the additional 100,000 units could only be supplied by reducing the supply to external customers. The minimum transfer price acceptable to the European subsidiary would be $95 as this would earn the same contribution per chip as external sales. At this price the American subsidiary would be paying $5 per chip more than from the external market and so would not be motivated to buy internally.

An average price for all 300,000 units could be set using $80 for the first 200,000 units and $95 for the remaining 100,000 units.

200,000 × $80 + 100,000 × $95 / 300,000 = $85.

It has already been seen in part (b) that this is the minimum price the European subsidiary would consider if performance was measured on profit. The American subsidiary would be saving $5 per chip.

A better solution may be to transfer 200,000 chips internally and purchase the remaining 100,000 chips from the external supplier. Assuming the transfer price is set at $80 this would result in a profit for the European subsidiary of 600,000 × $45 + 200,000 × $30 − $26m = $7m. The American subsidiary would reduce costs by 200,000 × $15 = $3m. Group profits would increase by $3m, an increase of $1.5m compared to using a transfer price of $95 (see part a).

At $80 all of the profit increase was in the American subsidiary. Depending on where the transfer price is set in the range $80 to $90 the increase in profit can be divided more equitably between the two divisions.

Performance measures

If performance is measured using profit then any price above $85, (for 300,000 units), but below $90 would allow both subsidiaries to increase profits. If return on assets is used however the minimum price that would be acceptable to the European subsidiary would be $92 (part b). The American subsidiary would be unwilling to trade at that price. It would be impossible to set a transfer price that would be acceptable to both divisions.

Conclusion

It would be beneficial for the group if 200,000 chips were transferred internally rather than the current practise of external purchase. Providing the external supplier is willing to supply only 100,000 chips at $90 per unit this is the preferred option.

A performance measurement system based on profit allows a transfer price to be set which would be acceptable to both subsidiaries. This is not the case if return on assets consumed is used.

(d) Multi-nationals may have some companies located in countries with high rates of corporate tax and others with lower rates. To reduce the overall tax charge the aim will be to keep profit as low as possible in high tax rate countries. This can be achieved by charging high transfer prices to companies in high tax countries purchasing goods and set low transfer prices for those companies in high tax countries supplying goods.

National tax authorities have taken action to discourage manipulation of profits. Internal transfers are examined closely and are expected to be at market prices, or where this is not possible, at cost. Heavy fines are imposed on companies suspected of deliberately manipulating transfer prices to avoid tax.